KV-577-466

The Legacy of Opera

Reading Music Theatre
as Experience and Performance

Edited by
Dominic Symonds and Pamela Karantonis

IFTR/FIRT
Music Theatre Working Group

Amsterdam - New York, NY 2013

Official Publication of the International Federation for Theatre Research/
Publication Officielle de la Fédération Internationale pour la Recherche
de Théâtre

Front cover image: Opera *Attila* by Guiseppe Verdi, performed at the "Stage of the
Ages" summer festival at Tsarevets Fortress in Veliko Tarnovo, Bulgaria, 31 July
2011. Image courtesy of Shutterstock: kpatyhka / Shutterstock.com

The paper on which this book is printed meets the requirements of "ISO
9706:1994, Information and documentation - Paper for documents -
Requirements for permanence".

ISBN: 978-90-420-3691-8
E-Book ISBN: 978-94-012-0950-2
©Editions Rodopi B.V., Amsterdam - New York, NY 2013
Printed in the Netherlands

6140120644

The Legacy of Opera

CM13003601
4 14
£50/40
782.1/ Sym

WITHDRAWN
Library and
Student Services
UNIVERSITY OF CUMBRIA

Themes in Theatre

Collective Approaches to Theatre and Performance

7

Series Editor:
Peter G.F. Eversmann

Editorial Board:
Temple Hauptfleisch
Hans van Maanen
Robin Nelson

TABLE OF CONTENTS

Acknowledgments   7

List of illustrations   9

Empty houses, booming voices   11
DOMINIC SYMONDS AND PAMELA KARANTONIS

1.   Is this still opera?
     Media operas as productive provocations   25
     BIANCA MICHAELS

2.   A new glimmer of light:
     Opera, metaphysics and mimesis   39
     NICHOLAS TILL

3.   The singing body in the *Tragédie Lyrique* of
     seventeenth- and eighteenth-century France:
     Voice, theatre, speech, pleasure   65
     SARAH NANCY

4.   Performing affect in seventeenth-century opera:
     Process, reception, transgression   79
     CLEMENS RISI

5.   The Violettas of Patti, Muzio and Callas:
     Style, interpretation and the question of legacy   103
     MAGNUS TESSING SCHNEIDER

6.   The tenor in decline?
      Narratives of nostalgia and the performativity of the
      operatic tenor   119
      PAMELA KARANTONIS

7.   *The Threepenny Opera*:
      Performativity and the Brechtian presence between
      music and theatre   131
      MICHAEL EIGTVED

8.   The *acousmêtre* on stage and screen:
      The power of the bodiless voice   149
      JEONGWON JOE

9.   Dancing in the twilight:
      On the borders of music and the scenic   165
      DAVID ROESNER

10.   Turkish post-migrant "opera" in Europe:
      A socio-historical perspective on aurality   185
      PIETER VERSTRAETE

11.   "Powerful spirit":
      Notes on some practice as research   209
      DOMINIC SYMONDS

      Abstracts   229

      Notes on contributors   239

      Bibliography   245

      Index   261

ACKNOWLEDGMENTS

This volume of essays has arisen from discussions by the Music Theatre working group of the International Federation for Theatre Research. Our thanks go to all members of the group, particularly those who shared their thoughts during initial discussions at IFTR conferences in St. Petersburg (2004), Maryland (2005) and Helsinki (2006), and at the inaugural *Song, Stage and Screen* conference at the University of Portsmouth (2006). We are very grateful to the host institutions and organisers of all of these events for facilitating ongoing international scholarship in this area. We would also like to express our thanks to the staff of Rodopi Press, and to the editorial board of this series for its support of this publication. In particular, our thanks go to Robin Nelson, Helen Gilbert and series editor Peter Eversmann. Finally, this publication owes its existence to Clemens Risi and Michael Eigtved, whose inspiration and drive during their tenure as convenors of the working group led to the inception of this collection.

LIST OF ILLUSTRATIONS

4.1: The farewell sequence from Monteverdi's *L'Incoronazione di Poppea* (1642) (Monteverdi 1967: 37-8), bars 423-433. © Mit freundlicher Genehmigung der UNIVERSAL EDITION A.G., Wien.

4.2: Claudio Monteverdi, *L'Incoronazione di Poppea*, production: Klaus Michael, Grüber, conductor: Marc Minkowski, stage design: Gilles Aillaud, costumes: Rudy Sabounghi, Festival d'Aix-en-Provence 1999, Nero: Anne Sofie von Otter, Poppea: Mireille Delunsch.

4.3: *L'Incoronazione di Poppea*, Festival d'Aix-en-Provence 1999.

4.4: *L'Incoronazione di Poppea*, Festival d'Aix-en-Provence 1999.

4.5: Claudio Monteverdi, *L'Incoronazione di Poppea*, production: Klaus Michael, Grüber, conductor: Marc Minkowski, stage design: Gilles Aillaud, costumes: Rudy Sabounghi, Festival d'Aix-en-Provence 1999, Nero: Anne Sofie von Otter, Poppea: Mireille Delunsch.

4.6: *L'Incoronazione di Poppea*, Festival d'Aix-en-Provence 1999.

4.7: *L'Incoronazione di Poppea*, Festival d'Aix-en-Provence 1999.

4.8: "*Pur ti miro*" from *L'Incoronazione di Poppea* (1642) (Monteverdi 1967: 246-9), bars 775ff. © Mit freundlicher Genehmigung der UNIVERSAL EDITION A.G., Wien.

4.9: Henry Purcell, *Dido and Aeneas*, choreography and production: Sasha Waltz, conductor: Attilio Cremonesi, stage design: Thomas Schenk and Sasha Waltz, costumes: Christine Birkle, Staatsoper Berlin 2005, Dido: Michal Mualem, Clementine Deluy, Aurore Ugolin.

4.10 "Ah Belinda" from *Dido and Aeneas* (1689) (Purcell 1889: 7-8), bars 1-58.

4.11: The choreographed arm movement of Aurore Ugolin as (the singing) Dido in Sasha Waltz's production of *Dido and Aeneas* at Staatsoper Berlin in 2005.

8.1: Giovanni Martinelli (1885-1969) as Canio in *Vesti La Giubba* (1926), Vitaphone No. 198 directed by Edwin B. DuPar.

8.2: Oedipus represented by the singer (Philip Langridge) with an extended mask above his head and the dancer-mime (Min

Tanaka) in Julie Taymor's Saito Kinen Festival production of Stravinsky's *Oedipus Rex* in 1992. This still image is right before Oedipus pierces his eyes.

8.3: Music scores on the table near the piano, in the piano lesson sequence from Marguerite Duras' *Nathalie Granger* (1972).

8.4: Nathalie's hands and her piano teacher's, in the piano lesson sequence from Marguerite Duras' *Nathalie Granger* (1972).

8.5: Armin Jordan as Amfortas lip-synching Wolfgang Schöne in Hans-Jürgen Syberberg's *Parsifal* (1982).

8.6: The "*Teatro Silencio*" scene from David Lynch's *Mulholland Drive* (2001).

9.1: "All is Vanity" by C. Allan Gilbert (1892).

9.2: Dancing in the factory in *Dancer in the Dark* (2000).

9.3: Level hand camera shot in *Dancer in the Dark* (2000).

9.4: Fixed camera shot in *Dancer in the Dark* (2000).

9.5: Bill (David Morse) having died…

9.6: …and having been resurrected, *Dancer in the Dark* (2000).

9.7: The police enter in a scene from *Dancer in the Dark* (2000).

9.8: Jeff watches the super-fictional dance in *Dancer in the Dark* (2000).

10.1: Poster for *Lege Wieg / Boş Beşik* (2010). Graphic design and photo by Maarten Mooren. Muziektheater Hollands Diep, 2010. Courtesy of Cilia Hogerzeil.

10.2: Poster for *Tango Türk* (2010). Photo by Matthias Heyde Neuköllner Oper, 2010. Courtesy of Bernhard Glocksin.

INTRODUCTION

EMPTY HOUSES, BOOMING VOICES

DOMINIC SYMONDS AND PAMELA KARANTONIS

> Why, then, for the love of opera? [...] Because from its very beginning, opera was dead, a stillborn child of musical art. [...] Opera *never* was in accord with its time—from its very beginnings, it was perceived as something outdated, as a retroactive solution [...] and as an impure art. To put it in Hegelese, opera is outdated in its very concept. (Žižek and Dolar 2002: viii-ix)

On October 13th, 2011, in the Sultanate of Oman's city of Muscat, His Majesty Sultan Qaboos Bin Said granted medals of honour to Franco Zeffirelli and Placido Domingo, the director and conductor respectively of the inaugural night's performance at the city's new Royal Opera House. The gala opening night production, featuring extracts from *Turandot*, *Carmen* and *Swan Lake*, launched the latest in a long line of new opera venues that have sprung up in recent years: Zaha Hadid's Guangzhou Opera House in China (2011), the Oslo Opera House in Norway (2008), the commercially-funded new Royal Opera House in Denmark (2004), and rebuilt venues at both La Scala, Milan (rebuilt 2004) and the Royal Opera House, Covent Garden (2000). The Omani venue has "the potential to include performances that highlight Omani art, as well as collaborations between leading Arab, Indian, Asian, African and Western artists", as Michael Kaiser puts it in the *Huffington Post*;[1] though with its stated intention to be "a towering beacon shedding light on the various trends of the Renaissance march towards growth",[2] it seems likely that much of the repertoire will wheel out the tried-and-tested staples of the operatic canon,[3] and that this venue—like many others—will simply become another monument to the institution of opera. Or perhaps an ossified display of operatic fragments—those precious jewels of the canon that suggest opera is always out of time and out of place.

This is an event that gives evidence of the ideological power of opera—not as an artistic form, but as a conservative Western cultural emblem that has been exported globally. Anthony Freud, the General Director of the Lyric Opera of Chicago and a board member of Opera America makes this much clear in an extraordinary claim relating to opera's global relevance: "without a significant infrastructure of cultural organizations, it is impossible for a city to claim the status of being major. An opera company must be an indispensible part of this infrastructure".[4] So in one spectacular gesture, Muscat announces itself as comparable to Paris, Milan and Los Angeles on the global scene.

Much discussion can be had simply about the infrastructure and managerial systems of the operatic apparatus, even before cultural, theatrical or musicological readings are applied to the works staged in its opera houses. In framing the field of opera in this way, its discourse becomes heavily prescribed to focus on genre and historical dialectics; our understanding of opera is often determined by a body of performance works that exist in relation to (or sometimes in defiance of) the operatic model of production. This is a powerful cultural and ideological force, and our discussions of music theatre—distanced only marginally and in a rather blurred way from opera—therefore become influenced, even contextualised by that power. Nevertheless, in moving beyond opera to a space that identifies itself as distinct, our book and our Working Group in music theatre[5] seeks a discursive freedom.

Franco Zeffirelli's views are a case in point, serving to underline how operatic innovation and conservatism are the dialectic of historical forces. "The Met", *Variety* reports, "recently started phasing out some of his classic productions" (*La Traviata, Tosca, Carmen*), and replaced them with what Zeffirelli has called "hippie crap", in "a terrifying cultural revolution". If these terms wash the director's perspective a particular political hue, he makes his position clear: "they aren't touching my *Bohème*", he snaps. More a petulant threat than a policy, one suspects, though we can rejoice that the generations of tomorrow will be safely encultured by the masterpieces of the past.[6] Meanwhile, innovation in operatic productions is as much a strategy for revenue raising and securing future audiences as staging conventional revivals. The acclaimed Canadian multimedia theatre-maker Robert Lepage was engaged by the Metropolitan Opera, New York to deliver his directorial vision for its 2012 season highlight of

Wagner's *Ring* cycle against a media storm relating to its monumental, machinic set design. Much of the criticism was levelled at the general director Peter Gelb who has "been a tireless promoter of theatrically innovative productions and the importance of replacing old productions with new ones. Both leave him open to fire from critics and traditionalists".[7] Although the particulars of the controversy did relate in part to some of the cumbersome moments when the set was prey to technical glitches, much of the critical discourse surrounding the work focussed on the Metropolitan Opera's vast budget and its political or philanthropic relationship to *Opera News*.[8] In this case, discussion of operatic innovation was completely overwhelmed by the cultural and financial apparatus that promotes The Met's New York "brand" of opera as a part of the cultural cachet of the city. This is even the case with the cinematic release of the Metropolitan Opera productions to global cinema complexes.

If preserving the repertoire and machinery of the apparatus is central to the cultural consumption of opera, it is certainly a project that is well supported on the other side of the Atlantic. In the United Kingdom, whose capital boasts two major opera houses (the Royal Opera House and the Coliseum, home to the English National Opera), opera is easily the largest beneficiary of government subsidy in the arts sector, with over £60 million of taxpayers' money donated annually to the four main companies (including Opera North and Welsh National Opera). Repertoires are fairly conservative, and although some incentive is given for new works to be produced, mainly by the regional companies, by far the greatest output privileges the celebrated classics ("about fifty operas from Gluck to Puccini", suggests Mladen Dolar).[9] The story is the same the world over, leaving the development of an alternative repertoire to take place in far less heavily subsidised conditions.[10] Is it any wonder small production companies working across many types of music theatre are tempted to add the words "opera" to their names for the chance of a subsidy?

A part of this cultural imbalance is undoubtedly due to the sort of aristocratising of culture about which Bourdieu has written so eloquently, one result of which is to fetishise certain aspects of the form. The voice—so central to the identity of opera—is a particularly potent victim of such fetishism. Thus unlikely celebrities are born out of gigantic figures (in every way) like Placido Domingo, Luciano Pavarotti and José Carreras, whose teaming up at the final of the 1990

FIFA World Cup was the culmination of seriously dedicated (and individually functioning) publicity machines devoted to promoting these artists as celebrities in the mainstream throughout the 1980s. However, when combined and re-branded as the "three" in 1990, the event catapulted these *bona fide* opera virtuosi to international fame with audiences more familiar with the chanting of the football crowd than the *bel canto* of the stage. Here the fetish becomes commoditised, separated from any form of event that even pretends to be a public concert, let alone opera or theatre, as, in a self-conscious display of echoed narcissism, the height of the divo's "kitschy pomp and show-off", in Dolar's words (4), is seen three-fold: Three Tenors, three clones, a trinity of vocal and authorial sublimation. Three Gods on Olympus with the baying multitude yelling in the terraces. Opera as paratext.

THE LEGACY OF OPERA

This book offers a diverse collection of writing that treats many distinct themes, all cognisant of the issues explored in this introduction, and all centred on an area and approach to performance that we label not "Opera", but "Music Theatre". These essays stem from the shared working practices and beliefs of a group of like-minded scholars from many different countries. Their beliefs have been explored in meetings of the Music Theatre Working Group of the International Federation for Theatre Research—a forum which does not preclude music scholars, but which because of its positioning under the aegis of the International Federation for Theatre Research emphasises the discourses of theatre studies rather than those of musicology. And this perspective makes a good deal of sense. Music and theatre, after all, share many principles of discussion—concepts of beat, pace, rhythm, pitch, voice and dynamics, for example. Moreover, at its most literal, theatre has almost always incorporated musical elements. A performance of the Japanese puppetry of Bunraku, for instance, is not complete without the musicians on the side of the stage; Shakespeare's plays bubble with the presence of characterising song; and theatre in its classical infancy notoriously merged the performance of language with the incantation of the voice.

But if music is, as many would argue, *integral* to theatre and performance, then why not simply discuss it as one of the languages of the stage? Why the need for a dedicated, as if discipline-bounded group? According to the Music Theatre Working Group's founding convenors, Clemens Risi and Michael Eigtved, the creation of such a forum was essential because the study of Music Theatre tended to fall between two stools: there was not enough discussion of music's importance in theatre studies, while musicology was lacking in an interrogation of performativity and other concepts growing from performance and theatre studies. This way of thinking assigns to the group a real self-consciousness about a disciplinary divide; not one that we seek to promote, but one that is perhaps borne out of the different cultures of scholarship that inevitably become entrenched in institutional and disciplinary domains. In recent years this lament has been challenged by developments in new musicology and post-dramatic theatre—both theatre and music have increasingly moved away from the cults of text and authorship, and more towards ecologies of performativity and interdisciplinarity. Nevertheless, there is still a sense of music theatre being somehow "in-between", causing timely reflection as new works demanding new vocabularies and approaches to analysis—such as "composed theatre", "musicking", "aurality"—increasingly emerge.[11]

Central to the working group's identity is a recognition that this "between" takes in a vast performative landscape. Music theatre is often the productive hybrid, an intermediary term, with its origins in the German *Musiktheater*, suggesting that new, interstitial forms can emerge from the two monoliths of theatre and music. But as we have explored at the beginning of this introduction, there is also a third monolith which already inhabits that territory, and which by the end of the nineteenth century had established itself as a powerful cultural edifice: opera.

Much has been said in this section already about the cultural, social and economic power of opera, and looking back over the long twentieth century, some might wonder what had become of the promise of opera. Endlessly regurgitating the European canon, crassly commoditising it into ways which insinuate themselves into a yearly calendar of "must-sees" for those who identify as its consumers, the studio-produced CD compilations, the desperately created new Christmas hits at "The Met" from a back-catalogue of pop arias and a script by Shakespeare—like *The Enchanted Isle* (2011)—the operatic apparatus in the age of post-modernity has never seemed so jaded. This is a far cry from the height of the nineteenth century, when the form really did represent the cutting edge and aesthetic hyperbole of sung expression. But was opera's lavish excess—Rossini on the one hand, Wagner on the other—really its final articulation of a symbolic death, its own *Liebestod*, as Slavoj Žižek and Mladen Dolar suggest in their book of two halves, *Opera's Second Death*?

To speak of opera today seems to conjure up that glorious colossus, to be sure, but seems also to reveal a displaced spectre of the arts, who in its day was the grand master, someone who still commands that nostalgic respect and for whom we keep staging farewell concerts, someone for whom all that remains is a legacy. As Dolar puts it in his half of *Opera's Second Death*, "Opera represents a corpus that is historically closed, finished […] a huge relic, an enormous anachronism, a persistent revival of a lost past, a reflection of the lost aura, a true postmodern subject par excellence" (Žižek and Dolar 2002: 2-3).

Žižek's discussion, which he hangs around the denouement of *Tristan und Isolde*, invokes the idea of the "second death": not only does Isolde die to the powerful musical strains of the "*Liebestod*", but also, in this evocative and widely celebrated musical moment, Wagner effectively "puts to bed" his long-term aspiration to write something that was, for opera, its definitive articulation. For Žižek, these deaths are inextricably linked, and just as opera was born through its own metaphorical power of music (the "Possente Spirto" of Monteverdi's *L'Orfeo*, discussed in our final chapter), so too it dies through metaphor in *Tristan und Isolde*: "She dies of singing, of immersing herself into the song; […] the culminating identification with the voice is the very medium of death" (Žižek and Dolar 2002: 105).

However, as this "cumbrous, expensive relic of the past [...] refused to fade away",[12] younger voices gathered, eager to follow on. Some were already speaking out—the disrespectful prodigal of populism chirped up as music hall, vaudeville and then musical comedy. Less brashly, youthful experimenters set up an exploratory avant-garde of music theatre as the new century emerged; meanwhile a worthy favourite dutifully continued the progenitor's tradition of opera, with an eye only for the legacy. And these three—the musical, music theatre, and opera-after-the-"*Liebestod*"—in their different ways took on the twentieth century: the changes of world order, the technological advances, the revolutions of modernity and post-modernity.

If it is Western material history that has constructed in that narrative the idea of opera as a *fin de siècle* cultural monolith and opera studies as an associated scholarly pursuit, these at least serve as reflecting pools for our own work; though the spirit of opera and the prism of opera studies are inescapable legacies that must be revisited in the wake of new work and new approaches to scholarship. So we work and practice in a field that seems to exist in the shadow of opera without quite being defined by its terminology: at times we feel like opera scholars, and feel that the object of our study is the same object that musicologists and historians of opera explore. At other times, we instinctively distance ourselves from the approaches of opera studies in its deferral to musicology and musical historiography and especially its dependence on the texts (the scores, the libretti) that form its literature. For these materials are the props of that grand master, without which he could not perform, but *without which* our whole new world comes alive. For ethnomusicologists, this is arguably a liberation in its field that came from the challenges of facing cultural alterity when abandoning the centrality of the score as a colonising instrument. But this debate is very much one that has been explored for decades in performance studies and theatre studies by scholars such as Richard Schechner, Peggy Phelan, Herbert Blau and Rebecca Schneider, in the binary of drama versus performance, play-text versus performance text, materiality versus ephemerality. For us, the first step to unlock our approach from that of opera studies is to challenge the dominance of the score and reveal the corporeal presence of the singer. This manoeuvre is one shared by many, including the avant-garde composer Sylvano Bussotti, who railed against the textual canon of opera in his dedication to pioneering vocalist Cathy Berberian, advising admirers of great opera houses and the traditional texts and scores they house to:

> lift their gaze carefully and observe the statues, the cornices decorated with the allegories of arts and crafts, the places crowded with theatres or temples: none ever displayed a monument to the Libretto![13]

This is an irreverence, like all other acts of the avant-garde that gives the impression here that the twentieth-century spin-offs from opera are its adolescent children: the precocious avant-garde, the intelligent chamber production and the populist profit-seeker.

There are undoubtedly elements of this critique that will appeal to some perspectives and challenge others, though while this perceptual genealogy may be a compelling idea, it may not be useful for us to view opera simplistically as a faded has-been and the younger forms as a hip new generation of trend-setters. A problem of terminology exists in the idea of such a legacy, since there is a paternalistic handing down from one generation to another that needs to be problematised. Maybe it is more appropriate to think of a single form, opera, having been wholesale "twentieth-centuried", as if it has responded to Theodor Adorno's compelling insight into Wagner's relevance in post-war Germany. Writing with the serious burden of operatic legacy in a Berlin of 1963, Adorno detected a fundamental tension at play between the iconoclastic impulse and the desire to preserve operatic forms: "If it is true about Wagner that no matter what one does, it is wrong, the thing that is still most likely to help is to force what is false, flawed, antinomical out into the open, rather than glossing over it and generating a kind of harmony". With this assertion, Adorno sanctioned the new generation, sounding vaguely Brechtian and offering a parallel to that which Brecht was to offer a different sort of theatre:

> only experimental solutions are justified today; only what injures the Wagner orthodoxy is true [...]. If Wagner's work is truly ambivalent and fractured, then it can be done justice only by a performance practice that takes this into account and realises the fractures instead of closing them cosmetically.[14]

While there are serious and very obvious political and historical stakes informing Adorno's comments on Wagner, his words grant some sort of validity to change, and retrospectively this could apply to most opera emerging since the early nineteenth century. However, it has been more noticeably the striking changes of the long twentieth century, from modernism to post-modernism and beyond, that have shaken the stability of so many of opera's guiding principles, exploding the previously monolithic into a multivalency of possibilities. Not only has the previously stage-bound form been remediated onto numerous new technological platforms, each with its own aesthetic possibilities, but the doctrines of narrative and dramatic structure have been fractured and repositioned; fundamental elements of an earlier period—like character, Act, and even aria—have in various new paradigms an uncertain presence. Almost as soon as Wagner brought the "total work of art" to the table, the *fin de siècle* shuffled the pack, and our understandings of "total", "work" and "art" were completely re-constituted.

Perhaps the most obvious casualty of this maelstrom has been the creator of the work (opus), the "opera-tor" himself (who was, after all, ever male). With a mighty flourish at the climax of one century, the final incarnation of this operator (or *über-writer*?)[15] hammered home the climactic ultimatum of an operatic legacy; and forthwith the myth both held and unravelled as the new century unfurled. This is not to say that the ego (or the patriarchal) has been entirely driven out: witness the many individuals—the Sondheims, Lloyd Webbers, Becketts, Brooks, Wilsons, Princes, Mackintoshes, Muellers and Bieitos—whose identities precede their creations. But even if these *auteurs* continue a tradition, their practices develop, and we speak more honestly of collaboration, more knowingly of the way pieces develop, and more confidently of the fact that—in Bruce Kirle's words—show business is always "unfinished" (Kirle 2005). In the slipstream of twentieth-century re-shaping linger many vestiges of an earlier time; indeed, a part of that re-shaping strategy has been to thieve like a magpie from previous sources, texts and styles.

In this way the death of the author for opera perhaps ruptures the form's identity more than for other practices, because opera has always carried in its expression a reminder of that monologism. Despite its capacity for spectacle and total art, the most emblematic and arguably the most prized element of opera has forever been the voice: a voice that dominates all, commanding both stage and orchestra (music and theatre); a voice that demands that we *attend* or at least listen to its importance; a voice that even vexes nature by the impression that it can capture time. Like a parody of its creation, opera again and again sites the singular voice at the apex of its presentation: centre stage the park-and-bark diva, accompanied by a massive throng of underlings; flown around the world to headline in "major" cities (as defined by Anthony Freud), rolling out the stock parts over decades; idolised by legions of fanatics pursuing the ineffable; defined by the high Cs.

If the twentieth century calls into question the voice of the author, it also takes a metaphorical scalpel to the larynx, the *sine qua non* of the operatic psyche. Perhaps first in the manipulation of technology, perhaps then in the distortion of convention, given permission by other voices of reason, and through the prisms of psychoanalysis, madness and decay, the vocal apparatus is gone. Now speaker systems attest to a larynx whose glory has been silenced, and the corporeal presence of one kind of master's voice is unnervingly ghosted into surround sound by another. While one voice dies with opera, another voice rises from the ashes; or perhaps, as if repeating the cycle, a new Orpheus descends to a new technological underworld where music can once again defy death.[16]

Such death-defiance responds to the brutal surgery in two ways: either it cryogenically resuscitates the corpse, re-instituting what was there before (as the loyal descendant would have it, as has happened from Oman to The Met); or it finds an alternative expression in the "post-operative", as Nicholas Till's witty moniker terms it, by embracing the new paradigms and their vast differences from the old, like a cyborg fuses the real with the technologised.

The first demand of a book such as this is to set out our stall: what precisely is at stake, and what are our collective intentions? If this appears to be something of a manifesto, that perhaps establishes our mutual politics as being radical, or at least "post": working to untangle historical residues, working to make visible entrenched assumptions and working to promote new perspectives. For us, collectively, the legacy of opera is one that is complex, being both the well-spring from which the source of so much fascination and creative material has bubbled, and the damp, mossy ground left as the well runs to a trickle. The legacy of opera—or indeed the spectre—looms large both as a creative energy and a delimiting force. That the term "opera" seems in the rhetoric of this introduction irredeemably shackled to the past forces new and sometimes destabilising terminology onto our discussion, though rather than engineer a codifying practice of consistency onto the disparate voices within this book, we have chosen to keep the play of terminology open. We are interested in critiquing why the terms "opera" and "music theatre" are used as if synonymous, sometimes by artists themselves and sometimes by scholars. It is almost as if at times attempts are made to revivify "opera" by applying its usage to current trends and contemporary practices. Our intention is to be mindful of the strategic use of the term "opera" to advance certain culturally and historically-loaded readings of music theatre works, and in turn to appraise the possibility that a music theatre discourse opens the dialogue for discussing ways of working creatively that may seem *materially* similar to "opera" but ideologically form a productive distance from the cultural apparatus of its legacy.

The book's chapters explore three broad areas relating to music theatre: first, it considers how opera has built a legacy enshrined in the ontological potency of operatic performance and the ideological structuring of the apparatus; second, it re-evaluates performance on the musical stage by considering the performativity of the voice and body of the singing actor and the affect of the performative encounter on audiences; third, it explores new forms and practices that have emerged through technological or paradigmatic shifts away from the operatic past.

Significantly, the book begins with a set of provocations that have arisen from discussions among the authors over successive working group meetings. Here we see them articulated in print—some considered briefly in this introduction, but others set out as explicit challenges in the first two chapters. In these, Bianca Michaels and Nicholas Till consider how music theatre in the twentieth century has functioned ontologically—both embracing and struggling with technological developments offered by new platforms, performative possibilities, and ideological assumptions that the operatic apparatus has reinforced about the metaphysical power of performance. Their chapters pose important questions as to what constitutes a twenty-first century audience and readership. Specifically Michaels explores some of the ways in which contemporary opera has incorporated small-screen mediality through the works of Robert Ashley and Steve Reich, defining these collective experiments as media opera. This establishes a discursive framework in our volume for the strategic deployment of the word "opera" in relation to work that could arguably be discussed as "music video" or "media music theatre". The reasons for the discursive power of "opera" in these discussions is elaborated upon in Nicholas Till's chapter, "A new glimmer of light: opera, metaphysics and mimesis", wherein he identifies some of the reasons why opera may be locked in the past. For him, it has become ideologically over-determined and therefore trapped in a set of metaphysical assumptions about music, text and performance. These conditions necessitate a re-appraisal of the term music theatre as a way of deconstructing those assumptions, a strategy that Till terms "post-operatic" or "anti-operatic".

Following these opening chapters, the volume presents four chapters (Nancy, Risi, Schneider, Karantonis) that shift towards what can be regarded as a primary language of music theatre in all its forms—namely, the voice. In this section the authors look back on pre-twentieth-century and recent vocal performance practice in opera and its corporeal and extra-theatrical potencies from a contemporary perspective. Sarah Nancy's work urges scholars and listeners to re-unite the voice and its corporeal origins in discussions of the listening experience that resonate with the wider readings of vocality and performance today. Similarly, Clemens Risi connects the transmission of music-dramatic "affect" in a traditional taxonomy of seventeenth-century stagecraft to the performativity of the body. Significant for a revisionist use of the term "music theatre" in relation to historical genres, Magnus Tessing Schneider investigates the vocal performance practices of three operatic divas as growing from concepts within theatre studies, continuous with theories of acting and directing on the theatrical stage. Finally Pamela Karantonis examines the issues of gender performativity as they might apply to performance studies or theatre studies within the contexts of vocal celebrity and the specific listening pleasures provided by the operatic tenor—significantly when singing outside the matrices of a staged opera. This section of the volume allows implicit methodological approaches to emerge that are key to our working group's understanding of music theatre: firstly, we look at the performance event and practice rather than "a text" *per se*; secondly, we use interdisciplinary perspectives to consider our subject; thirdly, we bring a post-structuralist questioning to existing assumptions about form and practice; and finally, we consider performance as a fundamentally human act that takes place in social environments, in cultural contexts and in diverse expressive forms.

The following four chapters (Eigtved, Joe, Roesner, Verstraete) consider how newer forms more readily identified as "music theatre" in terms of historical genre can be accounted for from the perspective of their audience(s). We take a broad sweep through some of the different audience situations presented throughout the twentieth century. First the paradigm shift of the Brechtian new dawn is considered by Michael Eigtved; then the psychologising shift brought about by the mediatisation of screen operas is discussed by Jeongwon Joe and David Roesner; finally, the cultural negotiation of diasporic communities engaging with music theatre in their non-native environs is explored by Pieter Verstraete. In its emerging articulations, music theatre provides models of spectatorship that borrow from the operatic entanglement with metaphysics suggested by Till and the ontological limits of mediatisation suggested by Michaels into new voices and experiences in the spaces between music and theatre.

In the final chapter of the book Dominic Symonds takes a significant twenty-first century mode of performance scholarship, the idea of practice as research, and uses it as a methodological tool to consider opera and its development over time as a long-term process and project. In this way, the traditional narrative and naturalisation of opera's "development" and the establishment of ideological assumptions is deconstructed, offering a fresh insight to the way in which we might re-conceive both a form and its identity.

So we begin and end with opera. opera can be regarded as contingent upon the stability of its elemental forms, music and theatre, and with their deconstruction, both by scholars and artists, emerges an interest in the efficacies of an interdisciplinary music theatre. Our work here contends that music theatre is now understood as a highly productive methodology and field of theory as much as an historically-placed genre.

It is this sort of contemporary and emerging understanding that we hope to bring to you our readers in our inaugural Music Theatre Working Group publication. In doing this, we explore how our case studies push beyond certain constraints in the discourse; but just as opera houses go up on one site and come crashing down on another, these elements are also prone to deconstruction in the development of our work.

NOTES

[1] See Kaiser 2011.

[2] See "Royal Opera House Muscat" 2012.

[3] Philippe Agid and Jean-Claude Tarondeau cite 37 operatic works they see as staples or "classics" of this canon. They elaborate on the sub-categories of these with the amusing nomenclature of "warhorses", "evergreens" and "blockbusters" as opposed to "rarities" (Agid and Tarondeau 2010: 20-21).

[4] Anthony Freud, cited from his foreword to Agid and Tarondeau's study (Agid and Tarondeau 2010: x).

[5] This book is a collection of papers drawn from discussions of the Music Theatre Working Group of the International Federation for Theatre Research.

[6] Vivarelli 2011.

[7] Wakin 2012.

[8] This publication decided to self-impose a ban on its review of productions at the Metropolitan Opera after the controversial public dialogue between its editorial staff and Peter Gelb: "*Opera News* has reviewed Met productions continuously since at least the mid-1970s [...]. While not frequent, negative notices have periodically made their way in, to the discomfiture of previous Met administrations. But no ban was imposed, at least in recent decades" (Wakin 2012).

[9] Žižek and Dolar 2002: 3.

[10] Battersea Arts Centre, one London-based venue that promotes new and experimental music theatre work through its Scratch initiative, its Burst season and its collaborations with festivals such as the Tête-a-Tête opera festival, receives by contrast just £700,000 in funding for an entire season.

[11] Terms such as "Composed Theatre" and "Musicalisation" refer respectively to two new major works in the field that is controversially labelled "post-dramatic": Rebstock and Roesner's *Composed Theatre: Aesthetics, Practices, Processes* (2012) and Hans-Thies Lehmann's *Post-dramatic Theatre* (2006). Further significant contributions to this area of study include Roesner 2010a, Roesner 2010b and Roesner and Kendrick 2011.

[12] Peter Conrad from *A Song of Love and Death*, cited in Agid and Tarondeau 2010: ix.

[13] Bussotti 2002 in Karantonis, Verstraete, *et al* 2013.

[14] This is a new translation, by Susan H. Gillespie, of Theodor W. Adorno's lecture of September 1963, given during the Berlin Festspielwochen in Adorno 2002: 600.

[15] If we are looking for an individual, the spectre of Richard Wagner looms ever large throughout this narrative, as an incarnation in a series of dominant Western male egos: Monteverdi—Purcell—Mozart—Gluck—Beethoven—Wagner—and so on, who, in a counterfactual history of the women and non-Western artists who have created opera, are unaware of the diversity of voices that have made opera.

[16] Žižek and Dolar 2002: 8.

CHAPTER 1

IS THIS STILL OPERA?
MEDIA OPERAS AS PRODUCTIVE PROVOCATIONS

BIANCA MICHAELS

"THAT'S NOT OPERA ANYMORE"

Several years ago, at the world congress of the International Federation for Theatre Research in Amsterdam (2002) I gave a presentation on CNN operas in the course of which I parenthetically mentioned the phenomenon of television opera. Television opera functioned as an example of operas that were musically, dramaturgically and scenographically conceived for the medium of television. One woman in the audience was visibly annoyed that the composers called their works for television "operas". For me, it was the first of several encounters with the seemingly widespread conviction that "that's not opera anymore". During my research on media operas—works that have been conceived and composed for audiovisual media—I realised that the term "opera" in this context seems to be so challenging that people feel obliged to protect the concept of opera from being abused. However, if—for example—a television opera such as *Perfect Lives* by Robert Ashley is not considered an opera, then what is a proper opera? Instead of proposing yet another definition of what opera is, the following article asks why some works that are called operas by their composers provoke opposition against the use of the term "opera". To contextualise this discussion, I will draw attention to a critical gap that I perceive in opera studies, whose conventional approach to scholarship resists discussing contemporary opera and music theatre: "despite impressive approaches", suggests Björn Heile, "there seems to be a lack of critical mass for a sophisticated sustained discourse to establish itself" (Heile 2006: 73).

This lack of theoretical discourse is already evident with experimental works, especially those performed outside of the opera houses, let alone with works that leave the conventional operatic stage in favour of alternative social and medial environments, such as, for example, television. In many cases, conventional musicology does not address the achievement of radical new forms, particularly if these experiments are performed outside of the ordinary, established institutions: if composers are not already well known as "serious" composers, those works are for the most part not visible on the academic agenda either. This affects contemporary works by American composers in particular.

Thus, the aim of this article is two-fold: after introducing what I call "media opera", the paper will explore the relationship of the term "opera" to its implied mediality, and the correlation between the mediality of opera as an art form and opera as a social and cultural practice. Summing up, I will propose some ideas about how media operas can serve as productive provocations for our everyday as well as scholarly understanding of opera and how they might open up a new perspective for studies in music theatre.

ON THE IMPORTANCE OF MEDIALITY, OR: WHAT MAKES THESE OPERAS PROVOCATIVE?

Opera—as with any other cultural work—does not exist in isolation from other media, nor in isolation from other social and economic forces. Thus it is a commonplace that opera and music theatre have always integrated new technological developments. Taking the recent historical dominance of the televisual into account it is no wonder that audiovisual media have had a major influence on the art form of opera. Whereas technological inventions in the past have mostly affected individual elements of the performance such as for example the orchestra or the scenography, the technological influences that are enabled by electronic media have led to developments that can fundamentally change our understanding of opera: they call into question our common understanding of this art form and at the same time oblige us to reconsider some of our familiar propositions.

According to Philip Auslander's widely-discussed publication *Liveness* (1999), the term "mediatised" indicates "that a particular cultural object is a product of the mass media or of media technology" (5). Thus, any mediatised performance "is a performance that is circulated on television, as audio or video recordings, and in other forms based in technologies of reproduction" (*ibid.*). The word "media" in this context refers to electronic media, and the term "mediality" refers to the conditions of communication between production and reception (Balme 2001: 483). I suggest introducing the term "media opera" for works that replace the mediality of the (conventional) operatic stage with its stage traditions and perception habits by a mediality that is based on digital and audiovisual media. Hence, the term "media opera" serves as a heuristically defined umbrella term for radio opera, television opera, video opera, internet opera, etc., to refer to works that are conceptually based upon technologies of reproduction such as audiovisual and digital media. For media operas, electronic media are part of the dramaturgical and compositional conception. Media operas such as, for instance, *Perfect Lives (Private Parts)* (1978-1983) by Robert Ashley or *Three Tales* (1998-2002) by Steve Reich are musically and visually conceived for audiovisual and digital media such as video, television and the internet, setting them apart from, for example, operas on film or the filming of stage operas that integrate those media at the level of performance.

Media operas emerged with the advent and wide dissemination of media technologies such as radio and television in the 1920s, and can now be seen in different forms that are intrinsically tied to radio, television, video, or the internet. After outlining a short survey of historical and contemporary media operas, especially by American composers, I will concentrate on how these works expose some of the crucial aspects underlying our common understanding of the term "opera".

The cultural context and the particular conditions in which opera institutions operate in the United States have had a significant impact on US composers and musicians: "The powerful impact of mass media on American opera composers extended beyond allowing their fresh visibility and outreach. Radio and television managed to rescue opera from large and imposing opera houses and bring it into American homes" (Kirk 2001:249). Apart from broadcasting opera performances,[1] the technological possibilities of radio gave rise to various experiments with these new media and led to works that were particularly designed for the conditions of radio. The radio opera is conceived for the conditions and particular constraints on the acoustic dimension of its medium. Its beginnings can be traced back to the early days of the first electronic mass medium with *Der Lindbergflug*

(Brecht/Weill/Hindemith, 1929), *The Old Maid and the Thief* (Menotti, 1939), etc.

Shortly after the development of television, composers also discovered this new medium for opera.[2] Television opera in this context is defined as opera particularly designed and commissioned for television in contrast to regular opera performances that are broadcast from opera houses. Television opera, it was hoped, would fill the gap between opera and the mass audience. The most popular television opera was Gian Carlo Menotti's *Amahl and the Night Visitors*, which was commissioned by NBC in America and which premiered on Christmas Eve 1951. Since then it has been restaged for television nineteen times and broadcast almost fifty times. The most important composers of television operas are Gian Carlo Menotti, Bohuslv Martinů and Heinrich Sutermeister. Even Igor Stravinsky (*The Flood*, 1962) and Benjamin Britten (*Owen Wingrave*, 1971) composed operas for television.

What Philip Auslander suggests for televised drama can easily be assigned to television opera: "the goal of televised drama was not merely to convey a theatrical event to the viewer, but to recreate the theatrical experience for the home viewer through televisual discourse and thus, to *replace* live performance" (Auslander 1999: 18ff.). Television opera combined the energy of the theatre with the proximity only possible with a camera lens, which led to an impression of heightened intimacy (see Barnes 2003: 7). After the successful premiere of the first television opera *Amahl and the Night Visitors* it was a common assumption that television opera would bridge the gap between the mass audience and the opera house and be able to develop a new kind of opera. However, because of high production costs television operas did not really succeed for long and gave way to direct broadcasts from opera houses in the 1960s.[3] Since the 1970s, experiments with multimedia theatricality have become increasingly common. Examples include various works such as *United States* (1983) by Laurie Anderson; Robert Ashley's *Perfect Lives (Private Parts)* (1977-1983) and *Atalanta (Acts of God)* (1982); Steve Reich's *The Cave* (1993); the work of Meredith Monk, including the "quasi-operatic" *Atlas* (1988-1991); and Pauline Oliveros's *Nzinga the Queen King* from 1993.[4]

One reason for the interest composers still have in the medium of television might be the fact that television has preserved its liveness and its real-time character from the period before it was possible to pre-record the programmes:

> The fact that television can "go live" at any moment to convey sight and sound at a distance in a way no other medium can remains a crucial part of the televisual imaginary even though that way of using the medium is now the exception rather than the rule. (Auslander 1999: 13)

Today new technologies continue to enable new forms such as, for example, various experiments with digital technology that lead to new forms of digital and virtual opera.[5]

Thanks to some significant developments over the last seventy years in the use of electronic and digital media within opera and music theatre, more and more elements of mediatisation have been integrated into music theatre performances. Relying fundamentally on audiovisual media, many contemporary operas not only cross the boundaries of different media but make the already problematic question of what the term "opera" actually means even more complicated. Thus, audiovisual media are also beginning to challenge our propositions and connotations of opera as a form of music theatre.

A CLOSER LOOK: *PERFECT LIVES* AND *THREE TALES* AS EXAMPLES OF MEDIA OPERAS

In order to clarify the term "media opera" I will illustrate it by means of two examples: the television opera *Perfect Lives* by Robert Ashley and the video documentary opera *Three Tales* by Steve Reich. I chose these two not only because of their particular mediality but also because both composers have considered very carefully the particular medial strategies of their works.

After experiments with multimedia theatricality in the 1960s, the American composer Robert Ashley began composing highly conceptual video and television operas in the 1970s that combined his interest in language with his interest in using audiovisual media to express musical ideas. One of the experiments to combine this with his interest in language was "Music with Roots in the Aether" (1976), a fourteen-hour production of video portraits of composers and their music. However, one of Ashley's most famous operas for television is *Perfect Lives*, which was commissioned for television by The Kitchen in New York, a centre for video, music, dance, performance, film, and literature in 1978. In the following years the different parts of *Perfect Lives* were shaped in live performances and toured extensively

throughout Europe and the USA. The television version, consisting of
seven episodes of twenty-five minutes, premiered on Great Britain's
Channel 4 on seven consecutive nights in 1984, has since been seen
on television in Austria, Germany, Spain and the United States, and
has been shown at film and video festivals around the world. To date
Perfect Lives is the only work of Ashley's that has enjoyed an
extensive broadcast life.

Perfect Lives—as all of his operas—differs distinctly from former
television operas and is distinctly American both in its subject matter
and its use of American language. Hence, the musicologist Allan
Evans called the work "nothing less than the first American opera.
[…] Works such as this put to rest any doubts [about whether] opera
can or should survive, and how" (Ashley n.d).

The opera consists of seven episodes titled "The Park", "The
Supermarket", "The Bank", "The Bar", "The Living Room", "The
Church", and "The Backyard". The events occur within these episodes
in a highly discontinuously reported way, with numerous visual,
textual and musical cross references. The basic theme is an

> over-the hill entertainer and his somewhat younger pal on the Midwest circuit,
> who find themselves in a small town, playing at the Perfect Lives Lounge,
> telling stories about the people of the town. They become friends with two
> local characters, the son and daughter of the sheriff. The four of them hatch a
> plan to do something that, if they are caught doing it, will be a crime, but if
> they are not caught will be Art. The idea is that the son of the sheriff, who is
> the assistant to the manager of the bank, will make it possible for them to take
> all the money out of the bank for one day. And then they will put it back.
> They've set themselves a challenge, but it's outside the realm of crime: it's
> not like Bonnie and Clyde. There's a kind of metaphysical meaning for the
> removal of the money. […] The stories in *Perfect Lives* are all stories about
> encounters between people who, to various degrees, know what's going on.
> (Ashley 1991: 153)

At first sight, the opera seems to be musically structured in a fairly
inartificial   way: Robert   Ashley   hinself   functions   as
narrator/entertainer (Raoul de Noget), who sings throughout the opera
a kind of monologic song-like speech against a background of
electronic music. In addition there are choir-like passages sung by Jill
Kroesen and David van Tieghem and passages of piano music by
"Blue" Gene Tyranny. According to Robert Ashley's highly
collaborative working methods,[6] the music was composed and

arranged by the above-mentioned performers alongside the producer Peter Gordon.[7]

Being probably the most thorough realisation of Ashley's concept of television opera, the musical and visual materials are very carefully arranged, insofar as they are coordinated through

> the use of templates, the term I've used to describe the subjective assignment of emotional values and moods to visual forms and corresponding musical structures. Within the rules defined by the templates, the collaborators, in all aspects of the work, are free to interpret, "improvise", invent, and superimpose characteristics of their own artistic styles onto the texture of the work. In a sense, the collaborators become "characters" in the opera at a deeper level than the illusionistic characters who appear on stage. (Ashley 1991: 180ff.)

The visual material consists of illustrations of the various domains or landscapes of the characters in the performance (e.g., the narrator, the piano player and the couple), the text itself and the characters themselves playing and singing in the Perfect Lives Lounge. The idea was that each episode should have a characteristic camera movement, a dynamic, and that the camera dynamic would be illustrated graphically in a pattern on the screen. For example, the

> first episode uses the bottom line of the six horizontals, the horizon, and the camera movement is a continuous pan left, a "seeking". In the second episode, there is the horizon *and* the triangle or pyramid of lines converging at the top. The dynamic is the "aggressive" zoom in. (Ashley 1991: 164)

According to the visual templates Ashley also uses metrical templates specific for each of the seven episodes that govern the rate of speech and the inflexion quality.[8]

The initial idea was that different directors could take the tapes which contained all the pre-recorded images for each episode and make different productions of *Perfect Lives* (see also Ashley 1991: 158). However, this idea could not be realised, so to date there exists only one video version. Although the television version of *Perfect Lives* was finished in 1983, this seminal work still seems to inspire new generations of artists: in 2011 a site-specific performance of *Perfect Lives* was staged by the performance group Varispeed, a collective of composer-performers, in Brooklyn in June, and as *Perfect Lives Manhattan* in November. The latter production was presented as part of the Performa 11 festival. This production—as

Steve Smith remarked in the *New York Times*—"was less an act of rescuing a work from oblivion than one of repurposing its materials to unleash latent potential, while remaining faithful to its textural integrity and structural rigor" (Smith 2011). In addition, in December 2011, a new Spanish version of the television opera, called *Vidas Perfectas* and directed by Alex Waterman in cooperation with Robert Ashley, opened in Brooklyn. Beside the live performances of *Vidas Perfectas*, which will be presented in several phases over the next few years, there will be a television production of this Spanish version of the opera that will also be released on DVD.[9]

Another example of a media opera I will briefly introduce is *Three Tales* (1998-2002) by the composer Steve Reich and video artist Beryl Korot.[10] *Three Tales* was co-commissioned by various noted festivals and premiered in May 2002 in Vienna with musicians of the Ensemble Modern and the Synergy Vocals, conducted by Brad Lubman and directed by Nick Mangano.[11]

Steve Reich calls *Three Tales* a documentary digital video opera in which "historical film and video footage, video taped interviews, photographs, texts, and specially constructed stills are created on the computer, transferred to video tape and projected on one large 32-foot screen. Sixteen musicians and singers take their place onstage below the screen" (Reich and Korot 1998-2002). The musicians and singers all perform synchronously with the video via the conductor. By means of three well known events from the twentieth century—the crash of the zeppelin Hindenburg in Lakehurst in 1937, the Atom bomb tests at Bikini atoll 1946-1954, and the cloning of an adult sheep in Scotland in 1997 as well as genetic engineering and robotics—the opera is presenting a debate about the physical, ethical and religious nature of technological development.

Although there are singers and instrumentalists present at the performance, the screen functions as the predominant space of performance. Whereas *Perfect Lives* leaves the operatic stage altogether, *Three Tales* keeps some of the inherited operatic conventions such as, for example, the—at least partial—co-presence of audience and performers. However, the singers neither incorporate the characters on the screen or play-act on stage, nor do they interact visually with the people and events on screen. Rather, there are almost continuous interactions between live elements and mediatised elements on the level of the music, between the live orchestra and the live singing and the pre-recorded sounds and samples.[12] Thus, the audiovisual elements function as an essential part of the performance.

OPERA: PROBLEMS OF CONCEPTUALISATION

The idea that a media opera or especially a television opera is not really an opera is a more or less reproachful objection many contemporary opera composers know very well.[13] That is why I would like to delve deeper into some of the limitations of the term "opera" when it comes to experimental forms and media. A closer look at common definitions of opera and music theatre and their shortcomings may illustrate the need for a systematic theoretical attempt to come to terms with this problem. Often being applied without theoretical reflection, the two terms "opera" and "music theatre" are frequently used synonymously, though with "opera" carrying more conventional connotations and "music theatre" a more progressive/experimental touch. Both words function as umbrella terms with implicit connotations regarding historical repertoire, apparatus and institutional frame, scale etc., and the currency of the term "music theatre" generally relates to all kinds of combinations of music and scene, as a synonym for director-dominated opera, "to characterize a kind of opera and opera production in which spectacle and dramatic impact are emphasised over purely musical factors" (Clements 1998: 528), and for particular manifestations and (counter-)concepts of opera presented since the 1960s. On the other hand, a well-founded systematic classification based on explicit criteria is still lacking:

> The present position is that "opera" is to some extent an evaluative term, used to refer to sung drama which is either "serious" enough, or traditional enough in form and technique, to be staged in an opera house. (Williams 1998: 676)

During the second half of the twentieth century, more and more works have emerged that defy even those very vague classification strategies and make the definition of opera even more complicated. They do so especially by including audiovisual media, new performance spaces, virtual design and a re-definition of the parameters of narrativity, words, music, scene and space. In particular, works that fundamentally rely on electronic or digital media seem to challenge what is commonly understood as opera. Thus, it seems to be appropriate to broaden the perspective of opera as an art form towards a notion of opera as a social and cultural practice.

OPERA AS A SOCIAL AND CULTURAL PRACTICE

Some media operas such as *Perfect Lives* not only integrate audiovisual media on a conceptual level but also leave the theatre stage and its conditions of communication between actors, musicians and audience. In those works the mediality of the traditional theatre with its physical co-presence of performers and audience is replaced by the communication situation of—for example—television or cinema. As numerous and sometimes unsuccessful attempts to classify opera illustrate, one crucial question within its discourse is that of perspective: discussing opera always requires us to identify which aspect of the term "opera" is the focus. As very rough distinctions, we can differentiate between opera as an institution, opera as a cultural practice and opera as an art form. Of course these perspectives overlap and interrelate but serve as a heuristic demarcation. Up to this point the focus of this chapter has been on the use of the term as an art form, and has largely ignored the implications of opera as a social and cultural practice, with specific institutional requirements and traditions. However, taking the mediality of many works into account I would follow Bernard Williams' comment that opera is somehow an evaluative term. Consequently, the following thoughts are based on the hypothesis that the prevalent "problem" of the term being applied to media operas is closely connected to the dimension of opera as a cultural practice.

According to Stuart Hall and his statement about the importance of the social field in which cultural symbols are integrated (Hall 1981), opera (as with any other cultural object) gets its meanings and qualities only from its social and cultural contexts. Thus the implicit social connotations of opera come into focus and underline Williams' remarks quoted above that the term "opera" refers to sung drama which is either serious enough, or traditional enough to be staged in an opera house. What he says illustrates how closely classifications are bound to our concepts of society and "high" culture. Opera seems to be a quintessential example of culture as a means of self-assurance, consolidating the status quo as opposed to challenging existing dynamics in an ongoing process of cultural evolution.

The particular communicative strategies of different kinds of media opera suggest that any opposition to the term "opera" in connection with—for example—television operas cannot be answered coherently on the level of the art form. Rather, what these operas call into question is the formerly unquestionable connection between the art form, the institution, and the cultural and social practice of going to the opera.

RÉSUMÉ: WHAT MAKES MEDIA OPERAS PRODUCTIVE?

The mediality of each of these works and the afore-mentioned early media operas differs significantly in terms of its liveness, the extent of its mediatisation and the existing/non-existing physical co-presence of singers/actors and audience. What they share is an allegiance to audiovisual media on a conceptual level and the abandonment of most medial conventions of the operatic stage. Media operas challenge a seemingly central although hardly mentioned implicit premise concerning opera: the liveness of its performance in the sense of its temporal simultaneity and the physical co-presence of the production and perception processes. Opera seems, by unanimous agreement, to be identified as a form of theatre. This widespread perspective appears to derive from historical forms of the past, and has the consequence that only works corresponding to those conventional associations can be considered—and valued—as "operas". Further, many attempts to grasp what the term "opera" actually means either take the theatrical stage and its conditions of communication for granted or ignore the mediality altogether. Dimensions of opera include (vocal) music, narrativity and *mise en scène*, but also the often neglected dimension of mediality, of the terms and conditions of communication between production and reception process. Opera—according to the common assumption—requires a physical co-presence between performers and audience. Nevertheless, this seemingly unshakable pre-requisite has already been questioned in numerous experiments with video- and internet-based performance. With the advent of electronic media, composers also started to challenge the theatrical stage as the natural location of opera, and with it the mediality of opera.

Media operas undermine the implicit assumption of opera *as* theatre and raise the question of whether the mediality of the theatre must be considered a pre-requisite of opera. Or, to put it differently: if you leave the theatre stage and its conditions of communication between actors, musicians and audience and replace it by those of, for instance, television or video, does that "deny" these works the essential "seriousness" of opera mentioned above by Williams? After taking a closer look at the phenomenon of media opera and the terminological difficulties concerning the term "opera", it seems that the mediality of a work cannot serve as a distinctive feature for the question of whether or not a work "deserves" the label "opera". Thus I would argue that the difference between them is not so much one between old and new forms, or between conventions and the avant-garde, but one of medial possibilities and limitations. The developments of the last century have revealed that opera—as with any art form—is historically contingent and that it is by no means restricted to the theatrical stage and to theatrical forms and conventions of the operatic stage. Instead, opera seems to be very active in enabling new forms that rest upon medial conditions that are closer to those of, for example, television and film than to the theatre and the (classical) operatic apparatus. The medial experiments of composers and producers—regardless of their respective successes—are evidence of the additional potential this art form has stood to gain thanks to new medial possibilities. The question of whether these forms are perceived as operas depends on their individual transition from unmarked to marked space, i.e., whether or not they have enough elements that are familiar to the context of opera.

In summary, media operas bring into focus an often neglected element of the form: its terms and conditions of communication, or mediality. In addition, these works draw attention to many of our implicit preconceptions about what opera should look like, ideas that we usually take for granted. In particular, this includes the ongoing question of what the term "opera" actually means. We tend to take the historical forms and their mediality as more or less rigid templates for the evaluation of contemporary developments, although we live today in a world that favours modes of communication totally different from those of 200 or 300 years ago. In most contexts, the term opera seems automatically to suggest categories deriving from historic forms of the past; consequently, only those works that correspond to conventional associations are considered to be operas. The indignation of the audience member mentioned at the beginning of this article that a television opera was not opera any more illustrates how opera—as opposed to the term music theatre that is often associated with provoking new forms—seems to fulfill a need for a reliable generic model. As Eric Fischer states from a discourse analytical perspective, opera in the more conventional sense—regarding the repertoire of the opera houses and conventional cultural practice—serves as a tool of cultural self-reassurance.[14] Having this in mind, it becomes clear in what way media operas are potentially provocative—largely irrespective of their musical language or their subject matter but merely because their mediality is significantly affecting the social and cultural contexts of a well-established cultural practice and its institutions. Media operas are just one example of how new works that challenge traditional definitions and concepts urge us to find a systematic approach to deal with operas that sit outside the existing, mainly historical categories. Thus, the idea of media operas can serve as a very productive tool with which to take a closer look at our "blind spot", at our underlying, often barely reflected premises and expectations concerning opera. Furthermore, their potential to challenge received opinion can help opera studies to become a discipline that increasingly incorporates the differing perspectives on opera as an art form, an institution, and a social and cultural practice.

NOTES

[1] How close the historic ties between the radio and the opera are, is underlined by the fact that the first public radio broadcast was an experimental transmission of a concert from the Metropolitan Opera House in New York City in January 1910.

[2] Generally, opera played an important role in the history of television itself: only eleven days after the very first broadcast by the BBC in November 1936, the British radio station broadcast scenes from Albert Coates' *Mr. Pickwick* from Covent Garden.

[3] See Barnes 2003.

[4] See Nicholls 1998: 533.

[5] The first virtual opera is Tod Machover's *Brain Opera* which the composer designed in 1996 at the Massachusetts Institute of Technology Media Laboratory, allowing members of the audience to be either present during the performance or connected through the internet. Another example of a digital opera is the "*Virtualis-Project*", which enables the user on his/her personal computer to interact with musical fragments, text and graphical 3D elements. For more information about this opera see Bonardi/Rousseaux 2002. Although digital and virtual operas can be called media operas, they raise extra questions concerning the role of the composer, the participation of the user, and the significance of the music. Hence, these operas will not be discussed in detail in this chapter. However, a special issue of the *International Journal of Performance Arts and Digital Media* (Spring 2012) deals with *Digital opera: new means and new meanings*.

[6] Concerning this matter, Ashley states: "For me it's almost impossible to make anything interesting if I make it by myself. I have to have a band—a group of people—to make music with" (Ashley 1991: 152).

[7] Video by John Sanborn, video synthesis and video tape editing by Dean Winkler.

[8] See Ashley 1991: 163.

[9] Whereas Robert Ashley starred in the original version as the narrator Raoul de Noget, the performing cast of this version will consist of Ned Sublette (as Raoul de Noget), Elio Villafranca (as "Buddy, the world's greatest piano player"), Elisa

Santiago and Abraham Gomez-Delgado. The composer Peter Gordon—who already collaborated with Robert Ashley on the original version of *Perfect Lives*, will return as music producer.

[10] This opera is very well documented on the composer's homepage: see Reich and Korot 1998-2002.

[11] A CD/DVD version of *Three Tales* was released by Nonesuch in 2003.

[12] Since the mediality of the performances of *Three Tales* was similar to that of a film, the composer stated in a public discussion after the premiere in Vienna in 2002: "It's just as much a movie as an opera. Maybe it's more a movie with a live soundtrack—a highly theatrical presentation of a movie" (Reich 2002).

[13] As Robert Ashley states: "The problem is that you don't have any words. I wish I had a different word so I didn't have to use the word opera because that causes a lot of confusion" (Ashley 2001: 7). The composer Mikel Rouse noted, "I have been very lucky with my pieces, but to be honest they could be much more successful if I didn't call them operas. [...] The answer is that if you think of opera in its truest sense in terms of scale and the goal to merge all the arts together, my pieces are operas. I am not just playing around with the word—it's what comes closest to describing what these pieces are" (Rouse cited by Blue 2002).

[14] See Fischer 1999: 99.

CHAPTER 2

A NEW GLIMMER OF LIGHT:
OPERA, METAPHYSICS AND MIMESIS

NICHOLAS TILL

Throughout the four hundred years of its existence opera is the art form that has, above all others, served to inscribe or figure some of the fundamental concepts of Western metaphysics. As Gary Tomlinson writes, opera's history may be seen as "the changing audible perception of a supersensible realm" (Tomlinson 1998: 5). In this chapter I want to suggest that the metaphysics of opera is ideologically overdetermined, and that any operatic practice that continues to subscribe to such metaphysics ignores the predominately anti-metaphysical tendencies of modern thought from Nietzsche through phenomenology and positivism to structuralism and post-structuralism. The implicit metaphysics of opera, which still haunt the form, are therefore maintained within a culture whose structures and thought systems no longer sustain such a metaphysics. To some extent this exercise brings up to date Adorno's still unaddressed pronouncements on the impossibility of opera after Wagner. Adorno also considered opera to be an inherently metaphysical form. But he was equally aware that the "glimmer of light that falls into the prison" that is offered by operatic metaphysics is merely illusory in an increasingly rationalised and instrumentalised culture, rendering the condition of opera in the twentieth century fundamentally aporetic (Adorno 1999: 21).

The ideological implications of operatic metaphysics are in general so engrained within the form that composers of the postwar avant garde who rejected the aesthetico-ideological apparatus of western art music tended to avoid opera altogether, seeking alternative ways of combining the musical and theatrical media from which opera is made. This anti-operatic tendency continues to fuel the energy of some of the most interesting contemporary forms of music theatre. But at the conclusion of this chapter I shall consider the work of three contemporary composers who, in related ways, appear to have found a way to re-engage critically with the formal apparatus of opera without being sucked back into its metaphysical sloughs, and whose work might be characterised as post-operatic rather than simply operatic or anti-operatic.

For Gary Tomlinson operatic metaphysics is intimately linked to modern ideologies of subjectivity and autonomy. Since in modern social and economic systems subjectivity and autonomy are at best epiphenomena of the systems that bring them into being, an art form based uncritically upon a metaphysics of irreducible subjectivity must be questionable. But the critique of metaphysics in modern western thought is more extensive than this, undermining all kinds of essentialism and universalism and exposing the binary ways of thinking that sustain such thought. In the arguments of Roland Barthes or Jacques Derrida, following Nietzsche, the pervasive metaphors of inside/outside, presence/absence, centre/periphery, fullness/emptiness upon which western metaphysics is built are brought into question. For Barthes and Derrida (amongst others), the concept of an irreducible human subjectivity based upon a distinction between invisible interiority (true) and visible exteriority (illusory) offers a persistent grounding for such a metaphysics. And both Barthes and Derrida also draw attention to the way in which figurations of the human voice have repeatedly served (as in both Aristotle and Hegel) as a metonym for interiority, the soul, and hence to the thread that links human subjectivity to the supersensible (Barthes 1984; Derrida 1967).

Tomlinson historicises his concept of the supersensible, showing that such notions always demarcate the subject's ontological relationship to the world. Tomlinson demonstrates how the location of the supersensible changes from the Renaissance to modernity, charting a passage that takes in Renaissance neo-platonism, the body-soul dualisms of Cartesian philosophy, the unknowable Kantian noumenon and the no less noumenal entities of Marxist exchange value and the Freudian unconscious. Tomlinson locates this supersensible realm in a number of places within the economy of operatic form: in the implied relation of cosmic, human and musical harmony in early opera; in the rift between language and meaning in seventeenth-century French opera; in the more general envoicing of a hidden interior subjectivity through the orchestra evident in late eighteenth-century, romantic and neo-romantic opera; in the invisible forces that determine the destinies of the characters in Wagner's music dramas.

A metaphysics of operatic form is, above all, essential to Wagnerian theory, in which music serves as the medium that reconciles the antinomies of the expressive "subjective" and the formal "universal" of art. In the discussion that follows I am using "Wagner" as a synecdoche for most late and neo-romantic opera, since, as Roger Parker has suggested, Wagner articulated many assumptions that other composers and critics broadly take for granted.[1] Wagner sets out to meet what Anthony J. Cascardi calls the fundamental challenge of modernity, which, having overthrown supernatural and traditional authority, must legitimate its new intellectual structures, demonstrating that they are necessary rather than contingent by proving their "essential" and "universal" nature (1992: 5). But it must also locate these universals within a human subject that is, in Derrida's words, a "self-present substance" that is "conscious and certain of itself" (1996: 97). In relation to music the concept of absolute music (autonomous; instrumental rather than vocal; formally self-justifying) that emerged at the end of the eighteenth century becomes the founding principle of musical modernity, offering a grounding of music in abstract forms that were supposed to replicate the structures of human consciousness. For Wagner, as for Hegel, music was above all the realm of interiority and subjectivity. But, unlike Hegel, Wagner had also to establish that music was not *merely* subjective, describing Beethoven's final symphony as "the redemption of Music from out of her own peculiar element into the realm of *universal Art*" (Wagner 1993: 54).

Hegel considered that the pure interiority of music meant that it lacked substance: "subjective inwardness constitutes the principle of music. But the most inward part of the concrete self is subjectivity as such, not determined by any content" (Hegel 1975: 320). Wagner also found that although Beethoven had liberated music to be itself, absolute music was at the same time dangerously empty (even if its emptiness was the guarantee of its universality). Music's sphere was that of "purest ideality", but "through her displaying herself as nothing but pure Form, —so that whatever threatened to disturb the latter, either fell away of itself or had to be held aloof from her... [she] might easily pass current for a mere agreeable toy" (Wagner 1995a: 154). In

Wagner's account of the development of music, Beethoven's choral conclusion to the Ninth Symphony, described as "a redoubtable leap from instrumental into vocal music" (*ibid*.:111) was a halfway step to music drama that Beethoven had been forced to take because of the emptiness of his music on its own. Wagner will follow Beethoven's pointer to music drama to restore content to music.

The autonomy of music is also exemplified for Wagner in the musical excesses of *bel canto* opera, in which a composer like Rossini can be seen, paradoxically, as the counterpart to Beethoven to the extent that drama serves Rossini simply as a peg for his musical exuberance. For Wagner, music must be a means to the end of drama and not vice versa. But although music aspires to the condition of drama, Wagner also needs to maintain a degree of autonomy for music so that it can serve to universalise the dramatic action. The orchestra therefore represents "the sphere of absolute music" in music drama (1995a: 77), conveying "endless, universal feeling" (1993: 102). Wagner has then to demonstrate that his return to the semantics of representational music in music drama, founded on his system of *leitmotifs,* is not merely contingent. And so he must establish a pre-semantic point of origin in which the motivic system can be grounded. Starting with his ideas for an opera called *Siegfried's Death*, Wagner famously worked backwards, building the rest of the tetralogy to explain the events that culminated in what became the conclusion to the *Ring* cycle, *Götterdämmerung*. His own explanation was that he needed to pre-empt the necessity for long narrative expositions—although given the preponderance of such expositions in the completed *Ring* this is hardly convincing. Thomas Mann suggested instead that Wagner had to invent a "prehistory"—his own myth of origin grounded in nature—for his leitmotivic system:

> He could not step into the music *in medias res*, for the music required its own prehistory, just as deep-rooted as that of the drama [...]. Back to the beginning, to the beginning of all things [...] It was not just the music of myth that he, the poet-composer would give us, but the very myth of music itself. (Mann 1985: 188-9)

For Wagner the music must be both autonomous (i.e., neither dependent upon socially agreed conventions of meaning nor contingent upon the dramatic action) and meaningful; to achieve this Wagner plays a wily game of *mise-en-abîme* in his deferrals of an absolute point of origin in *The Ring*. The cycle starts with a musical beginning that suggests both the very beginning of the world and, as Thomas Mann put it, the beginning of music: a low E flat, so low that it is barely audible, from which arises an ascending triad. Sandra Corse describes this moment as an allegory of the Hegelian process of individuation when the original self-identity of mind and matter turns to self-consciousness: the low E flat is sufficient unto itself, but the notes of the triad are also part of its own harmonic series, so that the primal rumble of the opening contains the material for its own antithesis, as "melody distinguishes itself from harmony and becomes a thing" (Corse 1990: 72-4). In narrative terms Wagner's temporal structure is more complicated, for after this primal opening it is revealed that there are already Rhinemaidens, dwarves, giants and gods populating the world; either the opening depicted the aeons between the beginning of the world and the moment in which the story begins, or it was merely a local beginning. Either way it then transpires that the opening may have been preceded in Wagner's historical mythology by the Earth Goddess Erda, whose motif when she appears later in the drama is clearly related to the opening Rhine music, and is described by Thomas Grey as being "recoined in a slow, darkened version" that "characterises Erda as an emanation of primal, natural forces" (2008: 99). Musical beginnings are not necessarily historical beginnings; the impossibility of creating meaning from nothing is pre-empted by the fiction of "that which went before" without actually coming before in performance time.

Perhaps Wagner could have saved himself such laborious sleight of hand. For although one narrative of the history of music (including Wagner's) tells of the emancipation of autonomous music, historically, opera may be said to have been one of the means whereby music had already semanticised itself before it could lay claim to autonomy. Nietzsche explained this very well when he wrote that "'Absolute music' is [...] symbolism of form speaking to the understanding without poetry after both arts had been united over a long course of evolution and the musical form had finally become entirely enmeshed in threads of feeling and concepts" (1986: 99). Musicologists such as Tomlinson and Daniel Chua (and indeed Nietzsche, *ibid.*: 101) suggest that the function of opera in the late Renaissance was primarily to humanise and semanticise a secularised music that had cut itself adrift from theological grounding. Susan McClary goes further when she demonstrates that this process of humanisation effects some very specific kinds of cultural work, defining rhetorical tropes for the gendering of musical gestures (1991). Having been thus semanticised, music may then assume its role as signifier of the supersensible, ideal or ineffable, thereby naturalising and universalising its newly acquired semantic meanings in an act of concealed signification. This is the process of ideological mythologisation, by which, according to Roland Barthes, "myth transforms history into nature [...] transforms meaning into form" (1973: 131). Nietzsche recognised this process, noting that "certain metaphysical presuppositions bestow much greater value upon art, for example, when it is believed that the character is unalterable and that all characters and actions are a continual expression of the nature of the world" (1986: 105).

Despite Nietzsche's warning, this process of mythologisation continues to be evident not only in opera, but in much critical writing on opera. In *Opera: The Extravagant Art* Herbert Lindenberger, for instance, suggests that:

> To the extent that the composer subjects human actions to the tight logic of musical form and seems to raise these actions to a mythical, more universal level than they achieve through purely verbal expression, opera impresses its audiences as ultimately more philosophical than spoken drama. (Lindenberger 1984: 56)

This universalisation/naturalisation of meaning sustains itself only by concealment: literally so in Wagner's case. Wagner's hiding of the orchestra at Bayreuth effaces the material production of the music: the music is now not the effect of physical effort but emanates from an otherworldly space. By displacing attention from the working musicians in the pit to the singers on stage, who inhabit a fictional space, Wagner brings about a phenomenal separation even as he insists upon the synthesis between music and drama. In effect, we might say that Wagner needs the very obvious physical materiality of the stage action for the orchestral music to perform its transcendent function. And he needs the dramatic narrative to provide the music with the meaning that it is supposed to lack, even if the content is always being sucked back down from the stage into the universalising machinery of the invisible orchestra. Nietzsche once noted that to achieve the modern way of experiencing music purely formally "a number of senses, especially the muscle senses, have been immobilised" (1998: 83). This is evident in Wagner's discussions of the relationship of music and gesture. In *Opera and Drama* Wagner claims that the meaningfulness of melody derives from its original association with bodily gesture; what gesture shows to the eye, melody communicates to the ear. But gesturally-derived melody must then be abstracted by the orchestra in a way that conceals its bodily-gestural origins (1995b: 319).

The metaphysical assumptions of operatic form seem to be inescapable, which does not mean that they are actual. A number of recent theorists of opera have dismantled the assumptions underpinning operatic metaphysics. Taking a deconstructive turn in her book *Unsung Voices* Caroline Abbate suggests that the convention that the musical world that the operatic character inhabits is in some sense "unheard" to him or her—what she describes as "noumenal"—is constantly punctured by the irruption of phenomenal—or "heard"—music in opera (as when a character such as Cherubino consciously sings a song, or when characters hear, or dance to, dance music on stage). Abbate also points out that even where the unheard music may not be positing an obviously metaphysical realm it is often given a particular authority as the voice of the omniscient narrator, the composer, who uses the orchestra to convey truths that are unknown to the characters themselves. Conventionally, Abbate suggests, such music is endowed with the "capacity to speak the ineffable and otherwise unknowable": "We generally assume that the message conveyed by that music—whatever form it takes—possesses absolute moral authority, that whatever falsehoods are spoken by the character, the music will speak across and thus expose the lies" (1991: 157). But Abbate also questions this assumption when she insists that the possibility of musical meaning arises from context; there is no essential realm of "truth" to which music has privileged access.

> When the Countess pardons the Count in Act 4 of *The Marriage of Figaro*, it is not that Mozart's music simultaneously gives voice to some more profound statement of or about forgiveness. Rather, it is the fact that there is a Countess, a Count, a specific dramatic situation, and ordinary words like "Contessa, perdono" sung out loud that has in quite precise ways predetermined the meaning to attach to Mozart's musical moment. (2004: 522)

And Abbate goes on to insist that "such phenomena undermine romantic notions about music's overriding force, seen as the power to do more than the verbal and the visible, to convey something beyond them, to transcend and survive their limits".

For Wagner the autonomy of music had rendered it incomplete; music (figured as needily female) required language and dramatic gesture to fulfil its potentiality. And the masculine word and dramatic action similarly needed the fertile womb of music to make them complete. As Laurence Kramer puts this belief: "to make anything more itself just add music" (2002: 4). Since the visual and linguistic sign are always depleted by absence, music seems to restore lived presence to what Kramer calls the "depleted image-text". But Kramer insists there is always a remainder that is "irreducibly ambiguous: always both gap *and* excess, lack *and* substance, it is a positive kernel of non-sense that keeps us coming back to the artwork" (*ibid.*: 171). This kernel of non-sense is what we may call the deconstructive rather than the metaphysical ineffable. In his book *Analysing Musical Multimedia*, Nicholas Cook offers some alternative explanations for the way in which music works in relation to other media. Most of the book is concerned with the relationship of music to film, but in one section Cook deals briefly with opera. And like other recent theorists such as Parker and Abbate, he wants to argue that the specific effectiveness of the different media of opera depends not upon their congruence but upon their friction. Cook cites a number of examples of critical assumptions that opera works best where there is "conformance" between music and drama, and shows that they inherently assume a priority of one or other of the media in play (e.g., that the music should, in some sense, "express" the pre-existent dramatic action or character, as if we could know what the dramatic action or the character *really* are without the mediations that occur through language or music). That which doesn't obviously conform is labelled as "dramatic irony" (1998: 98-126).

What is notable about Cook's discussion is that although Cook himself has challenged the way that musicologists have traditionally reified the musical score to encourage consideration of the more ephemeral aspects of performance, his discussion does not take into account the embodied nature of the media at work in opera: of the presence of musicians and singers in actual spaces, and their relationship to each other. In Cook's analysis "music" and "drama" are in some sense hypostatised as distinct media, rather than as media that (usually) share the common attribute of embodiment. Moreover, in a performance we don't usually experience "music" and "drama" or "music" and "words" perceptually as distinct elements that are in some sort of adjunct relationship to each other. In a song (and to some extent in opera) as listeners we more likely carve the joint not between words and music but between the sung words (or words and action in opera) and the instrumental accompaniment—as Wagner knew very well. But clearly there are other joints that we may not necessarily experience perceptually unless they are obviously disjunctive: "text" and "performance", for instance, whose relationship preoccupies interpreters, but may not be evident to an audience until there are obvious contradictions between the evidence of their ears and their eyes (reference to a sword when a character is clearly carrying a gun in an updated production). Moreover, the media in play are themselves not always perceived as unitary. In her study of subjectivity in modern opera Sandra Corse suggests that musical production and singing are already "self-divided" between their embodied materiality and the effect of immateriality, arguing that despite its clearly physical production "the voice is oddly dematerialized, projected out of the body" (2000: 20). In other words, not only is there a powerful naturalised metaphysics at work in the conventional forms of opera, but that metaphysics is sustained by concealment, and is moreover constantly at risk of being undermined by the intervention of rogue elements (such as "phenomenal" music) or the actual material constituents of the form. Wagner became increasingly aware of this as he struggled to realise his ideas theatrically, eventually expressing his horror of "all those costumed, stuffed creatures" on the stage, and famously suggesting that "after creating the invisible orchestra I would like to invent the invisible theatre!" (Wagner, C. 1977: 181-2).

Nietzsche attempted to imagine a non-metaphysical form of opera, and proposed Bizet's *Carmen* as an example, praising its frank sensuality and its cruel fatalism in contrast to the steamy idealism and redemptive narratives of Wagnerian opera (1899: 7). Nietzsche claimed, disingenuously perhaps, that it was "not solely out of sheer wickedness that I praise Bizet at the expense of Wagner" (*ibid.*: 1); Adorno felt no need to disclaim his own malice when he endorsed Nietzsche's reading of *Carmen*, arguing that in contrast to the metaphysics of Wagnerian redemption there is no transcendence in Bizet's characterisation of fate in *Carmen*. Fate is animal sexuality, pure and simple: "this prohibition on transcendence destroys the illusion that nature is anything more than mortal" (1998: 63). Other critics have noted the multiple voicings of Carmen herself, who often speaks (or sings—the ambiguity is deliberate) through assumed musical styles, not to convey the "metaphysical preconceptions" of the ambiguity between essence and appearance, as Adorno puts it, but to suggest a character whose essence *is* appearance—although, of course, Bizet contrasts Carmen's exteriority to the more typically operatic (and bourgeois) interiority of Jose and Micaela. But the epigones of romantic opera today continue to offer metaphysical fictions of subjectivity based upon self-presence and wholeness, conveyed through the unchallenged lyric voice. As we have seen, in Wagner's work, the expression of subjectivity lies at the core of music's contribution to drama since music conveys authentic feelings (whether known or unknown to the dramatic character) which have otherwise been made "unintelligible to ourselves by State-politics or religious dogmas" (1995b: 264). And for Wagner, singing is the means whereby music itself is humanised through the outpouring of the singer's feelings in melody (*ibid.*: 309). One of the effects of such singing, true perhaps of all modes of western art singing, is that it offers the illusion of the coherence of the subject. We hear this typically in the sought-after legato of the classically trained voice, able to hold itself together despite the depredations of linguistic articulation and musical excess. For Wagner it is indeed the vowel, or the "open sound", that, as the bearer of the melodic legato, represents "the whole *inner organism* of man's living body", whilst it is the consonant that acts as representative of the exterior social forms of language (*ibid.*: 266, 272).

But modernity does not in fact support subjectivities based upon uniqueness, boundedness, innerness, wholeness and autonomy, neither in the depersonalised mass identities and the fragmentation of the human subject's faculties in an instrumentalised society, nor in the era of post-Fordist consumerist post-modernity, in which subjectivity is recognised to be inherently inter-subjective, plural, and constructed. The fiction of autonomous subjectivity is indeed recognised as such in some of the key moments of twentieth-century modernist culture, since modernism is primarily a response to the alienations of capitalist-industrial society, and to the ideologies of liberal humanism that attempt to mask that reality. Modernist music "refuses to communicate the homely traces of the humane" says Adorno, which stems "from a correct perception of the reified alienation and depersonalisation of the destiny imposed on mankind [...]. Every self-righteous appeal to humanity in the midst of inhuman conditions should be viewed with the very greatest suspicion" (Adorno 1998: 256, 265). This does not mean that autonomous human subjectivity should not be an aspiration; simply that the conception of subjectivity that we have inherited from bourgeois liberalism is ideologically suspect, and, as Katherine Hayles has put it, "may have applied, at best, to that fraction of humanity who had the wealth, power and leisure to conceptualise themselves as autonomous beings exercising their will through individual agency and choice" (1999: 5, 286).

Modernist art movements respond in several related ways to the alienating forces of modernity. They may directly acknowledge and represent these forces, either celebrating the anti-humanism of modernity in an aesthetics of the machine and technology, or representing its alienations as such (as in Adorno's characterisation of authentic art). Or they may seek to defend art against the instrumental, reifying forces of modernity, safeguarding the autonomy of art by rejecting anything outside the aesthetic, turning to an objective abstraction that refuses the human in either expression or representation. In each instance the tendency is clearly anti-humanist: writing in 1925 the Spanish philosopher Ortega y Gasset tellingly gave his study of modernist art movements the title *The Dehumanization of Art* (Gasset 1968).

In the first camp the Futurists proclaimed the new machine aesthetics of modernity as a liberation from the sentimental humanist premises of previous arts. Marinetti proclaimed that "masses of molecules and whirling electrons are more exciting than the smiles or tears of a woman" (1971: 87). The machine ideology of Futurism is replicated by theatre artists such as Edward Gordon Craig or Vsevolod Meyerhold, who both sought to reduce the actor to a machine, as in Craig's theory of the *Über-marionette* or in Meyerhold's constructivist biomechanics. The anti-humanism of modernism is equally evident in music. Futurist musicians also dismissed romantic musical humanism, calling instead for an art of noise that would convey the sounds of the everyday urban world (Russolo 1973: 74-88). Soviet composers influenced by Futurism imitated the sounds of factories, and in 1924 Antheil and Léger collaborated on the film *Ballet Mécanique*, for which Antheil's music was composed for mechanical and percussion instruments. In 1926 Schoenberg expressed the view that new forms of musical automata would give the composer direct control over the realisation of his compositions, obviating the need for "primitive, unreliable and unwilling" human interpretation (1975: 328). But the neo-classicism of Stravinsky, and of the German *Neue Sachlichkeit* composers, was equally anti-humanist in intent, seeking a radical objectivity as, in different ways, does Schoenberg's serialism, which is an attempt to establish a set of objectively valid compositional rules for post-tonal music. In the post-World War Two period the second wave of modernism took these tendencies further in *musique concrète*, electronic music, the total serialism developed by Stockhausen and Boulez, and Cagean indeterminacy, whose aim is to let the sounding world speak for itself without human intervention. Subsequent developments such as minimalism and spectralism also imply an extreme objectivity: in minimalism an emphasis upon process rather than communication or expression; in spectralism and related forms upon the microprocesses of sound itself.

The anti-humanism of modernist music clearly presents problems for any form of opera that aspires to employ the languages of modernism to offer the consolations of humanist subjectivity; as Adorno observed, after Schoenberg had dismantled the humanist premises of nineteenth-century music his new serialism conveyed an alienated condition that was inherently tragic, and that was therefore quite unsuited to the domestic comedy of his first serial opera, *Von Heute auf Morgen* (Adorno 1976: 73). The aporia of Schoenberg's uncompleted *Moses und Aron* was that, as Adorno recognised, Schoenberg's dramaturgy remained essentially Wagnerian but that his musical language no longer supported such a dramaturgy or its metaphysics (1998: 245).

Twentieth-century opera composers who recognised and engaged with the condition of modernity, and with the resultant languages of musical modernism, had three valid options. Composers like Debussy, Bartók, Schoenberg, Berg, Shostakovich, Zimmerman or Britten employ dramatic narratives that thematise the alienated subjectivities conveyed by their music, thus still sustaining that aspect of operatic metaphysics that believes that music tells authentic truths about dramatic situations and characters. Composers like Stravinsky, Stockhausen, Birtwistle or Glass resort to the objectifications of myth and ritual, thus calling upon the other side of the metaphysical equation that musical form is able to universalise the contingent, although, unlike in Wagner, there are no longer any autonomous subjects in their operas to universalise. Adorno described this tendency as an "escape to presubjective objectivity" (Adorno 1976: 77), and found a similar belated "theological tendency" in Schoenberg's search for a systematic reconstruction of musical totality in serialism (1998: 232). Berg's resort to established musical structures in *Wozzeck* (suite, passacaglia, symphony) suggests a similar objectification that conveys a reified social world from the understanding of which the characters are excluded. Finally, composers like Stravinsky (in his neo-classical mode), Poulenc, Ligeti or Schnittke employ modernist parody to offer a different kind of alienation, in which the underpinnings of the universal are exposed as historically constructed. Opera is here knowingly trapped inside the now empty shell of an outmoded metaphysics with no way out. We may remember the exchange between the composer Leverkühn and the Devil in Thomas Mann's novel *Doctor Faustus*, an anguished investigation of how modernist anti-humanism led to Nazism, in which Leverkühn suggests the possibility of the composer "playing with forms out of which, as he well knew, life had disappeared", to which the Devil responds: "I know. Parody. It might be fun, if it were not so melancholy" (Mann 1968: 235). Parody is a typical strategy within that strain of modernism that is concerned to show that art can only ever deal with its own procedures, rather than saying anything about the outside world. And despite the evident difference between abstraction and parody, both tendencies are essentially self-referential.

What this surely leaves us with is a situation where composers who continue to work with the "joined-up" musical language and humanist dramaturgies of nineteenth-century opera (or parodies of these) have ensnared themselves in a three-sided trap of bad faith: on one side is an implicit metaphysics that endorses a now obsolete (and ideologically highly suspect) version of subjectivity; on the second side is the fact that this metaphysics is founded upon a system that is itself undermined by its reliance upon the suppression of the phenomenological and material aspects of performance; on the third side is the essential anti-humanism of most forms of modernist and post-modernist music. Moreover, the institutional structures of opera cement these forms—hierarchies of production, architectural fixing of the relationship between stage and orchestra pit, etc.—in a way that means that most artists wishing to explore new forms of music theatre prefer to work outside the straitjacket of the opera house so as to avoid the sticky metaphysical dramaturgies of conventional operatic form altogether.

Many works of post-war anti-operatic music theatre explored the possibility of a different relationship between subjectivity, dramatic action and musical accompaniment upon which the metaphysical

pretensions of opera are based. Instruments are often visible on stage
with the singers, although only a few composers went as far as, say,
Peter Maxwell Davies in *Eight Songs for a Mad King* (1969) in
incorporating the instruments into the narrative of a theatre work.
Most composers working within this genre continue to assume the
invisibility of the instruments they use even when they are visible, and
very few composers consider the physical appearance and cultural
meanings of the instruments they employ, or the performative
presence and gestures of those who play them, all of which are even
more obvious when the instruments are visible. Indeed, there is no
better evidence of the way in which classical western audiences have
been acculturated to ignore the physicality of musical performance. It
is only in more radical forms of anti-operatic music theatre that these
hierarchies, and the metaphysics they conceal, are fundamentally
challenged, whether in Cage's *Water Walk* (1959) that "wishes to be a
piece of music, but [...] can be experienced as theatre" (Kirby and
Schechner 1995: 60), the "instrumental theatre" of Kagel or Globokar,
"staged concerts", "visible music", or Fluxus intermedial events, etc.
In these works the physical presence of the musical instruments, and
of the performers who play them, becomes a signifying property of the
work. However, there is often a literalness in the relationship between
musical and dramatic effect: a duplication of dramatic and musical
idea that leads to redundancy rather than complexity. The depiction of
the tennis match in Kagel's *Match* of 1964 for two cellists (as players)
and percussionist (as umpire) soon ceases to be interesting either
dramatically or musically, and indeed before long Kagel drops the
initial proposition to develop the piece in more abstract, "modernist"
musical terms. It is only when composers like Heiner Goebbels or
Manos Tsangaris develop an extended theatrical language for
instrumental theatre, or when composers or composer-performers
work with unaccompanied voice (such as George Aperghis or
Meredith Monk), that the relationship between the performance
components permits complexity of meanings to arise between the
different elements of performance in a non-hierarchical way that also
acknowledges the material production of the music: the performative
here and now rather than the fictional there or then.

   I have described the predominant tendencies of modernism as
being anti-humanist. Yet at the same time these tendencies often retain
a clearly metaphysical allegiance to the universalising aspects of
musical form. Robert Fink (1999) characterises the "flatness" of

minimalism as offering the most challenging musical critique of the metaphysics of both subjectivity and form from a post-modern perspective—although ironically in minimalist opera the music often suggests a kind of interiority, albeit one of extreme solipsism lacking either development or the possibility of intersubjective relations. But I want now to consider instead a trio of composers whose work maintains a commitment to the critical premises of modernism and modernist music whilst refusing the consolations of the metaphysics of either subjectivity or form. These composers—Helmut Lachenmann, Salvatore Sciarrino and Olga Neuwirth—have all accepted most of the basic conventions of opera (character-based narrative, trained singing voices, the division between the fictional world of the stage and singers and the music that emanates from the "off-stage" instruments), but have re-worked those forms in ways that challenge the metaphysical hierarchies of opera without simply resorting to parody or pastiche. In each case these are composers who are more concerned with the materiality of musical sound in itself— with its production, its timbre, its penumbra, its physical placing in time and space, with the borders between music, sound and noise, even with the mimetic properties of music—than with musical sound's function as a conveyer of subjective expression or meaning, or as a vehicle for supposedly autonomous formal structures.

In the music of Lachenmann (b. 1935) musical production has its own inherent drama. Players visibly and audibly struggle to produce the sounds demanded of them, for in Lachenmann's works musical instruments present obdurate challenges which highlight both the materiality of the musical instrument itself and the hard labour of musical production in a fashion that directly contradicts the occlusion of production and labour in the Wagnerian orchestra. Lachenmann has described his process as *musique concrète instrumentale*,

> in which the sound events are chosen and organized so that the manner in which they are generated is at least as important as the resultant acoustic qualities themselves [...] listening, you hear the conditions under which a sound- or noise-action is carried out, you hear what materials and energies are involved and what resistance is encountered. (Lachenmann 2008)

Lachenmann's only theatrical work, *Das Mädchen mit den Schwefelhölzern* (1997), is based around Hans Christian Andersen's story *The Little Match Girl*, and is categorised as "music with pictures" by the composer. Lachenmann has consistently re-worked

Nicholas Till

historical genres such as the string quartet, believing that this is a more critically engaged option for the contemporary composer than to work with undefined forms. For Lachenmann no genre is more challenging formally, ideologically and institutionally than opera: "the renaissance of listening", he writes, "must always take place in the lion's den [...] and not in the complacently tolerated ghetto of the 'new music scene'" (2002: 41). In particular, Lachenmann knew that he had to engage with what he describes as the "traumatic" question of the singing voice, the most human and subjective of musical instruments, arguing that "a musical understanding that avoids the voice, or even excludes singing, is somehow not quite right" (*ibid.*).[2] In *Das Mädchen* Lachenmann seems determined to confront opera on its own turf, taking Andersen's miniature narrative of Wagnerian transfiguration (at the end of the story the little match girl ascends to heaven in the arms of her dead grandmother) as the basis for an expanded reflection on the ongoing cruelties of the modern world. Andersen's text, interspersed with other related texts, is presented as a narration by a group of vocalists rather than being embodied dramatically. Other aspects of the narrative are presented visually, with no clear privilege being given to one or other medium. Moreover, the text is so fragmented that it serves more as a collection of phonemes, plosives, sibilants and clicks for vocal exploration than as a conveyer of the story, the very materiality of the language blocking its communicative or expressive function. In Roland Barthes' famous essay "The Grain of the Voice" of 1972 Barthes makes a distinction between *pheno-song* ("all the features which belong to the structure of the language being sung [...] everything in the performance which is in the service of communication, representation, expression") and *geno-song* ("the body in the voice as it sings"; the "materiality" of the voice) which foregrounds the properties of the signifier over the linguistic signified, "meaning insofar as it is sensually produced" (Barthes 1984: 182, 184, 188). Lachenmann is clearly more interested in the *geno-song* than the *pheno-song*, highlighting the icy assonances and stabbing dissonances in the language itself as a way of conveying mimetically the glacial cold of the winter night and the chill tremor of the child's body, and metaphorically the no less icy hearts of the bourgeois revellers enjoying their Christmas feasts as the dying child looks in from the street outside.

The instrumental and electronic music for the opera, also no longer attempting to convey the meanings of the text or to mickey-mouse dramatic action, combines violent explosions (and implosions) of compressed energy with long, static tracts of noise and stuttering glitches and erasures that constantly deny the possibility of musical self-presence or structural integrity. Lachenmann believes that "expression is created on the reverse face of that on which the composer is working [...] destruction, deflation, and disintegration. But during this process expressive energy radiates out in the first instance like a creative serenity—freedom even" (Brodsky 2011). Adorno argued that genuine musical "expression" did not rely upon subjective psychologising or intention, insisting that musical forms themselves can be "saturated with expression" (Adorno 2002: 61), and in *Das Mädchen* Lachenmann manages to convey anger at the wrongs of a system that ignores suffering amidst plenty with an expressive intensity that avoids either sentimental identification with the little match girl herself, or evasive universalisation of her plight (as, indeed, does the dispassionate brevity of Andersen's original telling of the tale).

Theatre has been more fundamental to the career of the Italian composer Salvatore Sciarrino (b. 1947) than to Lachenmann. Sciarrino's music sets less heroic but no less demanding challenges than that of Lachenmann; like the late music of Luigi Nono, it often exists on the cusp between sound and silence, interspersing minimal (but often surprisingly fierce) gestures with long pauses that are full of dramatic tension (although these are in this respect unlike the silences of Nono, which seem instead like desolate absences without promise). Sciarrino's sound world is insistently material; the critic Jacopo Schilingi notes that, as in Lachenmann's music, the musical gesture in Sciarrino is always specifically instrumental (quoted in Restagno 2002: 37). Sciarrino himself explicitly dismisses "intellectual music, with its pretensions to universality" (1981), and the construction of his music does, indeed, often seem to be highly intuitive; Sciarrino insists that in his music "the universe of sounds is conceived as if it were living and not as if it is an ensemble of pre-constituted data" (Restagno 2002: 5). As with Lachenmann, it is music that seems to me to conform better than any I know to Adorno's concept of "musique informelle": "a type of music which has discarded all forms that are external or abstract or which confront it in an inflexible way", but which nonetheless constitutes itself "in an objectively compelling way, in the musical substance itself' (1998: 272). Sciarrino's method can seem disingenuously naïve. But his writings reveal a profound

philosopher of musical aesthetics, and like Lachenmann he always
engages with his musical materials conceptually and critically. In the
mid 1990s he declared that "the problem of vocality is central to my
recent production" (Fearn 1997: 213), and in a series of theatre works
written since the mid 1980s he has probed and re-probed this most
evidently worrisome constituent of operatic form. In *Lohengrin*
(1984), an "invisible action" ("invisible" because recounted rather
than shown) based on a scabrous parody of Wagner by the late
nineteenth-century French poet Jules Laforgue, all of the roles in the
drama are envoiced by the female singer who represents Elsa. The
form of the monodrama has been a favourite of modernist composers
since Schoenberg's expressionist masterpiece *Erwartung* (1909),
offering opportunities for extended vocal techniques to convey
extreme psychological conditions. But in Sciarrino's monologues
expression is never achieved. "Elsa" is seated amidst a small group of
musicians. She has a story to tell about a knight called Lohengrin, but
her utterances emerge like those of a medium ventriloquised by
conflicting spirit voices. The boundaries of inside and outside that
conventionally secure subjectivity are further troubled since she also
seems to be possessed by the jostling pathetic fallacies of Laforgue's
ironic narrative: the sounds of doves cooing, gusts of wind, bells
ringing. Where romantic and neo-romantic composers offered the
interpenetration of interior and exterior as a sign, as Raymond Knapp
puts it (2005), of an "intimate connection to the deep worldly
substance through which all such things are united and made to seem
parts of one single thing", or as "a depth shared between
consciousness and the world", in Sciarrino's music such
interpenetration is a sign instead of a porous, and often depleted,
subjectivity. And, as with Lachenmann, singing loses its
transcendence. Close-miked, the performer battles with the material
sludge of vocal production that classical singing seeks to expunge:
gulps, teeth chattering, saliva squelchings, lip pops. Clearly striving
for sustained melodic expression, the joined-up singing that in
operatic terms signifies interiority and self-presence, all she achieves
is to end up trapped inside the melodic loop of a Big Ben carillon.
Many of Sciarrino's characters seem to be thus confined within the
space of pre-linguistic vocality, employing infantile croonings and
babblings, or the religious glossolalia of Santa Maria de'Pazzi in
L'infinito nero of 1998. Such babblings do not suggest Wagner's pre-
linguistic authenticity, as they might have done in the extended vocal

techniques of an expressionist work (or a neo-expressionist work such as *Eight Songs for a Mad King*), so much as a failure to attain, or a desperate desire to fend off, the symbolic order.

In *Perseo e Andromeda* (1990*)*, based on another operatic parody by Laforgue, the self-absorption of Andromeda, who prefers to remain with her guardian dragon on the island which shapes her existence rather than to be rescued by the pasteboard hero Perseus, is conveyed through electronic sounds that construct an acoustic landscape, a barren island of clicks and howling winds. This sonic landscape can also be heard as a projection of the plosives, sibilants and glottals by which speech cuts across the otherwise seamless flows of breath striven for in operatic singing, for in Sciarrino's dramatic music the instrumental sounds often act as a kind of exteriorisation of the physical being of the singers, with the voice joining the instrumental sound world as another manifestation of somatic production. Composers often choose narratives that dramatise their own musical procedures ("musical acts made visible", to use Wagner's term) and here in *Perseo e Andromeda,* Sciarrino seems to find a scenographic expression of his own relationship to sound, silence and the natural world when he describes how in his music

> pulsating islands of sound brush seas of silence. Within this silence we find the sounds of our body, we recognise them as our primeval own and hear the smallest tensions of the intervals as will-o'-the wisps, which—devoid of all drama—light up gestures in the dark. (Quoted in Jahn 2000: 10)

Sciarrino says that he seeks to create "an ecology of listening" (2001: 249), wishing "not to construct the world but to restore its openness" (quoted in Restagno 2002: 10), and there is a sense in which Sciarrino recognises no real difference between the sounds produced by nature and those produced by humans: we hear the wind because it blows through an enclosed space, or across the reeds on a river, in the same way that the blow-hole of a flute or the reed of an oboe produce sounds from human breath, and human performers simply capture and replicate the processes of natural sound production. ("Sounds are Natural Phenomena" is also, tellingly, the title of Lachenmann's reflections on *Das Mädchen mit den Schwefelhölzern*). The Italian critic Enzo Restagno describes how Sciarrino creates "a sonorous universe in which the voice of the wind acquires the mysterious depth of ancient oracles" (2002: 6). Sciarrino recognises that the sounds of nature have, for the human listener, their own symbolic associations,

rather than being inert materials that have to be endowed with
semantic or expressive meaning by the composer.

Luci miei traditrici (1998) appears more like opera as we know it
than any of the quasi-operatic works hitherto discussed. Its text is
derived from a seventeenth-century drama by Giacinto Andrea
Cicognini, one of the most successful librettists of seventeenth-
century Venetian opera, based on the story of the composer
Gesualdo's jealous murder of his wife and her lover. The opera has
what is, in many ways, a conventional dramatic form, and the
relationship between dramatic narrative, character, singing and
musical accompaniment is also typical of operatic form. But Sciarrino
then manages to invert every assumption of the operatic. His secretive,
furtive musical style is figured in his choice of a drama of forbidden
passion and illicit eavesdropping. The opera is constructed as a series
of duets, in which the narcissistic sublation of difference of the
conventional operatic duet is constantly punctured by the voice of an
interloper. Rather than riding on the orchestra, it is the voices that
create the musico-dramatic impetus, the musical instruments offering
a sexuo-somatic aura of quickened pulses and heartbeats, sharp
intakes of breath, fluttering stomachs, rushing juices; acoustic
amplification of the bodily symptoms of passion and fear, which
Sciarrino himself describes as "the imitation or transmission of some
vital sounds of internal physiology [...] —a kind of objectification, a
speechless dramatisation of the heart and breath" (quoted in Jahn
2000: 9). The vocal style alternates between urgent, hushed recitative
and the artifice of an almost Rossinian *bel canto*; tense mutterings
suddenly flower extravagantly (the Italian word for vocal
embellishments is indeed *fioritura*) and then tail away—impulses
towards lyric plenitude that can no longer quite sustain themselves.[3]

The critic Gianfranco Vinay cites Giorgio Agamben's work on
human-animal relations to show how Sciarrino constantly blurs the
distinction between the human and the inhuman in his music (Vinay
2005). He could equally have mentioned Deleuze's and Guattari's
concept of "becoming animal", in which the human subject seeks not
to conquer that which is other than self but to transform the self in the
face of difference—a transformation that recognises both the profound
difference between human and animal (a difference that is occluded
when we anthropomorphise animals), and, given the animality of the
human, the human's essential biological affinity with the animal. This
relationship is exemplified for Deleuze and Guattari in Captain

Ahab's quest for the incommensurable whale in *Moby Dick*, where the whale is never "tamed" by Melville by being reduced to a metaphor or symbol for something other than itself (Deleuze and Guattari 1987: 246-341). Moreover, Deleuze and Guattari equate the state of becoming animal with the state of becoming music, describing the "becomings-animal of music" by which to inhabit music is a kind of dissolution of subjectivity (*ibid.*: 335). We experience more of this relationship between music and animality in the operas of the third of my trio of composers, the Austrian Olga Neuwirth (b. 1968), who, like Lachenmann many years earlier, was a pupil of Luigi Nono. In contrast to the rebarbative stutterings of Lachenmann, and the minimal scratchings and mutterings of Sciarrino, the music of Olga Neuwirth is maximally raucous, luring the listener into bad-trip labyrinths inside which faded memories surface through layers of drugged sleep to be ambushed by outbursts of psychotic ruckus. In Neuwirth's hands, sounds bend and slither underfoot, shapes drift in and out of focus, structures turn dropsical and flaccid, producing the musical equivalent of what the surrealist writer Georges Bataille celebrated as the *informe*, or "formless", in art (see Bois and Krauss 1997). Neuwirth's sound world is also disturbingly creaturely, evoking the skittering of rats beneath the floor, or helpless bleats and whimpers: intimations of animal urges and desires beneath the human surface. For Neuwirth, as for psychoanalytic theorists, the bounds of human subjectivity are constantly assailed by the impulses of such desire, her music conveying the post-human understanding of the subject as dispersed "desiring machine".

Weird, eerie, uncanny are the terms that recur when listening to Neuwirth's music, and she affirms the influence of surrealism, which often invokes a sinister world where things are never quite what they seem: "I always have the feeling with music that you can't touch it, it always escapes you. There's this uncanny thing because it's coming close to you but you can never have it".[4] But the untouchability of her music is not an effect of music's ideality; it is due, rather, to its slippery materiality. Slavoj Žižek talks of "the inertia of the Real" in modernity, where the "Real" must be understood, in Lacanian terms, as those aspects of existence that resist symbolisation: the dead weight of matter; the accumulating detritus of capitalist overproduction; the insistent tug of unacknowledged desires; unexplained feelings of guilt and loss; something sticky on the sole of your shoe. The music critic Ivan Hewett describes Neuwirth's unique ability to conjure "a texture that entrances and disgusts at the same time". Noting the "queasy" character of Neuwirth's music Hewett describes it as "like meat that has become 'high'" (Hewett 2002: 38), surely as vivid an impression of the materiality of the Real as any.

For her first opera, *Bählamms Fest*, written in 1998, Neuwirth turned to a story by the English surrealist painter and writer Leonora Carrington, whose own fierce imagination often drew upon the repressions of the English upper middle-class life within which Carrington grew up. The story was adapted for Neuwirth by the Austrian writer Elfriede Jelinek, best known for her novel *The Piano Teacher* (1983), another savage dissection of bourgeois social hypocrisy and repression. *Bählamms Fest*, described by Neuwirth as "a sadistic family story in scurrilous-surreal snapshots", is set in a Wuthering Heights-like English country house presided over by a tyrannical matriarch where, in Neuwirth's own words, "sadistic ice-age cravings of a psychic nature occur". In the icy wastes outside the house are violence and terror, whilst inside the house the no less frigid coldness of a bourgeois family collapses into "unappeased longings and desire" (Neuwirth 2003: 39), characterised by the metamorphosis of human and animal identities (the cast includes a dog, a werewolf, a spider, a fly, a cooked goldfish, and the skeleton of a rat).

As in so much surrealist art, Neuwirth constantly blurs categories and boundaries: between music, sound and noise; between acoustic and electronic; between vocal and instrumental; between animate and inanimate. These blurrings collapse the distinctions that sustain the metaphysics of subjectivity and its expression in conventional operatic form. She delights in instruments that dirty the purity of musical sound—hawaiian guitar, bavarian zither, ondes martinot or theremin, the latter often morphing into the human voices that they so uncannily resemble. Acoustic instruments employing smudgy multi-phonics mimic the frequencies of electronic sound, a technologising of the human that transgresses more familiar nature-culture distinctions. In *Bählamms Fest* diegetic ("phenomenal", in Abbate's terms) sounds of radio and telephone merge and cross over with the "noumenal" electronic and instrumental sounds. Like many women artists Neuwirth challenges the binary modes of western masculine thinking. The state of "in-between-ness", the blurring of categories and identities, is, Neuwirth suggests, a particular characteristic of female experience. "Women analyse their bodies and identities much more than men. You have to deal with roles that get put on you by society when you're fourteen or fifteen. So you have the feeling that you have several personalities, and that you are both part of nature and yet not".[5] It is this aspect of female experience, the mobile carapaces of social identity inescapably grounded by the female body's ties to nature—its flows and cycles, the insistent ticking of the biological clock—that characterises Neuwirth's music, with its restless, flickering transmutations of energy that constantly exhaust themselves against the entropic drag of time and gravity.

Neuwirth's second opera was an adaptation of David Lynch's neo-noir mystery thriller *Lost Highway* (2003), for which she once again worked with Jelinek as co-adapter for the stage. Lynch's film may be interpreted as a supernatural thriller of parallel universes and eerie *doppelgänger*, or as a psychological study of the condition of amnesiac fugue. Either way its spatio-temporal loops and conundrums and its brooding intensity invite the filmic cutting, spooky atmospherics and memory-defying labyrinths of Neuwirth's music. For *Lost Highway* Neuwirth creates a densely layered score that mirrors the slippages between different realities in Lynch's film, eliding live and pre-recorded orchestral material mixed with everyday soundtrack samples, bewildering the listener with lurching spatial and temporal dislocations. In romantic operas such as Weber's *Der Freischütz*, Meyerbeer's *Robert le Diable* or Wagner's *Der fliegender Holländer* supernatural elements often penetrate the real world, but the fundamental distinction between the natural and supernatural realms is always clear. In Lynch's work we can never disentangle real from unreal, and Neuwirth's score sustains this uncertainty. And like Lachenmann and Sciarrino, Neuwirth works with singing voices as if they were weird distortions of the normal human voice, similar to the micro-tuned scordatura and waa-waa vibrato or glissandi of her instrumental scoring. David Moss, for whom the part of the psychopathic mobster-pornographer Mr. Eddy was conceived, encapsulates the whole range of Neuwirth's vocal techniques in a virtuoso display of grunts, whistles, stutterings and falsetto hoots that are a long way from the seamless expressive legato of classical singing.

The dramatic theorist Peter Szondi described the primary structure of western drama as dialogic—an exploration of human subjects in their interactions with each other (1987). Until the nineteenth century, drama (and by implication opera) rarely engages the relationship of the subject to the non-human world. And when romantic composers *do* convey a symbiosis between human and natural worlds it invariably serves to universalise subjectivity or to anthropomorphise the non-human. The operatic works of Lachenmann, Sciarrino and Neuwirth all seem to present beings whose primary ontological relationship is with the material world (bodily or external) rather than with other human beings, existing within sonic envelopes that form (or sometimes assail) their subjectivity. John Croft has described Sciarrino's music as being "explicitly mimetic", noting how Sciarrino "moves between bodily mimesis and environment", blurring the boundary between them (2009: 33). The term "mimesis" used here by Croft refers to a concept that was a key component of the critical theory of both Walter Benjamin and Adorno.[6] Their use of it remains almost impossibly opaque, whether in its quasi-mystical form in Benjamin's formulations about mimetic modes of language, or in the *mise-en-abîme* contortions of Adorno's recursive refusals of positivity (in the sense of the opposite of negativity), which mean that any tentative gesture towards mimesis in art risks the charge of "positivism" (in the epistemological sense—"the artwork as mere fact", Adorno's critique of collage and montage, 1997: 61), or even the "barbaric literalness" of music that subscribes to what Adorno dismisses as "second naturalism" (*ibid.*), putting its faith in the material of sound itself, which thereby remains as mere "stuff" (1998: 281). For this reason, whilst Adorno admired John Cage's willingness to relinquish control over his material as a refusal of the "complicity of music with the domination of nature" (1998: 315), he considered that Cage's openness to natural sounds and his chance procedures were simply another form of positivism, and a surrender to determinism.

Nonetheless, difficult to pin down as it is, mimesis remains an important critical concept in contemporary theory. Far from being simply a process of constructive representation,[7] for both Adorno and Benjamin mimesis retained something of the archaic magic of resemblance before "ratio" had set in to separate humankind from nature and allow humankind to dominate nature. Mimesis allows engagement with the objectness of the world without abstracting or objectifying it (modes of modern engagement that, for Benjamin and Adorno, were the effect of the reifications of the commodity form under capitalism). As Michael Taussig puts it, citing Benjamin's essay "On the Mimetic Faculty", the mimetic faculty is "the nature that culture uses to create second nature, the faculty to copy, imitate, make models, explore difference, yield into and become the Other" (1993: xiii). For Adorno, mimesis is similarly "the nonconceptual affinity of the subjectively produced with its unposited other" (1997: 54), opening up a sensuous experience of the world in which the western distinction between subject and object is no longer firmly delineated. Rather than dominating nature through conceptualisation or anthropomorphism, in mimesis the human subject opens itself to the otherness of the non-human world. Thus Sciarrino suggests that the late music of Luigi Nono "supposes an openness to others and a reevaluation of subjectivity [...] a sort of journey to an 'elsewhere'" (2001: 250). Indeed, the capacity to open oneself to the non-human other (as also posited by Agamben and Deleuze and Guattari) would seem to be the prerequisite for opening oneself to the reified human other too, since for Adorno

> the subjective spirit which cancels the animation of nature can master a despiritualised nature only by imitating its rigidity and despiritualising itself in turn. Imitation enters into the service of domination inasmuch as even man is anthropomorphized for man. (Adorno and Horkheimer 1973: 57)

Only insofar as humans are able to recognise their affinity to nature as natural beings can the instrumental relationship between humans be overcome.

The mimetic impulse seems to be at work in both Lachenmann and Neuwirth as well as in Sciarrino: in *Das Mädchen* Lachenmann envoices the swirls of icy wind and the matchgirl's repeated striking of her matches to fend off the cold ("riiifff"); in addition to the pervasively "creaturely" aspects of her music Neuwirth presents morphed wolf howlings and the buzzing of flies in *Bählamms Fest*. All three composers share a kind of deliberately naive sonic mimesis of the natural world that is, nonetheless, never merely literal or objective (such that Adorno would have to reject it). Sciarrino, for instance, insists that at the heart of his music is the tension between realism and illusion, a tension that allows a play between the materiality of sound and its mimetic properties, and between imitation and symbolisation (Feneyrou in Restagno 2002: 13). All three composers offer what might be considered a post-human (rather than anti-human) subjectivity grounded in the mimetic faculty. Such a view of the human subject does not perpetuate the transcendent subjectivity of romantic (or neo-romantic) opera, nor does it reify or psychologise the abject subjects of modernity. Instead, awareness of the contingency of the embodied subject and openness to the non-human other makes possible a less dominative attitude to both the natural world (of which humans are inescapably a part) and human others. Following very different dramaturgical methods, and with entirely distinctive musical voices and processes, the post-operatic theatre works of Lachenmann, Sciarrino and Neuwirth seem to affirm that a non-metaphysical opera might be a musical-theatrical form that is capable of conveying different ways of being and of being in the world; that opera might not need be abandoned altogether after all.

NOTES

[1] "The manner in which we all evaluate opera still depends a good deal upon Wagnerian criteria" (Parker 1998: 291).

[2] Translation modified.

[3] John Croft suggests that Sciarrino's vocal *fioritura* in *Luci* may be a kind of distillation of early baroque vocal ornamentation found in music contemporaneous with the narrative, in particular the *ribattuta di gola*, "a slow trill in dotted rhythms". See Croft 2009: 33.

[4] Olga Neuwirth in an interview with the author, Graz 2003.

[5] Interview with author.

[6] The theory of mimesis is developed by Benjamin in "On the Mimetic Faculty" (Benjamin 1978). It is present throughout much of Adorno's later work, but most systematically in *Dialectic of Enlightenment* (1973) and *Aesthetic Theory* (1997).

[7] Derrida makes a crucial distinction between two concepts of mimesis in Greek philosophy, firstly mimesis as "the presentation of the thing itself", its unveiling, and secondly, mimesis as imitation, or adequation of one thing to another (1981: 193).

CHAPTER 3

THE SINGING BODY IN THE *TRAGÉDIE LYRIQUE* OF
SEVENTEENTH- AND EIGHTEENTH-CENTURY FRANCE:
VOICE, THEATRE, SPEECH, PLEASURE

SARAH NANCY

In her paper on the "operatic scandal of the singing body" for *The Cambridge Opera Journal*, Michelle Duncan points out how difficult it is to give an account of the experience of listening to opera, especially while considering the performer's body:

> [...] opera studies persist in thinking of the voice as extra-corporeal. Carnal voices are either lacking or absent, marked by what they do not do, operative through failure and negativity, or envisioned as supra-objects that are off the scale, excessively loud (and thus impossible to register or to be perceived as material) and potentially "violent". As for the body of the singer, opera studies has tended to ignore it altogether unless it possesses currency as the object of desire or of a fetish. And when this happens, both the body and voice become secondary to the affect or erotic desire of the spectator. (Duncan 2004: 285)

Duncan underlines that the singing voice, in opera studies, is not considered in and of itself. Even when it is imbued with some positive qualities, it is still considered as an element that is "off the scale", that always goes further, or even too far from our musical experience of listening. As such, it could only be grasped indirectly by the effects it projects upon the listener. This is the reason why the singing body disappears in opera studies: the real way the sound has been produced, by a real body, is not as important as the way it meets the listener's desire, which refers to a mysterious locus of risk and freedom within the listening subject.

To apprehend the voice as an excess is to experience the voice as almost magically transcending the body of the performer, as formidable and disciplined as that body may be. We know how psychoanalytic theory illuminates this scenario: by considering the voice as an *objet (petit) a,* replacing the maternal body as the unique and originating object of true affection, Jacques Lacan opened the way to understanding the experience of opera as *jouissance* (Lacan 1981). The voice would be the pure signal of what is before and also beyond the listening subject, before and beyond the self. Thus opera, especially with the role it gives to the female voice, as the summit of what is impossibly symbolised, would be dedicated entirely to this excessive, transgressive and affectively ambivalent quest. There is no doubt that today, this model of interpretation is the most acknowledged in studies concerning the lyrical voice (see, for instance, Poizat 1986; Quignard 1996; Vivès 2002). However, we also know that this model is attached to a specific moment, to a specific musical style: being "grand opera" of the nineteenth century, or in Nicholas Till's terms, opera as "metaphysical", an extraordinary system intended to glorify the voice, and thus lose the singing body through the alternatives of presence and absence, pleasure and understanding. But, in other places, at other moments, it is obviously distinct: for instance, we know that at the birth of the opera, the Florentine Camerata preoccupied itself with its words, with the clarity of their pronunciation; or in more recent twentieth century history, how Broadway musicals require bodies that sing and dance simultaneously, and even more recently we can hear how some contemporary performers try to "de-aestheticise" the female voice (Dunn and Jones 1997: 4): Laurie Anderson with the use of the vocoder, or Diamanda Galás with the scream. By considering the voice as the poetic[1] centre of the work, and naturalising the conditions of its presentation and production, and thus almost erasing them in order to overcome the listener, the nineteenth-century grand operatic tradition, whose legacy is still very evident in repertoires and expectations today, is without doubt a particularly striking moment in the history of music theatre, but nevertheless, a limited one.

Does that mean that we could rediscover the singing body by looking to operatic forms other than the nineteenth-century model of "grand opera"? Not exactly. But by considering this "grand opera" as a specific aesthetic moment, by relativising it, we can find new ways to think of the singing body. The first great French operatic genre, the *tragédie lyrique,* illustrated in about ninety works between 1673 and the middle of the 1760s, can help us do just that, with the strange silencing it seems to impose on the lyrical voice.

SINGING AND/OR/BUT ACTING

If the understanding of music theatre as entirely dedicated to the voice makes the singing body disappear, then the *tragédie lyrique* by contrast should make it re-appear. The latter form was actually thought of as theatre, and, as a result, the performer's body was fully taken into consideration because her/his singing is regarded as a challenge to her/his acting.

As Catherine Kintzler's analyses have determined, the first operatic genre in France was established alongside the rules of dramatic genre (Kintzler 1991) being rules that corresponded to a poetics for which the coherence of the fiction was the chief priority. Furthermore the French poetics of the theatre were predicated upon an Aristotelian view whereby coherence was guaranteed in the first instance by the story. As a part of the performance (*spectacle*), music was theoretically marginalised and looked upon as an obstacle to the mimetic representation (Louvat-Molozay 2002: 85-126).

As a consequence, the performer's first task was not to sing well, but to embody the dramatic fiction by playing a role. It is thus relevant to notice that the performer was called an "actor". This becomes apparent to scholars of the genre through the commentaries of the performances at the time. Nothing is said about the texture of the voices, their *timbre*; the audience, the commentators tell us, wants to understand the story and to believe in the characters. For instance, when Mme de Sévigné relates a performance of *Atys* (Lully and Quinault 1676), she complains that the preceding grotesque roles played by the main singer prevent her from believing in the hero: "Atys is this little person who played both the Fury and the Nurse; so that we always see these ridiculous characters through Atys" (Sévigné 1676: 285-286).[2] Meanwhile, the Councillor of the Grand Conseil and opera goer Ladvocat's impressions, conveyed to the young Abbé Dubos, are restricted to details of playing style, and simple descriptions of the staged roles. In a letter dated 16 April 1695 he wrote: "The rest of the actors executed their roles well enough, except Dumesnil who forgot to remove his sword in the fifth act, where he is to be sacrificed" (Ladvocat 1695: 48).[3] The role was more important than the voice. The source suggests that the bodies are described commensurate to their ability to give life to a character.

The singer's task was thus considered in relation to the actor's task. However, the difference is that the former was supposed to be more involved in her/his charge of conveying the character theatrically because her/his singing was seen as a handicap for expression, according to the aim of theatrical efficiency. When considering the different kinds of declamation, including the musical declamation that takes place in opera, Grimarest asserted:

> If the vocal music usually gives some pleasure, it is because the injury made to the words by the intervals of music is compensated by the actor's pleasant voice and art, who distances himself from musical time in order to approach as much as possible the correct way of expressing the passion (Grimarest 2001[1707]: 357).[4]

According to Grimarest, the performer must be able to follow his "feeling" and go further than the score in order to "compensate" for the lack of coherence of the musical representation. So, she/he is asked to play in her/his own singing voice. Two of the most obvious and common devices for this kind of involvement were *agréments,* that develop in a sort of lexicon that the performer can use in an individual way, and rhythmical *inégalités.* The *inégalités* aimed at slightly disturbing the strict divisions of rhythmical values by dotting some of them. As for *agréments,* they were a way of modifying the melodic design or the texture of the voice. Some of their names particularly suggest the involvement of the body, like the *tremblement,* a kind of trill, the *sanglot,* an expiration preceding the sound in itself, or also the *port de voix,* a way of guiding the voice while sliding from one note to another. It is thus obvious that singing was, in the context of the *tragédie lyrique,* considered a way of representing the physical symptoms of passions. In his medical and philosophical reflections, Cureau de la Chambre makes it clear when he comments about the way the *agréments* are usually situated on the melodic line:

> The *tremblements* are more frequent at the end of *cadences* and great *ports de voix* because this is where the breath decreases and loses itself. If they are done at the beginning and also in the progression of the voice, it is to mark the eagerness of the desire, the suffering and other similar passions that accompany love (Cureau de la Chambre 1647: 348).[5]

So, if the first French operatic genre drew attention to the singing body, or, we could even say, prevented us from forgetting it, it is because of its poetic mistrust of music as an ingredient of representation. The singing body was thus viewed as an acting body that sings, which translates into an acting body that created different ways of forming passions in that very voice.

THE BODY WITHIN THE VOICE AND THE VOICE'S OWN BODY

We cannot be surprised, then, that nobody seems to care about the singing body from a technical point of view in France from the end of the seventeenth century until the middle of the eighteenth century. Indeed, the few French treatises of the time discuss issues of pronunciation very deeply, but say nothing about the body as a singing tool: nothing about the larynx, the vocal cords, the muscles of the tongue and those of the lips, for which the mechanisms are rather well known (Dandrey 1990: 25-39). Despite this, what strikes readers the most is the fact that there is nothing written about the way for singers to manage the breath, at least not before the second half of the eighteenth century. This is meaningful because all of these aspects have very important sonorous consequences: that which is at stake includes the density of the sound, which in a sense relates to the way the body is inscribed in the sound. Artistically, the consequence of this absence of care for an efficient use of breath is indicated by the shortness of musical phrases. It is evident, also, that the French musician Rochemont claims this absence of care when he criticises Italian technique as a vain search for results, in that: "the less the voice uses air, the more it is able to serve the performer in the way he wants to play" (Rochemont 1754: 53).[6] The result of a lack of breath management is a texture less focused, more shady and evanescent. On this point, the comparative descriptions of French and Italian singing are very significant. From the French point of view, the Italian voice is "stronger, clearer, neater, and more sonorous" (Mersenne 1636: t. 2, 42),[7] and it plays with strong contrasts, between, on the one hand, the flights allowed by the "amazing easiness of the throw or singing exercises", (Saint-Évremond [1969]: 434)[8] and on the other hand, those sounds that seem to "die completely by the end of the breath" (Raguenet 1702: 93).[9] As such, the Italian voice recalls "*sanglots*" and "*cris*" (Saint-Évremond 1677: 100-102). The French voice, on the contrary, when appreciated once again from a French point of view, is thought of as "sweet", "charming" and "tender" (Mersenne 1636: t. 2, 42 and Le Cerf 1972 [1705]: 62) and is characterised by "grace", "tenderness of touch, and clarity" (Saint-Évremond 1677: 107).[10] While the Italian sound—characterised by excess and intensity—

seems to have autonomy and density, the French voice, on the contrary, is concerned with "*beau langage*" and politeness.

Thus, the absence of technical interest about the body in the first French operas leads to a specific kind of sonorous texture: not a full sound, giving the sensation of completion, but a more fragile sound, where the voice is never emancipated from language. Many foreign commentators were intrigued, if not annoyed by this link between the voice and articulate speech, with its audible prudence, hesitation, or even reluctance to use a loud and sonorous voice. For instance, the German musician Johann Joachim Quantz notices of the French musicians at the beginning of the eighteenth century that "their airs speak more than sing. They almost call for a more skilful use of the tongue than that of the throat, in order to pronounce the words" (Quantz 1752: 318).[11] As a consequence, he adds, "this way of singing is far from exhausting the power of the human voice" (*ibid*.).[12] But some other commentaries are much more cruel: Raguenet, who writes against Le Cerf, mocks the "little girls without lungs, without strength nor breath"[13] that he hears on the French stage (Raguenet 1702: 81) and observes that "the high voices have so little strength that if they were to further weaken, they would completely extinguish and they would not be heard anymore" (*ibid*.: 93).[14] As for the *castrato* Filipo Balatri, who travelled through the south of France at the beginning of the eighteenth century, his first encounter with the French singing style is depicted with sarcasm:

> She begins to say *Iris*, and on the *ris*
> Forces her voice so much, and dwells so long
> That it must have been heard from Lyon to London.
>
> I swear by Bacchus
> That this shriek bores into my brain.
> She takes up a higher note, and then a higher,
> And her *Iriiiiiiis* tears my heart to tatters. (Heriot 1974: 217)[15]

This commentary highlights a very important phenomenon: the preference of performers to neglect or refuse to use the body as a singing tool in order to stay close to ordinary spoken pronunciation may have had the paradoxical consequence of underlining the presence of the singing body, whereas the more elaborate Italian singing technique would have achieved a full and round voice that is perceived as having no relationship with the singing body, or as having its own body ignoring any social constraint. It is thus striking that the Italian voice is often described by images which refer to the fact of forgetting the human and social world, the world as it is shared with other people. For instance, Raguenet evokes the throats and the sounds of the voice of the nightingale (les "gosiers & [l]es sons de voix de Rossignol") and the "exhalations that can make you lose your sense of gravity and almost hold you back from breathing" (Raguenet 1702: 78-79).[16]

This gives us an insight into the degree of presence of the French operatic voice, and into what is at stake with it. It seems that refusing to let the voice "fly" in order to keep in contact with the body through singing is related to thinking of the operatic genre as theatre and thus prioritising the intelligibility of the text. In both cases, the presence that seems to be required from the performer is a presence *intelligibly* addressed to the audience.

THE LISTENING BODY
We can consider that the goal of this style of singing was to show that an effort was being made to keep some distance with the listener's body. In this respect, the remarks concerning the grimaces made during a performance are very revealing. The arrival of Italian opera in France at the beginning of the seventeenth century, and the subsequent birth of French opera paved the way for a *leitmotiv* in written commentaries from this time: the call to "sing without grimacing" ("*chanter sans grimace*"), a default even mentioned when it is avoided. For instance, the violist André Maugars appreciates that the famous Leonora Baroni, in spite of being Italian, knows how to "sweeten" and "strengthen" her voice "without effort and without any grimaces".[17] Bacilly, the author of the famous treatise about the *Art de bien chanter*, thinks that singing without grimacing is crucial for a singing teacher because it is one of those qualities that makes the strongest impressions in our minds (Bacilly 1679 [1994]: 73).

Obviously, these remarks do not show an ignorance of the body but, on the contrary, reveal an attention, a vigilance. Thus, control appears to be a requirement that the performer has to make visible and audible, not only a defence, a protection, but also like a positive gesture addressed to the listener. This is all the more striking, if we make the connection between these remarks and some prescriptions given in other arts of speech, such as rhetoric or conversation. For instance, René Bary, in his *Méthode pour bien prononcer un discours*, seems to remember that Erasme had said that "closed and tight lips used to be perceived, a long time ago, as a sign of righteousness" (Erasme 1977 [1530]: 60)[18] and explains that it is necessary to consider that those to whom we speak are close enough, "reasonably distant, because honest people never speak with the mouth largely open" (Bary 1679: 45-46).[19] Of course, this is much more than practical advice given in order to develop good speech. What it illuminates is the strategic role of the mouth, as a visible place of transition between interior and exterior, which, as such, can awake phantasmatic fears about what the historian Georges Vigarello refers to as the "porosity" of the body (Vigarello 1985: 15-25). Indeed, the fear for seepage and contagion is particularly strong at a time when the "process of civilization" (Elias 1973) is developing, building between bodies "this wall made of fearful modesty and emotional repulsion" (*ibid.:* 360). [20]

From that point of view, connecting the beauty of singing to the control of the body has nothing to do with ignoring the body. On the contrary, it is a way of considering it intensely in its ability to link people. Hence, the technical disinterest in the singing body has directly to do with the care for its social value. It can be related to François Couperin's advice on the way to "touch the harpsichord": moving beyond technical considerations, he suggests that the musician should "fix the grimaces of the face" ("[corriger] les grimaces du visage"), and display a look that is neither too fixed nor too lax[21] (Couperin 1716: 4) - all this for the benefit of the "company" for whom we play (*ibid.*: 5-6). We see it clearly: the body concerned in musical and vocal performance is held under the same rules as the body in society.

Hence, the way the singing body is forced to be "contained" in the French operatic singing style reveals an ideal conception of the listening body: withheld, self-conscious, and, as such, able to keep in touch with the other listeners in an intelligible way. This is what depictions of the audience show. Le Cerf de La Viéville, for example, describes his experience of watching Lully's *Armide*:

> When Armide is driven to stab Renaud in the last scene of Act Two, I have twenty times seen everyone struck with fear, breathing no more, motionless, the entire soul in the ears and in the eyes, until the air of the violin which ends the scene gives us permission to breathe; then breathing returns with a humming of joy and admiration [...] This unanimous movement of the people told me that the scene was certainly ravishing (Le Cerf 1972 [1705]: 139).[22]

We see here that the listeners quiver together as the plot thickens, finally meeting in a feeling of admiration through sonorous expressions that create a "humming". In *Persée* (Quinault and Lully 1682), as Le Cerf also narrates, the listeners "show one another the pleasure that the duo of Phinée et Mérope made them feel by slightly leaning their heads forward".[23] Finally, he notices that, in *Hésione* (Danchet and Campra, 1700), when Anchise vows his obedience to Venus, the women in the audience "look at each other and smile".[24] Smiles, looks, gestures, "humming" noises that circulate *between* (*"entre"*) them: we see that bodies are in touch through signs that they share. In fact, we can precisely recognise what Géraud de Cordemoy, in his *Discours physique de la parole*, designates as "signs of institution" (*"signes d'institution"*): signs that are linked arbitrarily to a thought or an emotion, and which can be acknowledged by all, as opposed to the spontaneous and thus uncontrollable productions of the "natural" voice that are activated by the passions, and which depend on particular and individual cases (Cordemoy 1677: 67, 86, 131). It is as if the fact of being together, for the listeners, was given to be shown itself as performance, and as such feeding the consciousness of forming a group.

The contrast with the depictions of the Italian audience makes it all the more striking. An editor of the *Mercure de France* says how the Italian reactions to the singers surprised him by their intensity, as if the listener had been completely captured by it:

> It is quite a pleasant thing that as soon as the women have finished a grand air, or as soon as they go out of the theatre, the Baracols [*sic*] (those who navigate the gondolas), and a number of other more respectable people, cry with all might *Viva Bella, viva, ah, Cara ! Sia benedetta.* (*Mercure Galant* 1683: 243-245)[25]

The description made by Raguenet is even more radical. According to him, when we listen to Italian opera:

> We are in an ecstasy of pleasure; we must shout in order to release ourselves, no one can help it; we are impatient to reach the end of each air in order to breathe; often, we cannot wait for the end, we stop the musician with cries and everlasting applause. (Raguenet 1702: 58-59)[26]

In this example, the listener is possessed by a kind of pleasure that affects his body in an extreme way. Between the listener and the performer, the exchange is not organized: her/his cries do less to answer to the singing but more to merge with it. The audience seems to then form a mass, a crowd, an undefined group where singularities are expunged.

We find the same phenomenon later, when French singing evolved towards a freeing of the voice, an exacerbated lyrical style in the later eighteenth century. Under the effect of the full and round voice, playing with excessive contrasts, the listener seems to lose himself. We can see it for instance in the portrait of the Delbar, the playwright Piron's wife, made by La Mettrie, when he theorizes the human "machine":

> See the Delbar [...] in a box in the Opera: she looks pale and red alternately, she beats time with Rebel, she is touched with Iphigénie, becomes furious with Roland. All the impressions of the orchestra show through her face, as on a painting. Her eyes sweeten, convulse, laugh or arm themselves with military courage. People think she is crazy. She is not, unless it is crazy to feel pleasure (Offray de La Mettrie 1748: 37-38).[27]

The listener's body is subject here to the musical impressions, and, as such, isolated and dependent on an accelerated rhythm that takes it away from the world around us. And it is clear that it is the effect searched for by the new singing style.

Thus, the first French singing style confirms its singularity: with it, everything seems to be done in order to keep the listener's body in an intelligible system of signs, in order to fit an ideal conception of the audience as a structured body, with distinct members. There is no doubt that it enhances the fact that the audience, the "public", in an aesthetic sense, does not yet completely exist (Merlin-Kajman, 1994). As a matter of fact, this conception of the audience reminds us of the search for order, and of the consequent fear of dislocation that goes hand in hand with the production of efficient speech, as is evident, for instance, in Le Faucheur's reflection. The predicator, author of the first treatise on the eloquence of the body, writes:

> What God did in the creation of the Universe, which he divided into different species without which it would be a confused mass and without form; and what he did in the production of our bodies, which he composed from different parts without which they would be an ugly, hideous mass of flesh, we must do in our public discourses, not only for invention, for disposition, and for elocution, but also for pronunciation (Le Faucheur 1657: 90-91).[28]

But of course, singing is not eloquence. So what is suggested by the fact that opera, like eloquence, preoccupies itself with the organisation of the audience is less a dependence upon the social preoccupations conveyed by operatic singing, but more the social and maybe political dimension that is given to this activity of pleasure. Thus this singing style brings out something that will often become invisible once the aesthetic is defined by autonomy and gratuity at the end of the eighteenth century (Agamben 1996): it brings out the fact that the singing body has always something to do with the body politic.

So, focusing on the first French operatic stage helps us find our way out of the theoretical impasse that tends to make the singing body disappear, with these three solutions:

(i) By remembering the fact that the singing body is also always an acting body, we are invited to question the distinction and the articulation between one and the other, and thus to seek the singing body through the embodiment of the character.

(ii) By illuminating the paradoxical relationship between, on the one hand, the physical investment of the performer through singing, and, on the other hand, the perception of the body by the listener, we can re-consider the way the body is present within the voice: the weaker the technical investment, the more audible the body within the voice. From that perspective, we can consider that there are tendencially two different kinds of voices: one that tends to let the body appear only at the margins of language, and one that seems to have its own body.

(iii) Finally, by recognising the way that *tragédie lyrique* takes the listeners' bodies, and, by doing so, the audience *as a body* into consideration, we are reminded of the fact that the singing body always concerns the listening body in a communal way.

We see then that examining and appraising the listener's desire does not lead to the fatal theoretical disappearance of the singing body, as we may have first thought with Duncan's remark on its "secondary" status for the listener. On the contrary, a detour through seventeenth-century France, in re-evaluating the poetic dominance of the singing voice emblematized by "grand opera", helps us to think about the way the listener experiences himself during the performance both as a desiring subject and as a social subject. Different systems of values become apparent in the history of music theatre: sometimes, what is praised is the compatibility between the two of them, and at other times, it is the way pleasure can rapture the listener from her/his social identity. In the latter case, the singing body is at the very centre of an aesthetic perception, as is shown in the cult of the diva in subsequent centuries, who has relied upon an interpenetration of life and art that was and is achieved within the body of the singer.

In other terms, by helping us to consider how music theatre links the aesthetic body to the public body, this historical detour invites us to reflect upon what philosopher Jacques Rancière calls the "sharing of the sensible" (*"partage du sensible"*)[29], by referring to the way the aesthetic experience organises space, and thus affects the way we live together (Rancière 2000). From that point of view, music theatre appears not only as a non-evident, heterogeneous, and complex aesthetic object, but also as a way of performing something in society, and experiencing relationships with others.

NOTES

[1] Here and throughout the article, I use the adjective "poetic" in its link to *The Poetics* (Aristotle) thus meaning "related to the organisation, the functioning of the work".

[2] [Editors' note: the English translations of relevant historical sources throughout this chapter have kindly been provided by author Sarah Nancy and the original French text is presented in this notes section]. "Atys est ce petit drôle qui faisait la Furie et la Nourrice; de sorte que nous voyons toujours ces ridicules personnages au travers d'Atys".

[3] "Le reste des acteurs exécutèrent assez bien leurs rôles, hormis Dumesnil qui oublia d'ôter son épée au cinquième acte, où l'on le doit sacrifier".

[4] "Si la Musique vocale cause communément du plaisir, c'est qu'on est dédommagé du tort que les intervalles font aux paroles, par la voix agréable, et par l'artifice de l'Acteur, qui quand il a le sentiment juste, s'écarte des mesures de la Musique pour approcher le plus qu'il peut de la manière dont la passion doit être exprimée".

[5] "Les tremblements sont plus fréquents à la fin des cadences et des grands ports de voix, parce que c'est là que l'haleine se diminue et se perd. Et s'ils se font dès le commencement et dans le progrès de la voix, c'est pour marquer l'empressement du désir, de la Douleur, et d'autres semblables passions qui accompagnent l'Amour".

[6] "Moins [la voix] dépense d'air, plus elle est capable de l'exécution qu'il [l'interprète] en exige".

[7] "Plus forte, plus claire, plus nette, et plus sonore".

[8] "Facilité de gosier surprenante pour les passages".

[9] "Mourir tout à fait à la fin de l'air".

[10] "Douce", "charmante" (Mersenne 1636) "tendre" (Le Cerf 1705); "la tendresse du toucher, et la propreté" (Saint-Évremond 1677).

[11] "Leurs airs sont plus parlants que chantants. Ils demandent presque plus d'habileté de la langue, pour prononcer les paroles, que d'habileté du gosier".

[12] "Loin s'en faut qu[e le chant français] n'épuise, pour ainsi dire, le pouvoir de la voix humaine".

[13] Les "petites filles sans poumons, sans force, & sans haleine".

[14] "Les Dessus ont si peu de force que, pour peu qu'ils vinssent à les affaiblir, ils s'éteindraient entièrement & on ne les entendrait plus du tout".

[15] "Comincia a dir *Iris*, e spinge tanto / Su quel *ris* la sua voce, e dura tanto / Che da Lione a Londra saria andato. / Cospetto di Baccone, Bacconacio, / Che quel strido mi trapana 'l cervello / Riprende un tuon più alto, lascia quelle, / E c'è un *Iriiiiiiis* fa de mio cuore un straccio".

[16] Les "gosiers & [l]es sons de voix de Rossignol"; "haleines à faire perdre terre & à vous ôter presque la respiration".

[17] "Adouci[r]" et "renforce[r]" sa voix "sans peine et sans faire aucunes grimaces" (Maugars 1639: 26).

[18] "Que les lèvres jointes et serrées passaient jadis pour un indice de droiture".

[19] "Raisonnablement distants, parce que les honnêtes gens ne parlent jamais la bouche extrêmement ouverte".

[20] "Ce mur fait de pudeur craintive et de répulsion émotionnelle".

[21] Il ne faut pas "trop fixer la vue sur quelque objet, ni avoir l'air trop vague".

[22] "Lorsqu'Armide s'anime à poignarder Renaud, dans cette dernière Scene du 2. Acte, j'ai vu vingt fois tout le monde saisi de frayeur, ne soufflant pas, demeurer immobile, l'âme toute entière dans les oreilles & dans les yeux, jusqu'à ce que l'air de Violon, qui finit la Scene, donnât permission de respirer; puis respirant là avec un bourdonnement de joie & d'admiration. [...] Ce mouvement unanime du peuple me disait fort sûrement, que la scène est ravissante".

[23] "S'entremarqu[ent] l'un à l'autre par un penchement de tête, le plaisir qu[e le duo de Phinée et Mérope] leur avait fait" (*ibid.*).

[24] "S'entre-regarde[nt] & souri[ent]" (*ibid.*).

[25] "C'est une chose assez plaisante, que du moment qu[e les femmes] ont fini quelque grand Airs, ou qu'elles sortent du Théâtre, les Baracols [*sic*] (ce sont ceux qui conduisent les Gondoles) & même quantité de personnes plus considérables, s'écrient de toutes leurs forces, *Viva Bella, viva, ah, Cara ! Sia benedetta!*"

[26] "On est extasié de plaisir; il faut se récrier pour se soulager, il n'y a personne qui puisse s'en défendre; on attend avec impatience la fin de chaque Air, pour respirer; on ne peut souvent se contenir jusqu'au bout, on interrompt le Musicien par des cris & par des applaudissements infinis".

[27] "Voyez la Delbar [...] dans une loge d'Opéra; pâle et rouge tour à tour, elle bat la mesure avec Rebel; s'attendrit avec Iphigénie, entre en fureur avec Roland, etc. Toutes les impressions de l'orchestre passent sur son visage, comme sur une toile. Ses yeux s'adoucissent, se pâment, rient, ou s'arment d'un courage guerrier. On la prend pour folle. Elle ne l'est point, à moins qu'il n'y ait de la folie à sentir le plaisir".

[28] "Ce que Dieu a fait en la création de l'Univers, lequel il a distingué en tant de différentes espèces qui s'y voient, sans quoi ce ne serait qu'une masse confuse et informe; et en la production de nos corps qu'il a composés de tant de diverses parties, sans quoi ils ne seraient qu'une masse de chair laide et hideuse: nous le devons faire

en nos Discours publics, non seulement pour l'Invention, pour la Disposition, et pour l'Élocution, mais aussi pour la Prononciation".

[29] [Editors' note: this phrase has been translated equally as the "sharing" or "distribution" of "the sensible" in English-language sources].

CHAPTER 4

PERFORMING AFFECT IN SEVENTEENTH-CENTURY OPERA: PROCESS, RECEPTION, TRANSGRESSION

CLEMENS RISI

It was not only Athanasius Kircher who, in his *Musurgia universalis* of 1650, raised the question of "whether, why, and in what way music has the power to move the human soul" (Kircher 1650 [Volume 1]: 549).[1] The discussion about the musical and theatrical representation of affect, as well as its transference to the listener was *the* central theme of the newly emerging performance genre around 1600: opera. The first reflections on the new style of composing have proved in hindsight to be formulations of an explicit theory of reception, which accompany the history of opera to this day. Inasmuch as the transfer of affect occurs as a process between performers and perceiving listeners/spectators, it pertains to the paradigmatic moments of opera's performative dimension.

In the following, I would like to shed light on this performative core of opera from two directions. To begin with, from an historical perspective, from which I would like to reconstruct the supposed mechanisms for the transfer of affect and the transgression of these rules, focusing on seventeenth-century physiological and anatomical knowledge. Secondly, by means of two examples from recent productions (Monteverdi's *L'incoronazione di Poppea,* staged by Klaus Michael Grüber, conducted by Marc Minkowski, in Aix-en-Provence 1999; and Purcell's *Dido and Aeneas*, staged by Sasha Waltz, conducted by Attilio Cremonesi, in Berlin 2005), I would like to attempt to identify the causes as to why, at present, an increased interest in the performance of the affect-oriented music of the seventeenth century can be observed.

Now to proceed with the particular theories of reception and affect in music theatre at the turn of the seventeenth century; which is to say, let us regard the theory of the newly emerging operatic genre. Claudio Monteverdi had this to say about music and affect:

> I know that it is the contradictions (of affects), which greatly move our soul—good music must have the goal of moving the soul. (Monteverdi 1638)[2]

The Jesuit priest, polymath, and authority on and above all things relating to affect, Athanasius Kircher, similarly formulated his view in 1650 in his *Musurgia Universalis*, specifying his interest as to "whether, why, and in what way music has the power to move the human soul" (quoted in Scharlau 1969: 549).[3] In the phrases "*ad animos hominum commouendos*" or "*movere l'animo nostro*", a crucial change manifests itself in the concept of musical aesthetics from that of the sixteenth to the seventeenth centuries. Music is no longer only about representing affect in the sense of "*demonstratio*", "*repraesentatio*", or "*significatio*" ("demonstration, representation, signification") (Dammann 1995: 221, 225). In lieu of "*exprimere*" (expression) (*ibid.*: 227), there is excitement ("*excitare*" in Kircher, quoted in Scharlau 1969: 218), the stimulation of affect in the listener and spectator. Music intends to put people off balance, to put them beside themselves (Kircher 1650 [Volume 2]: 202).[4] Athanasius Kircher reports incidents of very successful audience responses in this respect in Rome's music theatre scene: "what theatrical music today in Rome has in terms of miraculous effects / is indescribable: the movement is often so great and severe / that the auditors stentorially begin to scream / sigh / weep / particularly in *casibus tragicis* [...]" (Kircher *ibid.*: 546).[5] He further writes that the "auditors" could often not control themselves ("*contineri nescij*"), breaking out into screams ("*clamores*"), wails ("*gemitus*"), sighs ("*suspiria*"), and tears ("*lachrymas*"). He observes bodies erupting into strange movements ("*exoticos corporum motus erumpentes*") and inner stimulation ("*interiorum affectuum*") displaying external signs ("*signis extrinsecis*", Kircher 1650 (Volume 1): 546).

Federico Follino, artistic director of the 1608 festivities in Mantua, reports something very similar on the occasion of Francesco Gonzaga's marriage with Margaret of Savoy, for which Monteverdi composed his opera *Arianna* which has been lost to us except for one piece:

The Lament was performed with so much affect and in such pitiable fashion that each listener found his heart softened and each lady spilled tears at Arianna's beautiful lamentation. (Quoted in Becker 1981: 27)[6]

Yet how could such reactions occur? With what physiological assumptions can one explain the occurrence of this emotional transfer to the listener?

The seventeenth century, euphoric with new discoveries in science, paid particular attention to questions regarding the transfer of affect and the required strategies to achieve this transfer. In the wake of a desire for experimentation and science, all the known and newly acquired knowledge about human physiology was collected and considered in order to answer the questions regarding the mode of emotional stimulation-response in listeners and spectators, as well as the transfer of (instrumentally or vocally) represented affect from a performer to her or his observer/listener.[7]

Kircher based his theory of affect on the intertwining of two theoretical concepts: Hippocrates's humoral pathology and temperament theory on one hand (passed down by Galen), and the theory of resonance or sympathetic strings on the other. As an illustration of the theory of sympathetic or resonance strings, Kircher refers to an experience in Mainz Cathedral (between 1624 and 1628). There, he heard that with certain tones from the organ, the string of a lute hanging on the wall resounded without this string having been touched (Scharlau 1969: 31 and 157). He later observed the same phenomenon in two string instruments, which were not far from one another in a room; when one was plucked the other also sounded (Dammann 1995: 248). With that, it was now easy for Kircher to explain the process of the transfer of affect: the musical vibration (i.e., an external movement of the air) touches the eardrum, it is transferred by resonance to the so-called animal spirits or *"spiritus animales"*[8] within the listener which communicate the vibrations to the brain, and the brain determines the production of one of the humours accordingly. The fluid thus produced dissolves into steam, mixes itself with the animal spirits, and at last creates the emotion. An acceleration of the animal spirits leads to a joyous affect, whereas slowing them down brings pain and sorrow. The feelings of the soul are communicated to the heart, the centre of the animal spirits. The spirits stream from the heart into the muscles, thus provoking visible physical reactions (Scharlau 1969: 222-4).[9] Having understood this mechanism first, it then becomes easy to find the corresponding musical means that can achieve a desired effect. Kircher not only elaborated this theory in detail, he also listed musical guidelines to be followed in order to represent and stimulate particular emotions. For example, to produce the affect of joy, major thirds, purposeful intervallic leaps in major, accelerated tempi, triple dance meters, bright tones and high registers, energetic dynamics and arpeggios should be employed (Dammann 1995: 258). Sorrow was considered an unusual affect; therefore, for its musical representation, it required unusual means, such as dissonance, non-harmonic relations, and prohibited intervals (*"intervalla prohibita"*, *ibid.*: 258, 386). As the smallest interval in use and the shortest distance between tones, the half-step was of particular interest to Kircher. According to his theory, chromatics and enharmonics draw the animal spirits together and slow their movement. The uniquely tender and relaxed effect of the half-step makes it appropriate for the expression of sorrow (Scharlau 1969: 255).[10] And therefore, it hardly seems surprising that in the only surviving piece from Monteverdi's opera *Arianna*, the *Lamento d'Arianna* (*"Lasciate mi morire"*), showcases chromatics and unusual dissonances which play a central role in constructing and evoking the affect of sorrow. The exceptional aspect of this scoring is the use of dissonance with which Monteverdi takes far greater liberties than his contemporaries for the purpose of expressing and transferring affect: the use of extraordinary means to express this extraordinary affect of sorrow.

Thus seventeenth-century developments in music theory and anatomical knowledge allowed composers to believe that there were mechanisms of control and action to transfer affect. A composer could think that he was able to guarantee the success of a desired effect at any given time with the correct application of means.

It now appears as if the euphoria for the decoding of the human body and behaviour is being repeated today under new, more intensified auspices. Hardly a week goes by without new findings in neuro-scientific research being published in the daily or weekly newspapers. What is love? How does learning function? How does memory function? Why is forgetting important for remembering? What is creative listening? Can so called "mirror neurons" be understood as a form of sympathetic resonance in human emotional responses? The race for decoding the human genome, as with the interpretation of the sovereignty of human actions granted by research on the brain explicitly allows a new (thoroughly frightening) positivism to appear in the surveying of humankind. A new belief is propagated and practiced that can explain everything with the help of the "hard" sciences (genetics, neuroscience, neurophysiology, etc.)—a steadfastness in the belief in science that also distinguished the seventeenth century. What does it mean that, in this very similar (science-euphoric) climate, the old form of Baroque opera is celebrating a new triumph? Are we capable, as present-day spectators, of relating to the system of rules and standards for the Baroque transfer of affect since we are already pre-determined (genetically, physiologically through our brains) in all of our perceptions and actions? Is it therefore the right form for the right time?

It is evident that every form of theatre—possibly opera even more intensely than spoken theatre—is defined by a multiplicity of scripts (libretto, score) and a control system of strategies to create a particular effect. In this respect, the opera stage may serve at first glance as suitable experimental ground for the scientifically inspired mechanism of affect transfer. However, as soon as one takes the concrete, singular performance into consideration, the question is prominently posed, in the theatre and particularly on the opera stage, about the influence of the incalculable and unpredictable, about the productive excess of the performative that threatens to eliminate the basic rules for each attempt at standardisation, as each transfer of affect only happens in the unique and unrepeatable situation of the performance. Kircher himself had to concede that the success of the affect transfer can fail due to subjective differences (Dammann 1995: 252-3; Scharlau 1969: 230, 246). He observed that due to temperamental disposition, people responded differently or not at all to a particular affect. Likewise, the climate of a country also determines the effect of a specific affect. The property of a room (too small, too narrow, too intricate, too full and too large) is also responsible for music conveying its desired effect. Of most interest, however, is what Kircher had to say about the unpredictability of both main figures responsible for the process of transferring affect, the performer and the listener:

> So prevalent even in [music] is the vice of vanity—commonly called singers' temperament—which in certain people is the greater the less their education. Some of them join to their want of skill or aptitude an insufferable arrogance, which makes them value themselves so highly that in a large choir they wish only their own voice to be heard; hence they are wont quite deliberately to drown out those of the rest with indiscriminate noise, straining their voices so

disgustingly that you think you are listening to the music we hear when the bray of asses accompanies bleating sheep; which in all ways offends against the laws of decorum. I shall say nothing here of the absurd bodily posture that singers display while singing; you can see a number of them purporting to beat the time by moving their whole bodies in the most unseemly manner. You may see some now raising their heads at each interval, now bowing them, now shaking and twisting them from side to side—you would say they were actors—and, so as to omit no unseemliness in a seemly practice, you may not without laughter espy them changing the appearance of their mouths, now round like a cooking-pot, now protruded like a trumpet, and distorted into one shape after another. If to this should be added that most unsightly movement of the eyes, and the capricious puckerings of the brows, one can hardly say to how much laughter, guffawing, and mockery they expose a composition otherwise beautiful and skillfully written; so that some people were right to hold that musicians should be shut away and not seen by anyone.[11]

Here, Kircher himself gives a most striking example of how even the best or most well-meant adherence to the principles of the doctrine of affections is undone by the reality of performance. In the face of such conditions, how can a doctrine of affections be effective? To resolve this conflict, it is necessary to consider the situation from the opposite viewpoint: only the performative reality is capable of expressing and conveying affect. This does not mean that the negative examples, cited by Kircher, would be capable of conveying a particular affect; but the examples focus on what is being discussed here: there can be no effective communication beyond the act of performing affect. A transfer of affect takes place only in the moment of performance. Kircher himself seems to be well aware of the contradictions between theory and practice, i.e., the bad habits of the singers that undermine his clearly and thoroughly formulated theory, or the fact that the stimulation is very individual and situation-dependent undermining his conviction that the stimulation can be formulated as a way of a mechanism following objective rules.

The contradictions in theory point to that quality of transference, which according to my understanding would be described as performative—each transfer of affect is concerned with a performance of an unsecured and therefore unpredictable course and outcome.

Seventeenth-century music theatre practitioners overtly took account of this knowledge of the event's openness [contingency] to transference. A few years before Kircher, Claudio Monteverdi confronted this basic condition of performative processes in a surprising and unique way. With the *Lamento della Ninfa* from his eighth madrigal book (1638), he shows how conscious he is that only through performance, different with each singer, can the desired effect occur: that is to say, through the individually-felt affect and the individual performance of this feeling. Therefore, he allows the person singing the part of the nymph to determine her tempo. In the heading to the printed score, Monteverdi clearly expresses:

> The three voices (in the frame story) sing at the tempo of the (conducting) hand; [...] the nymph's lament should be sung to the tempo of her soul's state and not the conducting hand. (Monteverdi 1638 [1967]: 286)[12]

Here, an understanding of the unpredictability and elusiveness of the crucial moment of transference is revealed, in which the unforeseeable in the transfer of affect is embedded in the score as a gap. The nymph's lament is not to be sung in a fixed tempo but rather to the tempo of her soul's state, "*a tempo del'affetto del animo*".

This knowledge, I would claim, has not only inscribed itself in historical scores but can also be identified as an impulse in contemporary theatre praxis to deal with these seventeenth-century scenarios of emotional expression in new stagings over and over again. If this is the case, we have to ask how the performance and staging praxis handle the strongly formalised musical means of seventeenth-century opera in combination with the scenic dimension.

Early seventeenth-century opera distinguished itself in that it transferred a declamatory style of speaking into music in order to produce a quasi-endless chain of recitatives. Claudio Monteverdi is primarily to thank for enhancing this sequence of recitatives through other forms—in part from earlier musical eras—thereby creating a music theatre form comprised of recitative sequences and closed forms—a sequence that we consider as characteristic for Baroque opera. A kind of mixture of both styles—the earlier use of recitatives with the earlier style of aria—can be found in the first large scene between Nero and Poppea in Monteverdi's opera *L'Incoronazione di Poppea*, which premiered in 1642 in Venice. The Roman Emperor Nero has just spent a romantic night with his socially inferior lover Poppea whom he would like to make his Empress, which would first require him to expel his wife Octavia. In the relevant scene, Nero and Poppea reassert their love for one another although Poppea expresses her doubts since, because of her status, she is not certain to remain the object of Nero's permanent affection. After a musically rich and lively exchange of arguments, the Emperor and his lover must take leave of

Figure 4.1: The farewell sequence from Monteverdi's *L'Incoronazione di Poppea* (1642) (Monteverdi 1967: 37-8), bars 410-433. © Mit freundlicher Genehmigung der UNIVERSAL EDITION A.G., Wien.

one another for which Monteverdi wrote a repeating farewell sequence, equally beautiful as formal. Both repeat *"A Dio"* as well as the other's name several times (figure 4.1).

The structure of the repeated cadences makes the musical gesture of parting very formal; accordingly, director Klaus Michael Grüber (in 1999, in Aix-en-Provence, and under the musical direction of Marc Minkowski) also encouraged both of his protagonists—Mireille Delunsch as Poppea and Anne Sofie von Otter as Nero—to move their bodies onstage in a joined form. Like two statues in proximate S-curves, they remain virtually immobile at a distance that allows contact through gaze and gesture, but not touch. Only the hands and arms move together in a dancerly, serpentine pose, and extend out in succession, in an interplay of seduction and attraction. They remain in this pose for almost the entire duration of the eight *"A Dio"* repetitions (figure 4.2).

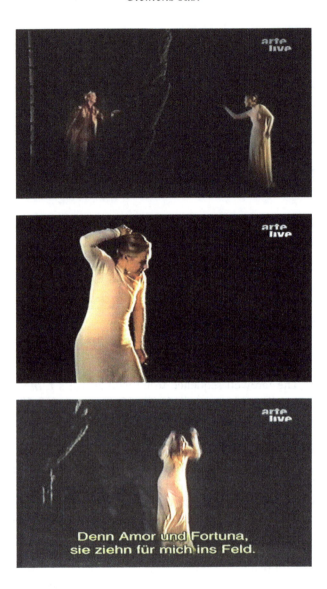

Figures 4.2, 4.3, 4.4: Claudio Monteverdi, *L'Incoronazione di Poppea*, production: Klaus Michael, Grüber, conductor: Marc Minkowski, stage design: Gilles Aillaud, costumes: Rudy Sabounghi, Festival d'Aix-en-Provence 1999, Nero: Anne Sofie von Otter, Poppea: Mireille Delunsch.

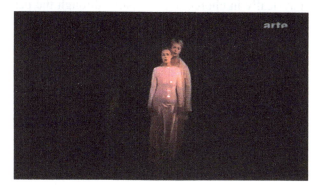

Figures 4.5, 4.6, 4.7: Claudio Monteverdi, *L'Incoronazione di Poppea*, production: Klaus Michael, Grüber, conductor: Marc Minkowski, stage design: Gilles Aillaud, costumes: Rudy Sabounghi, Festival d'Aix-en-Provence 1999, Nero: Anne Sofie von Otter, Poppea: Mireille Delunsch.

After Nero's departure, Poppea finds herself in a new emotional situation, expressing feelings that she has perhaps until then repressed: a hope for social advancement coupled with a confirmed self-assurance that with the help of Amor and Fortuna she will reach her goal. The striking contrast between Poppea's euphoric expression of hope and her exaggerated determination are magnified through Monteverdi's music and the gesture and movement of the scene. Here, in Grüber's staging, a kind of corporeal emotional eruption was achieved as she let her hair loose, breaking out of the "corset" of her hairstyle (figures 4.3 and 4.4).[13]

As if for the finale, the production wanted to bring Poppea's seemingly uncontrolled eruption of emotion back into a stylised, choreographed form once again, in the famous final duet *"Pur ti miro"*, which produced the impression of being a carefully calculated study in movement. In this duet, generally acknowledged as not being by Monteverdi himself (but by Benedetto Ferrari), Poppea and Nero sing to each other, yet frequently in reciprocal imitation, parallel intervals, while coming together—*unisono*—only seldomly (see figure 4.8).

The performers are likewise choreographed in a way that corresponds to this compositional ambivalence of affective closeness and distance. The sharp, successive, calculated vocal phrases are translated physically in choreographed paths through the performance space; the tension of the distance, maintained both spatially and in the movement, is provided by the music through the numerous, exquisitely suspended resolutions in the voices. Successive movement towards one another, past one another, emphasises the movements through juxtaposition and opposition. Both voices attempt to entangle one another, to fuse, until at last with the final note, the climax, they are actually one voice, spatially, at least optically, standing one before the other, being fused and merged into one figure (figures 4.5-4.7).

This process of conveying the strict form of the musical presentation of affect in movement patterns can become even more intense when choreographers undertake the staging of operas from this time, as with the 2005 staging of Henry Purcell's opera fragment from 1689, *Dido and Aeneas* by choreographer Sasha Waltz at the Berlin State Opera Unter den Linden. With Dido's very first aria "Ah Belinda", we see yet another way to convey musical form through choreography. In this aria, where Dido is torn between the vow of fidelity that she swore to her deceased husband and giving expression

1) La figura ⌢ non permette una interpretazione esatta. Essendo la parte strumentale "a tempo,, puó darsi che valga 12 quarti oppure che il fa vada tenuto sino alla fine della bat-.tuta seguente.

2) Qui finisce il taglio. Vedi Nota N⁰ 28.

3) Questo duetto finale non si trova nel libretto stampato.

XIII

Figure 4.8 (preceding pages): *"Pur ti miro"* from *L'Incoronazione di Poppea* (1642) (Monteverdi 1967: 246-9), bars 775ff. © Mit freundlicher Genehmigung der UNIVERSAL EDITION A.G., Wien.

to her burning love for Aeneas, Dido appears on the Staatsoper's stage in three different forms, in the body and voice of the singer Aurore Ugolin, and in two additional bodies, those of dancers Clementine Deluy and Michal Mualem. In an interview, Sasha Waltz took the following position on this conception: "I do not only want to tell the story through the singers but also through the images and gestures, through the entirely personal language of dance that the music complements. It is the attempt to merge the various levels of performance without one dominating the other".[14]

Figure 4.9 Henry Purcell, *Dido and Aeneas*, choreography and production: Sasha Waltz, conductor: Attilio Cremonesi, stage design: Thomas Schenk and Sasha Waltz, costumes: Christine Birkle, Staatsoper Berlin 2005, Dido: Michal Mualem, Clementine Deluy, Aurore Ugolin.

The three Didos are almost dressed the same, and all three follow a formalised vocabulary of movement, including the singer (figure 4.9). In the choral scene directly before the aria (as well as in a number of other scenes) we can experience the most fascinating moment of

Sasha Waltz's work: the singers and dancers merge with one another, and it is frequently not clear (or only with a second glance) who is "who" or who is "what". And yet—with all the merging—it is the difference in the materiality of voice and body that is responsible for the visual and acoustic appearance of the individual subject—the performer. Despite or perhaps because of the attempt to convey the performers' phenomenal corporeality in a choreographed collective my perception always switches back and forth between the choreographed, merged triad of singer and dancers, the collective of three, the choreographed form on the one hand and the continually glimpsed difference of corporeality on the other which takes in the differences of stature, bearing, and movement, as with vocality. Despite the clearly effective, harmonising and defined coordination, each individual corporeality and vocality of those involved is brought to the foreground in the musical as well as the visual (in the layer of movement). It is precisely this interplay of a collectively ordered set of rules and its transgression by individuality which is responsible for the particular appeal of this scene, as with the entire performance.

Arguably, this doubling in the expression of affect, the establishment and observation of rules and their simultaneous transgression, is already informed by Purcell's score. As in the case of Monteverdi, in Purcell' s setting of the aria "Ah Belinda", it can be said that the concession towards transgressing rules found its way into the musical score. Noticeable in this aria is the simultaneity of two differing levels in organising song on the one hand and instrumental accompaniment on the other. The bass follows a clearly and severely formalised structure of repetition: a four-bar phrase that is repeated a total of sixteen times. It is a *chaconne*. The bass chaconne's main characteristic is the tension between the bass and the soprano, the singing voice as it is presented here in "Ah Belinda"—namely the tension between the strict musical form on the one hand (the bass) and a soprano voice which can seem rhythmically and melodically set free within this framework, as with the singular, short motifs (the irregular, interrupted, and near to spoken declamation) and the sighs, repeatedly heard on the word "A-ah" (figure 4.10).

This doubling of the expression of affect is exactly what fascinated the production's conductor Attilio Cremonesi, in this aria particularly. He noted in an interview that:

With the aria "Ah Belinda", [...] it was important for me that the singer sings with great agitation—under which at the same time there is a stable structure. [...] She is troubled, she does not know how she should handle this situation. There is this strict meter, this norm, and she struggles against it.[15]

The musical layers between instrumental bass and singer already produce a tension of rules and transgression; thus, Sasha Waltz adds a

Figure 4.10: "Ah Belinda" from *Dido and Aeneas* (1689) (Purcell 1889: 7-8), bars 1-58.

further tension at the level of the singer through her choreography in that she allows the singing Dido to repeat a formally strict movement of the arm precisely with her irregularly placed "Ahs", in which the right arm, bent in a curve, is guided to the side (figure 4.11). The subjective eruption of affect, sworn in the sung text, is reshaped into movement in the choreography, contrasting the vocal eruptions with a newly established set of rules in the choreography.

Figure 4.11: the choreographed arm movement of Aurore Ugolin as (the singing) Dido in Sasha Waltz's production of *Dido and Aeneas* at Staatsoper Berlin in 2005.

The confrontation of seventeenth-century theory with contemporary performance practices reveals a connection over time in the interplay of rules and their transgression. The tension between formalisation on the one hand and eruption and freedom on the other, between the physiologically founded mechanisms of control and action on the one hand and the transgression through each individual body and voice in performance on the other, challenges today's performances, realising this exact tension on multiple levels of performance. Current examinations of seventeenth-century emotional scenarios are interested exactly in scrutinising and challenging the seeming validity of knowledge about the body. The most intense experiences of affect transfer occur in particular when the performance transgresses the strategies of the staging. It is precisely this interplay of asserted and staged rules and their transgression, that caused seventeenth-century theoreticians and composers, as well as the present theatre world, to be fascinated with affect and which characterises opera as a special place of great affection.

NOTES

[1] [Editors' note: Clemens Risi has kindly provided English-language translations of numerous early-modern texts in this chapter and the original text sources are provided in this notes section]. "Vtrum, cur, and quomodo Musica vim habeat ad animos hominum commouendos".

[2] "Sapendo che gli contrarij [dei passioni, od'affetioni, del animo] sono quelli che movono grandemente l'animo nostro, fine del movere che deve havere la bona Musica" (Monteverdi, Claudio. 1638, 1967. *Madrigali guerrieri, et amorosi. Libro ottavo* (Venetia 1638) in *Tutte le opere di Claudio Monteverdi* (ed. G. Francesco Malipiero), Vienna: Universal Edition: VIII).

[3] "Vtrum, cur, e quomodo Musica vim habeat ad animos hominum commouendos". Also cited in Dammann, Rolf. 1995. *Der Musikbegriff im deutschen Barock*. Laaber: Laaber: 215-396.

[4] "Animam extra se rapere".

[5] Kircher, *ibid.*, 546. Hirsch, Andreas. 1662. 1988. *Philosophischer Extract und Auszug aus deß Welt-berühmten Teutschen Jesuitens Athanasii Kircheri von Fulda Musurgia Universali*. Kassel: Bärenreiter-Antiquariat: 134. The original reads "*autores*" instead of "*auditores*" (quoted in Dammann 1995: 228).

[6] "Il lamento […] fu rappresentato con tanto affetto, e con sì pietosi modi, che non si trovò ascoltante alcuno, che non s'intenerisse, né fu pur una Dama, che non versasse qualche lagrimetta al suo bel pianto".

[7] See also Risi 2005 and Risi 2007.

[8] See also Descartes' "*esprits animaux*".

[9] Even before Kircher, Zarlino (1558) endeavoured to explain in his *Institutioni harmoniche* how music achieved its effect with the help of the animal spirits, or the humours.

[10] See also Dammann, 274: "vicinitas ad unisonum mollitiem inducit".

[11] Kircher 1995.

[12] "Le tre parti, che cantano fuori del pianto della Ninfa […] cantano al tempo della mano; […] il pianto [della Ninfa] va cantato a tempo del'affetto del animo, e non a quello della mano".

[13] Although there is no evidence to suggest that this symbolism was familiar to Monteverdi or common to seventeenth-century staging praxis, it has been fixed in visual memory since the early nineteenth century as a representation of madness and every other generally uncontrolled eruption of emotion in opera.

[14] Waltz, Sasha and Attilio Cremonesi. 2005. 'Liebe in Zeiten des Krieges': Sasha Waltz und Attilio Cremonesi im Gespräch mit Caroline Emcke' in *Staatsoper Unter den Linden* (prod.). *Dido & Aeneas*. Programme Booklet for premiere. 19 February 2005. Berlin Staatsoper Unter den Linden: 6.

[15] *Ibid.*: 7.

CHAPTER 5

THE VIOLETTAS OF PATTI, MUZIO AND CALLAS: STYLE, INTERPRETATION AND THE QUESTION OF LEGACY

MAGNUS TESSING SCHNEIDER

Whereas the field of musicology, in principle, embraces both the study of the musical score and the musical performance, little interchange has traditionally taken place between these two branches. Students of the great composers rarely combine close readings of the scores with examinations of how the music has been performed historically, and students of performance practice rarely use their knowledge of the history of singing, the development of the musical instruments, etc. for in-depth analyses of the classics. As a student of the original productions of operas by Monteverdi, Mozart and Verdi, I have been surprised to learn how much is actually known about how many of the original singers played and sang their roles, and even more surprised to realise how little impact this has had on how the scores have been analysed and interpreted.

Perhaps this is where the approach of theatre studies is called for because one of the traditional virtues of the dramaturge is the trained ability to read a dramatic text as more of a theatrical script—one containing an infinite variety of scenic possibilities—than as a finished work of art. If operatic singing is indeed a stage language on a par with the actor's delivery, a musical performance in the theatre is a theatrical performance, too, and one could even argue that the history of operatic singing cannot be properly understood without regard to the history of acting. It is striking, at least, when one examines the history of vocal art through the lens of the theatre historian, how closely the development of operatic singing reflects historical changes in the theatre.

In the following, I intend to demonstrate my point by comparing the performances of three famous sopranos—Adelina Patti, Claudia Muzio and Maria Callas—in Verdi's *La Traviata.* We may get an idea of their portrayals by studying reviews and other eyewitness accounts in the light of contemporary scenic and vocal performance practice.

ADELINA PATTI (1843-1919)

Without any doubt, the most celebrated Violetta of the nineteenth century was Adelina Patti whose fame was so overwhelming that the 1860s, 70s and 80s are sometimes referred to as "the reign of Patti". Emma Calvé compared Patti's voice to "a string of luminous pearls, perfectly matched, every jewel flawless, identical in form and colour" (Calvé 1922: 161), Nellie Melba found the timbre of her voice "exquisite, the diction crystalline" (in Cone 1981: 1), George Bernard Shaw praised "her unsurpassed phrasing and that delicate touch and expressive *nuance* which make her cantabile singing so captivating" (1932 Vol. III: 4) and William J. Henderson believed that her name would stand out on the pages of musical history "as that of a singer in whom luscious beauty of voice, admirable facility in florid music and exquisite, ravishing beauty in pure cantilena were happily united" (Henderson 1968: 296, 298).

While praise for Patti as a vocalist was unanimous, opinions regarding her abilities as an actress differed to a striking degree. One of those least impressed with her histrionic powers was Shaw who found that her

> offences against artistic propriety are mighty ones and millions. She seldom even pretends to play any other part than that of Adelina, the spoiled child with the adorable voice; and I believe she would be rather hurt than otherwise if you for a moment lost sight of Patti in your preoccupation with Zerlina, or Aida, or Caterina. [...] Patti will get up and bow to you in the very agony of stage death if you only drop your stick accidentally. (Shaw 1950: 354)

According to Clara Louise Kellogg, Patti

> never acted; and she never, never felt. As Violetta she did express some slight emotion, to be sure. Her "Gran Dio" in the last act was sung with something like passion, at least with more passion than she ever sang anything else. [...] But her great success was always due to her wonderful voice. Her acting was essentially mechanical. (Kellogg 1913: 130-1)

These views, characteristic of the attitude around the turn-of-the-century towards earlier generations of opera singers, stand in marked contrast to those of some other commentators. A review of the eighteen-year-old singer's London debut as Violetta mentioned the "striking display of histrionic genius with which she delighted the public", describing her performance in the last act as "truthful and beautiful",[1] and more than thirty years later another reviewer considered Patti "the most fascinating Violetta that ever trod the boards".[2] Herman Klein noted that even the great Sarah Bernhardt, who counted the Lady of the Camellias among her greatest roles, had wept over Patti's Violetta when she heard her in Paris (Klein 1931: 35).

Patti herself took the acting dimension of her art very seriously:

> I love the stage. I love to act and to portray every species, every shade of human emotion. [...] I care not whether it be comedy or tragedy, so long as I feel that I can devote my whole energy, my whole being, to realizing the character that I have to delineate. (Klein 1903: 313-4)

According to Klein, who witnessed some of the private pantomime performances to which Patti devoted herself enthusiastically after her retirement from the lyric stage, the "mobility of her facial expression, the aptness and significance of her gestures, the litheness of her movements, her capacity for delineating character and portraying difficult scenes without uttering a sound—all these afforded new and striking evidence of her Italian origin" (1931: 44-5).

The contrast in opinions seems to reflect a change in theatrical tastes. As implied by Klein, the diva's acting seems to have been closer to the classical style of the eighteenth and early nineteenth centuries in which the character was represented more as a type, i.e. as a set of dominant passions that did not change during performance, than to the naturalism of the late nineteenth century. The classical actor concentrated entirely on his effect on the audience through a nuanced delivery of text and a careful selection of gestures and facial expressions appropriate to the character and the relevant moment. Accordingly, the "independence of the psychological unity of the role, the relative emancipation from the character represented [...] made it easier for the actor [...] to exploit a situation to the maximum" (Christiansen, S. 1975: 164).[3] This included the virtuoso improvisations and extra-dramatic bows to the audience, which Shaw, the devoted Ibsenite, considered "offences against artistic propriety". An early review of Patti's Violetta gives us a glimpse of the classical performer's use of contrasting, clearly defined passions in the delineation of character:

> Mlle. Patti represents Violetta as one who, under other conditions, might have adorned a very different sphere from that in which she is unhappily destined to move. [...] Her gaiety in the earlier scenes is continually under check. Now and then a gesture, a movement, a mere look, shows plainly that, while striving to brave it out, she is ashamed of and really detests her position; and that even the idea of disinterested love for Alfredo, ultimately leading to redemption, breaks upon her, from time to time, as an illusion to the emptiness of which she becomes thoroughly alive [sic].[4]

In the context of this debate, it is interesting that Giuseppe Verdi considered Patti "an artistic nature so complete that her equal has perhaps never existed"[5] elsewhere describing her as "perfect organization, perfect balance between singer and actress, a *born* artist in the fullest sense of the word".[6] Among the roles in which he admired her was Violetta: on one occasion he described her execution of the Act One cavatina as an "incomparable performance" (*ibid.*) and Patti wrote to Klein after having sung *La Traviata* at La Scala in 1893 that the

> enthusiasm was so great throughout the performance that Verdi [...] actually wept tears of joy and delight. It appears that he said to Bevignani [Patti's accompanist] that my phrasing was too touching for words and that I sang divinely! (Quoted in Klein 1920: 313)

Interestingly, Verdi always had to defend his view of Patti as a great actress against those who saw her "merely as a good executer of notes",[7] an opinion that appears to have held strong with the Italian public, "which pretends to so much, [but] has not wished to understand, till this day, that she is a marvellous actress as well, comparable to anyone, and that she has, moreover, a charm and a naturalness that no one else has!" (*ibid.*)

Patti's "classical" performance style seems to have been Verdi's ideal, and even critics with more naturalistic ideals confessed that she was successful in *La Traviata*. Gino Monaldi, who found that "her heart was not in anything", conceded that she succeeded in moving the audience with her Violetta: "'Addio del passato', as sung by Patti, descended onto the soul like a fairy's melodious weeping: her admirable notes seemed sorrowful; they were caresses by velvet hands" (Monaldi 1929: 119). A similar point was made by Henderson who found that Patti, although she "displayed in all her impersonations about as much passion as one of the ladies on the frieze of the Parthenon", was Verdi's ideal Violetta "because she attended strictly to her business of singing the music into which the immortal master had translated the soul of the courtesan glorified by love" (Henderson 1968: 415-6).

There appears to be some truth in Henderson's claim that all the successful singers of the part had "reached their ends by pure singing, not by pantomimic demonstrations, gasps or coughs" (*ibid.*: 416), when we consider that Verdi, in connection with his *Macbeth*, had explicitly condemned extra-musical vocal effects in his singers. While praising the actress Adelaide Ristori as Shakespeare's Lady Macbeth for her "death-rattle", he emphasised that, in music,

> that must not and cannot be done; just as one shouldn't cough in the last act of *La traviata*; or laugh in the "scherzo od è follia" of *Ballo in maschera*. [...] The piece [Lady Macbeth's mad scene] should be sung with the utmost simplicity and in *voce cupa* [a dark voice] (she is a dying woman) but without ever letting the voice become ventriloquial.[8]

Apparently, Verdi did not consider "pure singing" enough to realise his characters theatrically: the voice needed to be coloured. According to Luisa Tetrazzini, who prided herself on having moved Patti to tears with *her* Violetta, the last act of *La Traviata* requires the use of "the white voice", a vocal colour achieved by employing a head resonance alone "without sufficient of the *appoggio* or enough of the mouth resonance to give the tone a vital quality". In the last act of *La Traviata* the white voice should suggest "utter physical exhaustion and the approach of death" (Tetrazzini 1921: 316-7).

The "dark voice" of Lady Macbeth and the "white voice" of Violetta may be considered vocal equivalents of the classical actor's mask-like representation of the emotions. This serves as a reminder that opera was formerly an auditory rather than a visual theatre, in which the delineation of character occurred primarily on an acoustic level. Like classical acting, dramatic singing was "dependent on the rhetorical requirements of the language" (Christiansen, S. 1975: 164), for which reason major attention was given to clear enunciation, vocal ornaments the purpose of which was to highlight the text rhetorically, a nuanced phrasing expressive of the passions of the words rather than of the psychological subtext of the role, and a timbre investing the words and musical lines with inner life and capable of changing its colour, chameleon-like, according to the character, the dramatic situation, or the meaning of the words.

To Patti and Verdi, no less than to Monteverdi, dramatic singing was the natural extension of the actor's speech, the passions residing *in* rather than *behind* the word. From the mid-eighteenth century onwards, the subservience of music to speech was gradually replaced by an upgrading of autonomously expressive music, just as the classical acting style was replaced by a more visual, i.e. extra-verbal, acting style, but this development seems to have occurred much later in Italy than north of the Alps. Italian singers and composers maintained an artistic ideal rooted in rhetoric, resulting in a markedly declamatory singing style, and Verdi still fought for this ideal when casting and directing his operas. Evidently, his favourite soprano must have possessed these qualities to a high degree.

CLAUDIA MUZIO (1889-1936)
One of the most admired Violettas in the first half of the twentieth century was the Italian soprano Claudia Muzio who was almost identified with the role of the tragic courtesan in the mid-1920s. She is regarded by many as the greatest soprano of the so-called *verismo* style—the operatic equivalent of theatrical naturalism—her most famous role being Violetta. In the words of Adriano Belli,

> Muzio [...] in this opera, which she lives in a really startling way, shines with a vocal and dramatic sincerity that intensifies the expressiveness of both singing and acting. And the suffering character leaps out of the stage picture with a reality so lifelike and convincing that we can only wonder if we are hearing a performance by a singer or the interpretation of a great dramatic actress. (Quoted in Gualerzi 1986: 647)

It is hard to imagine a greater contrast to Adelina Patti's classical performance than Muzio's full-blooded naturalistic identification. Whereas Patti kept a distance to the role that permitted her to exploit the theatrical potential of a situation, what marks the naturalistic actor:

> is that all his artistic effects are used for the delineation of character, that he never allows himself to be carried away by the individual words or situations. The naturalistic actor bases each of his characters on an internal psychological

line of development which he follows with an almost hypnotic determination.
(Christiansen, S. 1975: 163-4)

This was how Muzio acted. Whereas the review of Patti's Violetta quoted above does not mention any psychological development in her acting of the role (but rather focuses on the recurring clashes of contrasting passions), Muzio was reported to have focused specifically on Violetta's gradual development. "At first", said Frida Leider "she was the very beautiful great lady[;] then she changed slowly as the tragedy developed. I have never heard the last act so poignantly performed" (quoted in Richards 1968: 205).

The naturalistic focus on the character's psychological subtext led, within the spoken theatre, to a downgrading of the poetic dimension of language, the motivation of the words tending to replace the music of the words. But this new theatrical convention conflicted fundamentally with Italian opera's traditional conception of song as a poetic stage language, resulting in the musical aspect of opera tending to detach itself from its theatrical aspect.

This change in the hierarchic relationship between music, words and theatre appears clearly from a comparison of Patti's and Muzio's working methods. Whereas Patti, on principle, stayed away from rehearsals, which she found vocally taxing, apparently paying little heed to the performances of her fellow singers, Muzio prepared a new role with meticulous attention to the external and internal atmosphere of the overall illusion. She would study the relevant historical period of the opera before turning to the libretto, and only then would she open the score, studying not only her own part, but the music of the whole opera. She subordinated everything, including her singing, to the dominant atmosphere of the setting, replacing the virtuoso solo performance with the psychologically and environmentally informed ensemble performance.

To Patti, song had been the extension of speech, but Muzio reduced both words and music to being an effect of the subtext. She was in perfect agreement with the tastes of her generation who conceived the ornaments, the sculpted phrasing, the idealised tone, the rhetorical employment of vocal colours characteristic of the old school as cold, un-dramatic and artificial, preferring a more "raw" conveyance of the emotional subtext—or, perhaps, one could talk of the "sub-music". That the *verismo* singing style appears fraught with interior conflict, is due to this separation of surface and subtext, of music and expression, which also seems the reason why commentators often referred to what *underlay* the music in Muzio's performances. This is evident from Belli's reference to her "fascinating inner and deep intensity" and Giacomo Lauri-Volpi's talk of her voice as "made of tears and sighs and restrained interior fire" (quoted in Christiansen, R. 1984: 302), as well as from Vittorio Frajese's description of her Violetta as "gifted with an incredible strength of passion which achieved the most unexpected effect extremely simply without ever betraying or distorting Verdi's music" (quoted in Gualerzi 1986: 647). Surely, the very idea of passion being at odds with music would never have occurred to anyone in relation to Patti, and besides, not everyone agreed with Frajese. For instance, in her famous 1935 recording of "Addio del passato", according to Jürgen Kesting, "one does not experience a genuinely musical delivery, but a dramatically overexcited one" (1986 Vol. I: 490) and Rupert Christiansen describes the same recording in these terms:

> Muzio exploits the use of short breaths—not sobs, so much as an effortful intake of air—until the memory of "l'amor di Alfredo" brings out a full passionate grief for what has been lost. A constant seesaw between *crescendo* and *diminuendo*, within both single notes and full phrases, further intensifies the feverishness. At the end the little spasms of breath return inexorably, culminating in a perfectly pitched scream of agony, cut sharply off into silence. (Christiansen, R. 1984: 304)

In other words, the underlying passion poses a constant threat to the music through the lacerating dynamic shifts, the short breaths, the spasms and the near-screams, which follow the "internal psychological line of development" rather than the shape of the phrases. In this *verismo* Violetta, the subtext is on the verge of dissolving the music.

MARIA CALLAS (1923-77)

Surely, the most famous Violetta of the twentieth century was that of Maria Callas. Originally, she had declined to sing the role, arguing that Violetta should be sung by a lighter voice, but her performances of *La Traviata* in the 1950s changed the general conception of the role entirely, not least through the six live recordings and one studio recording of the opera, which amply document the development in her interpretation.

Much of the literature on Callas deals with her significance to the history of opera, which has been characterised as a break with the light coloratura sopranos of the late nineteenth century (Patti) as well as with the *verismo* sopranos of the immediate past (Muzio). Traditionally, she has been described as a wide-ranged and expressive dramatic soprano trained to master the coloratura technique of the light soprano, whereby she revived the vocal ideal of such legendary singers as Maria Malibran and Giuditta Pasta who shone in the operas of Rossini, Donizetti and Bellini in the early nineteenth century. In the words of Rodolfo Celletti "Callas's voice was certainly ugly in natural quality", and yet he believed that

> part of her appeal was precisely due to this fact. Why? Because, for all its natural lack of varnish, velvet and richness, this voice could acquire such distinctive colours and timbre as to be unforgettable. (Celletti quoted in Lowe 1987: 84-5)

Expression through ugliness is an ideal as far removed from Patti's flawless "string of luminous pearls" as from "the fundamentally beautiful, round, ample, sensual, and limited *verismo* voice" (Segalini 1987: 119) characteristic of Muzio, but according to Celletti, Malibran had possessed a "flawed voice" too, and he claimed that "naturally beautiful voices, content to wallow in their own beauty, rarely produce anything of significance and are often boring" (Celletti 1987: 91). This view, which evidently conflicts with that of Verdi, was shared by other Callas fans who made Patti and her generation largely responsible for a decline in operatic singing. According to Teodoro Celli, the light soprano was merely "an instrument able to create continuous arabesques of sound devoid of true or intimate relationship with particular states of spirit, and was therefore practically incapable of true dramatic expressiveness" (1959: 44) and according to Sergio Segalini, Patti was the result of an evolution that "had brought the *bel canto* scores in line with the taste of Victorian salons, lightening the emission, changing the timbre, diminishing the volume to a sort of singing that contained more fin-de-siècle coquetry and disfigured the original spirit of the works". Callas, on the other hand, "had learned to restore to *bel canto* her power of emission, her breadth of timbre, her dramatic profundity" (Segalini 1987: 115). The ideal opera for the voice and art of Maria Callas, therefore, was *La Traviata*, according to Celli, because it contained

a role for a dramatic *soprano d'agilità* in which the separate capabilities of
this type of voice are employed separately: its agility to suggest the frivolous
aspect of the character in the first act, the dramatic or pathetic character
thereafter. The Verdian Violetta, which in the "adaptations" initiated at the
end of the past century has been divided between two interpretative
traditions—that of the light sopranos, who sing the first act well, the others
insufficiently, and that of the dramatic sopranos who sing the first act badly,
the others better—receives from Callas's art a truly unbetterable
interpretation. (1959: 60)

Despite Verdi's praise of Patti, critics like Celletti, Segalini and Celli
contended that Callas represented the truer art of Verdian drama. In *La
Traviata*, according to Stelios Galatopoulos, she had "penetrated
deeply down to the roots" of Violetta and had explored the role only
to give it back "afresh and without compromises, as Verdi had
conceived it through his musical genius" (1976: 208).

But did Callas really launch the return of a lost ideal? In some
respects, at least, she seems to have been closer to the Method actors
of her own generation than to the classical actresses of the nineteenth
century. "When I work on a character, I always ask myself: 'If I were
in her place, what would I do?'", she said in an interview, adding that
one "must transform oneself while remaining oneself" (Banzet in
Lowe 1987: 52), thus echoing the descriptions of Muzio's
psychological impersonations. Galatopoulos' description of her
performance of the final act of *La Traviata*, in which she "makes us
believe that she has indeed been ill in the bed for months and months,
dying, abandoned and forgotten", also rings of *verismo:*

> The way she drags her weak body from bed to sit once more at her dressing
> table, her arms useless, is almost frightening in its realism: the human being
> we knew has now become a living corpse. [...] as she senses the approach of
> death, she looks in the mirror and sings "Addio del passato" [...] so movingly
> that it is no longer merely an aria, but a sigh from the depths of a once frail
> but now purified soul. (Galatopoulos 1976: 261-2)

Yet for all her realism, Callas was not a *verismo* singer. When asking
Augusta Oltrabella, who belonged to the previous generation of
sopranos, why Callas had disappointed him in such pieces as
Giordano's *Fedora* and *Andrea Chénier*, Lanfranco Rasponi was told
that *verismo* "was not for her":

because despite what everyone says, she was an actress in the expression of the music, and not vice versa. In *verismo* the music is often secondary, and one must know how to create an atmosphere apart from the score. (1984: 584)

This probably explains why, especially early in her career, critics sometimes found Callas' theatrical appearance lacking in dramatic expression. When she sang Violetta in Venice in 1953, some spectators were "shocked by her lack of feeling in the part",[9] and in the opinion of the soprano Gina Cigna, Callas could not touch Muzio: "With Muzio you suffered agonies with her heroines, with Callas never" (Rasponi 1984: 209). According to one of her more sensitive critics, Callas' acting as Violetta "is of the simplest and she appears to make no effort to dramatize the situation physically, as the color of her voice depicts every emotion and sensation she is experiencing",[10] and a similar conclusion is drawn by Kesting in his comparison of Callas' recordings of "Addio del passato" to that of Muzio: "Maria Callas sees the piece more from the viewpoint of song: she moulds the words to the sound" (Kesting 1992: 100).

Callas' dramatic art was, unlike Muzio's, primarily a musical one. She replaced the latter's "bella voce" *accompanied* by psychology with "bel canto" *merged* with psychology. Though she greatly admired Muzio and often listened to her recordings, her way of approaching a role was quite different, as is implied by the allegation that she never read Alexandre Dumas' *La dame aux camélias* on which *La Traviata* is based. She always began with the music:

> I had to go by the music, by the libretto. The music itself justifies it, so the main thing is not the libretto, though I give enormous attention to the words. I try to find truth in the music. (Quoted in Galatopoulos 1976: 202)

With Callas, every aspect of the music became psychologically motivated. Whereas with Patti, vocal ornaments served to highlight emotionally laden words, with Callas they became directly expressive of the subtext: "even the *fioritura* and trills, all the coloratura things have a reason in the composer's mind, [...] they are the expression of the *stato d'animo* of the character—that is, the way he feels at that moment, the passing emotions that take hold of him" (quoted in Maguire 1968: 49).

Consequently, all aspects of Violetta's character had to be translated into musical terms. "I see the role, and therefore the voice, as fragile, weak and delicate" (quoted in Wisneski 1976: 84), she said in an interview, and she elaborated on this point after having abandoned the part:

> I had strived for years to create a sickly quality in the voice for Violetta; after all, she is a sick woman. It's all a question of breath, and you need a very clear throat to sustain this tired way of talking, or singing, in this case. And what did they say? "Callas is tired. The voice is tired". But that was precisely the impression I was trying to create. How could Violetta be in her condition and sing in big, round tones? It would be ridiculous.[11]

The creation of a "sickly" voice for Violetta recalls Verdi's insistence on vocal colour rather than extra-musical effects, but unlike Luisa Tetrazzini, who applied the "white voice" to her Violetta in the manner of a typified emotion, Callas' voice for Violetta emerged as the result of a deeply personal work with the character, whereby she sought to live up to her dictum: "One must transform oneself while remaining oneself".

To characterise Callas as a modernist performer may sound strange to some, but in certain respects she did reflect the aesthetic ideals of post-war modernism. Unlike many of her fans, she herself was even conscious of her singing as different from that of the nineteenth century:

> In a sense, [...] opera is today an old-fashioned form of art. Whereas before you could sing "I love you" or "I hate you", now you can still sing about it but you must express the corresponding feeling through music rather than through the words. It is our duty to modernise our approach so that we can give opera a bit of fresh air—cut lengthy repetitions (repetition of a melody is usually not much good; the sooner you come to the point, the better it is), cut redundant movement so that it must become credible to the audience. (Galatopoulos 1976: 213)

Cutting "lengthy repetitions" and "redundant movement"—Callas argued that one should always omit the second verse of "Addio del passato", since it "adds nothing; in fact, it would only detract from what you have done" (Ardoin 1987: 169)—was certainly a result of her psychological approach to the music. To Adelina Patti, repetitions were invitations to draw full effect from the central emotions of a scene, in open acknowledgment of the performance situation, by ornamenting the vocal line, but to Callas who, like Muzio, based her characters "on an internal psychological line of development" musical repetitions were simply an obstacle to the drama.

No less striking in the above quotation is Callas' view of musical rather than verbal communication as essentially "modern". This recalls the oft-heard descriptions of her singing as "instrumental", and indeed she characterised *bel canto* as "a schooling of the voice so as to develop it as an instrument",[12] describing herself as "the first instrument of the orchestra",[13] and to many critics, Callas' coupling of the instrumental with the emotionally expressive was the central feature of her revival of the *bel canto* style.

From the letters of Bellini and Verdi, however, it appears that their vocal ideal was declamatory rather than instrumental. Indeed, I have not come across a favourable comparison of a singer's voice to an instrument in Verdi's letters. To ears used to the pregnant psychological expression of Claudio Muzio and her generation, the cooler, more ornamented and technically perfected singing of Adelina Patti may indeed appear instrumental, but this does not appear to be how her contemporaries heard her. Rather, later generations have wrongly taken agility and emotional distance for an instrumental ideal.

But Callas' ideal was instrumental. In her singing one may hear a musical reflection of the modernist ideals of shape and line, of structure and clarity, which also seem to underlie Walter Legge's telling description of her legato as "a telegraph wire or telephone wire, where you can see the line going through and the consonants are just perched on it like the feet of sparrows" (Schwarzkopf 1982: 198). But few have realised as clearly as André Tubeuf that Callas did not, in truth, revive the vocal ideals of the *ottocento*:

> She owes her musical imagination to the orchestra of the end of the nineteenth century. It is not in singing that one should seek her masters and models. It is in instruments. In the detail of her *Traviata*, of her *Sonnambula*, of her *Norma*, look for the sudden color and presence of the oboe, or flute, or even clarinet—under the conductive legato, that outline of the viola d'amore. [...] To a music that one believed outdated, Callas brought this sensibility of timbre and inflection polished in later eras. [...] Callas managed to be born without a singer's roots. She was born a German musician. (Tubeuf in Lowe 1987: 109-10).

In Tubeuf's opinion, Callas' true medium was the record, modernism's most essential contribution to musical culture:

> Her verve, her vivacity were purely musical, and in no way theatrical. By abolishing the theatre and its ostensible movements, records liberated and

magnified that pure mobility; it made of it a Racinian truth, complex in meaning, pure in accent. (Tubeuf in Lowe 1987: 110-11).

Callas' translation of psychological expression into musical form points to a final aspect of her modernism, i.e. her almost obsessive respect for the letter of the score, which showed her to be a child of an age focussed on musical structure and form. According to Callas, the first duty of a singer "is to try and feel what the composer wanted" (Galatopoulos 1976: 213); she was famously uncompromising in her attempt to sing the notes exactly as written, giving them what she considered to be the intended expression.

Faithfulness to the letter of the score was a late invention. It was never one of Patti's greatest virtues, to say the least, but the heavy ornamentation to which her Bellini recordings bear witness never drew a critical remark from Verdi (though it did from Rossini). To Patti, the score was less a sacred text than the basis of a performance, and it was exactly her freedom of interpretation that enabled her to make use of the musical repetitions that Callas cut.

The revival of historical performance practices will always be filtered through the sensibilities of modern performers, and just as Claudia Muzio discovered the violent expressionism of her own time in *La Traviata,* Maria Callas found in the same score the transparent musical structure coupled with psychological precision that so accurately captured the fascinations of the post-war period. Both interpretations may be said to exist as potentials in the opera, though neither of them actually reflect Verdi's stated intentions, and all three interpretations reflect the proximity of the histories of singing and acting.

NOTES

[1] *The Musical World*, 6 July 1861, quoted in Klein 1920: 83.
[2] *The Sunday Times*, 16 June 1895, quoted in Klein 1920: 449.
[3] All translations into English have been made by the author.
[4] *The Times*, 5 July 1861, quoted in Klein 1920: 407.
[5] Letter to Opprandino Arrivabene of 27 December 1877, quoted in Albert 1931: 205-6.
[6] Letter to Giulio Ricordi of 5 October1877, quoted in Busch 1978: 407.
[7] Letter to Giuseppe Piroli of 27 December 1877, quoted in Luzio Vol. IV. 1947: 129.
[8] Letter to Léon Escudier of 11 March 1865, quoted in Rosen and Porter 1984. 110.

[9] Cynthia Jolly, review in *Opera*, 1953 in Lowe 1987: 155.

[10] Peter Dragazde, review in *Opera,* 1952 in Lowe 1987: 152.

[11] Interview by Derek Prouse, London *Sunday Times*, 19 March 1961, quoted in Wisneski: 85.

[12] Interview in *The Observer*, 8 and 15 February 1970 in Lowe 1987: 63.

[13] Radio interview by Norman Ross, Chicago, 17 November 1957, quoted in Jellinek 1960: 317.

CHAPTER 6

THE TENOR IN DECLINE? NARRATIVES OF NOSTALGIA AND THE PERFORMATIVITY OF THE OPERATIC TENOR

PAMELA KARANTONIS

> A Doleful tale prepare to hear
> As ever yet was told:
> The like, perhaps, ne'er reach'd the Ear
> Of either Young or Old.
> This of the sad and sudden Death
> Of one of mighty Fame
> Who lately hath resign'd his Breath—
> Old Tenor was his Name.
> (Joseph Green, 1750)

The verse above may have been better suited to the untimely (and still somewhat mysterious) death of the legendary German tenor Fritz Wunderlich in 1966 at the age of 32, but equally its "old tenor" is the point of departure for this chapter, written at a moment in history when the operatic world has moved beyond an artist of stature (both vocal and corporeal) as Luciano Pavarotti, who died in 2007. He was a tenor who became the ambassador for opera in the late twentieth century "who ha[d] [...] brought the gift of opera to millions world wide—many of whom might never have known what an aria was, or have been bothered to find out" (Bonvincini 2007: 199). Accordingly, this chapter will examine some key concepts concerned with the performativity of the operatic tenor over the past one hundred years. Attendant to this are issues of masculinity, the visceral appeal of the voice as against the dramatic imperative of representation, the blending of popular cultural and operatic genres and the cultural power of vocal pedagogues. It will also examine the nature of the listening audience, who range from consumers of opera and film to fans of the tenor *per se* (this latter kind will continue to enjoy a tenor's sound, despite the theatrical, musical or technological matrixing of the artist). Furthermore, this chapter will suggest that the preference of audiences for the visceral presence of the tenor, as opposed to the representation of the musical and theatrical languages which he serves, has a significant impact on the culture of music theatre. The conclusions suggest that commentators on the voice, who are prone to particularly emotive narratives about the tenor and his decline, may be betraying related narratives which extend to theories of listening, pleasure, masculinity and cultural power.

In 2004, a documentary was produced in Great Britain entitled *Pavarotti—The Last Tenor* (Hanly 2004). Featured in the documentary are a number of iconic male Hollywood celebrities such as Dustin Hoffman and Michael Caine and rock legends Bono and Brian May. What is curious about this documentary as a part of the performance archive, is that the tenor, too, is cast in the role of *machismo* display with the "high art" connotations of opera being moderated to read as a muscular athleticism that links masculinity, virility and cultural power in the West. It begs the question as to why the operatic tenor needs to be flanked by these icons of masculinity, when opera fans might assume his celebrity has arisen from a mastery of musical languages and finely adept dramatic characterisations. The answer might be suggested by the hypothesis that the commodification of the operatic tenor and the pleasure of that commodity's consumption through the twentieth to twenty-first centuries are fraught with a much less empowering model of gender politics than in the raising to divadom of women, namely, of the operatic soprano. As the diva is often venerated by audiences who associate her soprano *fach* with historically tragic genres, the inescapable metaphysics of her repeated sacrifice in varying dramatic texts is matched by the vulnerability and femininity of her singing body, with its overt and sublimated maternal sonic properties. However, the tenor has a far more demonstrative visceral history—escaping the knife of castration—his virility is sublimated in the moment in 1829, when the first full-throated high C rings out in a production of *Guillaume Tell*.[1] So by the end of the nineteenth century, when the tenor and soprano are paired as partners in the musical language of dominant operatic texts (such as those of Verdi, Wagner and Puccini), this diva-worship is matched by a worship of the tenor who forges a celebrity based on his paratextual appeal (Genette 1997). What is meant by the "paratextual" here is that it is evident throughout the twentieth century, starting most notably with the recording career of Enrico Caruso, that the operatic tenor has made particular efforts to accrue a fandom, beyond the textual limits of the operatic repertoire to which he is ostensibly committed. Consider the claims of Pavarotti's extroverted New York manager Herbert Breslin (who conveniently forgets that Enrico Caruso enjoyed popular cultural status as a tenor several decades earlier):

> When Luciano came along, sopranos ruled the opera world: Callas, Tebaldi, Sutherland. I shifted the attention of the opera world from rampant diva-dom to a tenor. Then I brought that tenor out of the opera house and into the arms of an enormous mass public. Nobody else had ideas like that [...]. Together we changed the landscape of opera. (Breslin and Midgette 2004: 13)

While there might be some hyperbole to the claim of unprecedented tenor celebrity, Pavarotti's non-operatic career trajectory does offer an interesting study in using the tenor to "make opera" of non-operatic contexts (with the added teamwork of Placido Domingo and José Carreras to complete the marketing coup of "The Three Tenors") in the masculine, working-class domain of football games such as the 1990 World Cup in Rome.

The study of the operatic tenor, as a unique lesson in gender performativity, needs to begin in the eighteenth century, when he is overshadowed by the *castrati*. In his inception, the operatic tenor, as we know him in the Western recording-artist tradition, operated as an intervention in cross-gender performance, for reasons that are both dramatic and musical. To this effect, John Rosselli[2] builds a case for opera's inception as being predicated upon gender confusion, with the examples of French and Italian traditions of the counter-tenor utilising either falsetto or an unnaturally high range of normal vocal registration:

> In French opera, the *haute-contre* who sang many leading parts was—rather than a countertenor such as we now hear—a tenor with an unusually high extension [...]. *Haute-contres* might sing the part of a fury or some mythological being, like the frog-nymph in Rameau's *Platée* [...]. Human cross-dressing was thought against "good taste", but for an old convention whereby tenors could sing the parts of old comic women [...]. In Italian serious opera, tenors had limited scope: they played the parts of fathers or rulers [...] were esteemed and paid less than the castrato and *prima donna*. Only at the very end of the eighteenth century did they start to outdo the castrato in both prestige and fee. (Rosselli in Potter 2000: 91-92)

The subsequent history suggests that French and Italian audiences were enjoying a fortified and dramatic tenor sound in the *tenore di forza* (Rosselli 2000: 98), who were nationalised champions, similarly accorded transcendent qualities of a more "masculine" or "chesty" sound than the counter-tenor of the eighteenth century:

> The earliest Italian heroic tenor, Matteo Babbini, spent time in Paris during the Revolution and later impressed audiences with his dramatic ability and vocal power in "republican" parts. (Rosselli 2000: 98)

The phenomenon of the tenor voice as a gender intervention might be explained from a pedagogic perspective. Ultimately, the tenor voice is a consummate blending of opposing vocal qualities—light and heavy, masculine and feminine (which are culturally negotiated). These qualities can take on the power of a personality in the voice, which can be chaotic in training but fruitful in the mature career:

> Most beginners tend to sing either all heavy or all light. If they are conscious at all of the other register, they are schizophrenic about it. The *unused register* [...] is like a different personality to the beginner, something into which he lapses only by accident. He must be taught to use a *full voice,* a blending of both heavy and light quality. With men, the unused register is *falsetto.* Ever since their voices changed, most men (with the exception of some tenors) have been so afraid they might sound effeminate that they have cultivated a tense, heavy production. (Vennard 1967: 73, 76)

The very word *falsetto*—a technical phenomenon which should not be confused with the *castrato* as it can be achieved by an *un*castrated male—can remind the listener of the visceral reality of the singer's sex, and in the root of the word, implies an artificiality of vocal production and is something which is modified. The ideal is the alternative tonal concept of the "head" voice, championed by *bel canto* era pedagogue Manuel Garcia (Vennard 1967: 77). However, it is at this crisis point of gender signification in the voice that the operatic tenor can be most instructive as to how masculinity is performed by a "taming" of the upper regions of the voice. In a feat of vocal trapeze artistry, the head voice of the tenor pulls him back from any historical associations with the sexual ambiguity of the counter-tenor and into a new but fragile celebrity. Ultimately, it could be argued that the operatic tenor is a marginalised form of masculinity, for his ability to conquer "the unused register" and risk emasculating himself in the process.

In his account of overcoming such vocal challenges, the Mexican tenor Francisco Araiza identifies that his naturally prominent "Adam's apple" (or thyroid cartilage, Vennard 1967: 52) was an impediment. Once he mastered exercises to open up the pharynx and allow less upward movement and prominence of the thyroid cartilage, his voice became more resonant (Araiza in Matheopoulos 1986: 23). Significantly on the visual level, the "Adam's apple" is an unmistakable marker of the male sex and one which betrays cross-gender impersonation. By modifying its movement and visual prominence, the tenor produces a sound with less register breaks, so that the "effeminacy" of falsetto is avoided, while this visual icon of masculinity is suppressed: a matter of anatomical necessity in making an operatic sound.

To add another layer of complexity, discourses about the tenor which form the popular imagination and biography cast him in a hyperbolised terrain of masculinity. The tenor voice becomes indexical to phallic power and a popular cultural appeal to heterosexual narratives of conquest. It is not too imaginative a leap to regard the tenor as "a playboy" or "risk-taker", given photographic images of Jussi Björling speed-boating on the Stockholm archipelago or the mysterious circumstances surrounding the deaths of both Fritz Wunderlich and Mario Lanza. Consistent with this celebration of the tenor's corporeality, in the popular imagination, is an extended fantasy, that the listener may enjoy his vocal power and its attendant virility vicariously. The vicarious pleasure of the listener is augmented by fantasies of heroism and adventure when it comes to the tenor voice. As Simon Frith argues: "the voice as direct expression of the body [...] is as important for the way we listen as for the way we interpret what we hear: we can sing along, reconstruct in fantasy our own sung versions" (Frith 1996: 192). This notion of vicarious pleasure in the listener is also crucial to Wayne Koestenbaum's work, though his focus is on sopranos, rather than tenors, for reasons which have both psychoanalytic and sexuality-related validity (Koestenbaum 1993).

The specificity of the listener's desire for the tenor voice is something which ties somewhat mysteriously to discourses of vocal pedagogy, with their increasingly scientific emphasis and categorisation of the tenor voice much like the description of competitive athletes and appraisals which have nationalistic or cultural resonances, almost identical to sports fanaticism. The listener's interest in the tenor becomes a complex matrix of desires. Such examples of categorisation in the Italian School include *tenore robusto* (or *Heldentenor* in German), *lyric, lyrico-spinto* (or singing-thrust), *tenore serio* (or dramatic tenor), which are identical in dramatic and dynamic properties to the female counterparts (Vennard 1967: 263) with the exception of the German *Heldentenor*, which is often regarded (sometimes problematically) as an extended baritone (Vennard 1967: 79). While many of these categories are common to *all* voice types, issues of vocal weight, stamina and range have particular resonances for the tenor's performativity, because it underscores the appeal of his corporeality. This is fed by the tenor's representation in the popular media. In 1933, British journalist Richard Capell described Beniamino Gigli's British recital début at the Albert Hall in London, with a none-too-subtle use of metaphor: "Gigli is a superb singer. He is a little man, a bantam fighting cock. He sings with the whole force of his body, as naturally as a game cock fights" (Douglas 1994: 88). To reprise an earlier example, but in light of this sporting fetish, the World Cup performance success of "The Three Tenors" led to a much-publicised and reproduced concert in Rome in 1990. The issue of paratext arises because there is no tenor trio in Western operatic literature, therefore a new repertoire was fashioned to suit the performative act of pitting three tenors against each other. Underscoring the anticipated experience for the listener was the model of "compare and contrast" in the consumption of tenor sounds. This was a fact knowingly exploited by the participating artists in a "sporting" esteem:

> We also had to fight off some lunatic ideas. Before the concert one of the producers though it would make the evening more interesting if a panel of judges scored each of us as we sang, just as they do for Olympic athletes. Thank heavens this idea did not go very far. I am all for competition [...]. The competition between the three of us makes us all put forth our greatest effort. And who benefits from that? The audience of course. (Pavarotti 1995: 65)

As well as comparing and contrasting individual tenor sounds, much pleasure is derived in emphasising the tonal and linguistic differences implicit in various "National Schools" and, by extension, a suggestion of supremacy of one style over the other.[3] In fact, the more globalised and internationalised the world of opera becomes, the more laboured the narratives on cultural differences appear. In recent decades, the Spanish tenor, Alfredo Kraus observed the challenges of singing French repertoire as a native Spanish speaker:

[The French style] demands good taste, subtlety, finesse, sensitivity and control [...]. And to Italian and Spanish voices, the French language sometimes seems anti-musical, anti-singing, because it seems to go against the natural musical and vocal line. This always displeases the French, although they, themselves, are the first to admit it. (Kraus in Matheopoulos 1986: 113)

While this argument is essentialist and often unsupported, these generalising comparisons add to the performativity of the tenor, who is seen to overcome the hurdles of cultural difference on the world stage. Furthermore, this kind of supreme intelligence in the artist is narrated as increasingly rarefied, if we are to believe the pedagogic predictions about the "decline" of the tenor voice.

Edgar Herbert-Caesari's *The Voice of the Mind* is such a pedagogic text. It favours the Italian training of the singer, but with a scientific emphasis. The author argues: "There is no such thing as a [...] national mechanism" (Herbert-Caesari 1978: 44) when it comes to vocal technique, though instead chooses to identify immutable scientific principles in the Italian *bel canto* tradition. He warns of the decline of good singing, through both poorly-acquired technique and vocally unsuitable repertoire (which translates usually to pop music). Herbert-Caesari casts the net wide in apportioning blame for the decline of a beautiful singing tone, when he writes in 1951:

[the] culture of the arts is heading slowly and surely for a chaos of ugliness, a retrogression to the first feeble attempts of primitive man. Witness the slant today in terms of the surrealist daubs, sculptured monstrosities, and architectural atrocities. Is it the deliberate cult of ugliness? Or incapacity? (*ibid.*: 38)

Despite the questionable political undertone to this observation, an interesting question is raised: could modernist architecture or experimental visual arts be destroying the classical voice? Is the tenor voice in danger of losing its balance of dark and light that is a painterly chiaroscuro aesthetic? Herbert-Caesari argues that it is *aural* culture's deterioration that destroys the classical voice, as much as poor vocal instruction. Could the cult of the *tenore di forza*, with his upward thrusting chest sound (and dare I suggest its phallic connotations?) be destroying this fine balance of tenor voice production?

Despite his protestations, Herbert-Caesari is also a scholar and fan of the technical tradition followed by the Italian, Gigli, whose career was also augmented by cinematic and pop-song activities, particularly the title song from the film in which he starred in 1941, *Mamma* (Brignone 1941). Rather than being the exception, Gigli's on-screen appearance indicated a new matrixing of tenorial presence. To this effect, the performativity of operatic film star Mario Lanza was complex and emblematic of the interdependence of performance media for the tenor's celebrity. The 1951 MGM film *The Great Caruso* was given greater box office appeal due to the dual factors of Lanza's screen success in *The Toast of New Orleans* (1950) as well as his recording success, from the film's soundtrack, of the pop single "Be My Love" (Brodzsky, 1950). *The Great Caruso* loosely traces the life of Italian tenor and star of the Metropolitan Opera, Enrico Caruso.[4] In the film, Lanza plays the title role, alongside other Metropolitan stars. The irony of Lanza's success in this role is that he will always be eulogised as a tenor who did not realise an operatic stage career, but in the public imagination, his visual and aural performance was always metonymic for opera. Lanza's recorded popularity of Lara's "Granada" (Lara 1998) is an example of the hybridity of his visceral sound, before a theory of the "cross-over" artist was really formulated. The tonal quality alternates between a full-throated, operatic, pharyngeal resonation and an American nasality of squeezing the voice into spoken vowels, so that the larynx moves upward and emulates a flattened, pop-singer sound.

Some fifty years later, the question remains as to how much the listening public risks being fetishistic in its enjoyment of the tenor sound. An iconic example of this is the genre experimentation of the 1980s, when Placido Domingo recorded a collection of pop songs with country-and-western star, John Denver, entitled *Perhaps Love* (Denver 1981). Criticism of him, from a fellow tenor, was expressed as "Domingo wants to be the Leonardo da Vinci of opera" (Matheopoulos 1986: 75), although the back-handed compliment betrayed the risks of the experiment. The cross-over tenor could be our evidence of "decline", if we believe Simon Frith on "bad music", which includes: "tracks involving genre confusion [...]. I'd add almost any opera singer performing almost any rock song. And, come to that, the Kiri Te Kanawa/José Carreras recording of *West Side Story*" (Frith 2004: 18). While Frith is able to debate the contingencies of cross-over success or failure, some conservative commentators simply bemoan the cultural mobility of cross-over artists and their over-exposure in the media. According to a review by Rupert Christiansen in Great Britain's *Daily Telegraph,*

Russell Watson is a New Zealand tenor plucked from the working men's clubs [and] signed to Decca [...]. At the heart of his mystique—parroted in endless celebrity magazine interviews—is the notion that he is a dead ordinary cheeky chappie who can do "Nessun Dorma" and "Vesti La Giubba" like Pavarotti. (Christiansen 2002)

Rather than objecting to these tenors on the basis of their musicality or vocal powers, opposition to this kind of celebrity tenor goes to the heart of the commodification of classical music, with the crucial issue of marketing priorities in recording companies, which allow "the Russell Watsons" to "burn up the marketing budgets of the so-called classical labels on which they appear [...]. Crossover is not an aid to classical renewal, rather an act of classical euthanasia" (Lebrecht 2001).

With increasingly sophisticated recording technology, tenor "boy-bands" such as Il Divo threaten to dissolve the aural cultural threshold of pop and opera. Their recordings of "easy listening" romances indicate very little interpretive or dramatic matrixing—but suggest that twenty-first century popular culture is accommodating of a tenor simulacrum, which sees its defining vocal features as a high range and upward thrusting chest sound or even falsetto. Furthermore, the sheer numbers (or collectives) of solo tenors who can be marketed as grouped divo-soloists, rather than a choir, is increasing, with the recent celebrity of "The Ten Tenors" from Australia, with an album titled *One is Not Enough* (Morley 2003). Conversely, popular musical theatre is seeking to emulate the full-throated solo operatic sound, if we regard the more recent musical theatre character of Jean Valjean that gives the heroic lead of Boublil and Schönberg's *Les Misérables* a fortified visceral presence in his command of head-voice tessitura repertoire (Boublil 1985) that has very recently transferred to cinema. The ever-morphing repertoire of operatic cinematic-singing too, can be regarded, rather than indexical to staged operatic scores, as a discrete musical canon, if we are to consider examples such as Roberto Alagna's homage to French screen legend Luis Marino in a collection titled *C'est Magnifique!*

To return to the title of this chapter, an appreciation of the operatic tenor rests upon a consciousness in the public, of *nostalgia* for the cultural spaces the historical tenor has inhabited as increasingly rarefied. Ultimately the resting place of the tenor is in the performance archive. Peggy Phelan's theory of the performativity of the archive itself is that a performance must disappear in order for the archive to rise in status (Phelan in Schneider 2001: 105). This is supported by the power of historical revisions in the listening experience, advocated in Sarah Nancy's chapter on the *Tragédie Lyrique* in this volume. As museums for tenors such as Jussi Björling and Fritz Wunderlich spring up across the world, it seems logical to ask if we are eulogising a performance style and culture rooted in the past? The most informative piece on Mario Lanza's career, for instance, is a US documentary, which plays up the logic of this nostalgia—*Mario Lanza: The American Caruso* (Musilli 1983).

To conclude, the performativity of the tenor exists within a matrix of complicated and competing narratives about his decline and celebrity, within a culture in which appreciation of the operatic tenor is in apprehending a sound-object that is as overtly masculine as it is thrillingly unusual. What has not been addressed here is the indeterminate nature of the tenor's subjectivity in that process. However something is suggested about those who listen to, and commentate upon, on the tenor's performativity and audiences who experience a personal engagement or attachment to the visceral appeal of the singer. There is arguably a psychoanalytic element to this attachment, where the *jouissance* of the listener is under threat when their attachment object produces a sound that is no longer virile. To give this a greater sense of urgency, when listening to a voice becomes an addiction, much can be threatened by its natural decline. It can distort the listener's perception of the entire textual fabric of aural culture. Perhaps it can be suggested that the decline of a singer is vicarious to the aging process of the listener and not aural culture itself.

However, nostalgia, historiography and the archive cannot be dismissed so easily as to be labelled experiences in psychological attachment. They do chart a progression of the listening culture of the operatic tenor over the past one hundred years which diverges quite decidedly from the musical and dramatic literatures for which the tenor ostensible rose to celebrity, legitimated by a connection to "opera". Commentators continue to be divided over the artistic consequences of our tenor-related listening pleasures and desires.

EPILOGUE

Finding a new way of presenting Verdi's most popular aria "La Donna e Mobile", from *Rigoletto* is a challenge to directors. [...] This week I saw Lindsay Posner's terrific production of *Rigoletto* at Opera Holland Park [...]. In the bar where the tenor sings the aria, there was a television showing Pavarotti performing. The tenor shrugged and turned it off as he commenced the song [...] it was something of a mixed blessing for the tenor singing the role of the Duke in this production to have the audience's heads buzzing with memories of Pavarotti (Lister 2011).

NOTES

[1] I am indebted here to Clemens Risi who points out the public premiere of this High C in chest-mix sound by a tenor in Rossini's work and for directing me to John Rosselli's scholarship on the tenor.

[2] Articles by John Rosselli consulted here are "Grand Opera: Nineteenth-Century Revolution and Twentieth-Century Tradition" and "Song into Theatre: The Beginnings of Opera", which both appear in Potter 2000.

[3] The late American tenor and vocal pedagogue Richard Miller makes a case for the Old Italian School of singing and its principles as a standard by which to assess German, French, English and North American approaches to breath management, phonation and desired tonal qualities in Miller 1997.

[4] Arguably, the popularity of this film is testimony to the fact that many tenors in the twentieth century have measured their vocal success in relation to Caruso's, as well as seeking to imitate his voice.

CHAPTER 7

THE THREEPENNY OPERA:
PERFORMATIVITY AND THE BRECHTIAN PRESENCE
BETWEEN MUSIC AND THEATRE

MICHAEL EIGTVED

"I strongly recommend people who suffer from chronic sleeplessness a visit to the Theatre at Schiffbauerdamm" was the sarcastic reaction of one reporter sent out to review the opening of *The Threepenny Opera* on 31 August 1928 (quoted in Wyss 1977: 50).[1] Representing the *Neue Preussische Kreuz-Zeitung*, and thus probably far from Bertolt Brecht and his ideas, the reporter managed to make his unwillingness to agree with the political or ideological statements in the performance totally overshadow the fact that he had been part of what most others have described as a triumphant and almost hypnotic experience. Monty Jacobs in *Vossische Zeitung* did however not attribute this to Brecht, he found that what really made the evening worthwhile were the ballads. He notes that they

> are casually scattered throughout the Penny Opera, [and] are what determine the triumph of the evening. Their introduction into the play is one of the merits of Erich Engels' outstanding staging. (*Ibid.*: 52)[2]

What both journalists managed to avoid—at least when reporting on the evening—is what Brecht had hoped for: that the performativity of the performance would trigger an urge to (political) action in the audience. And perhaps this scope of Brecht's work was simply not as obvious for the 1928 audience witnessing *The Threepenny Opera*, as traditional theatre history has since argued. "Not a trace of modern social or political satire",[3] scoffed the reporter from the communist paper *Die Rote Fahne*.

In his "Anmerkungen zur Oper Aufstieg und Fall der Stadt Mahagonny" from 1931, Bertolt Brecht states: "In the provocative we

see reality re-established".[4] But being put to sleep—or just enjoying
the songs—is probably not exactly what *The Threepenny Opera* was
supposed to provoke in the audience. The following is based on an
interest in trying to show that the performance did indeed provoke
reactions in the audience, but not necessarily the kind of experience
that Brecht had planned. My main interest is in looking into the
relationship between the theoretical framework Brecht provided for
his work, the time and circumstances under which *The Threepenny
Opera* was written and produced, and the specific performativity
involved in the first presentation of the show. The specificity of
theatre, and of performativity in it, will inevitably be part of this
discussion. Erica Fischer-Lichte writes in an article from 1995 that
theatre (unlike everyday life) provides an experience of the

> very process of construction and the conditions underlying it. While
> constructing a reality of our own [in theatre], we become aware of doing so
> and begin to reflect upon it. Thus, theatre turns out to be a field of
> experimentation where we can test our capacity for and the possibilities of
> constructing reality. (Fischer-Lichte 1995: 104)

It is in other words the process rather than the content that constitutes
something as theatrical. It is the construction of a new reality rather
than of a fiction that makes theatre into theatre. And that corresponds
very well with the ideas of Brecht and his epic theatre.

The use of song and music in Brecht's early works is a significant
element of his developing aesthetic. The music provides variation, and
perhaps more significantly, the use of music offers the possibility of
creating "poetic theatre" in the midst of sharp political messages.
Brecht is aware of the fact that this might undermine his own idea of a
theatre without hypnosis (1993: 241), but he believed that music could
act as a "double", that the quotation marks he himself heard in popular
music would be present for the audience as well. And this in fact relies
on the performativity of the show, on what Brecht labelled the *Gest*.

The performing artist must be able to produce this doubleness: on
the one hand projecting the emotional content of the popular song,
thus honestly illustrating its sentiment, and on the other hand
maintaining a distance so that the audience becomes aware of the
double purpose of the song. It is not a question of revealing the
character's inner life, but of demonstrating certain processes of life
which take place in society. Brecht did not want to leave behind the

pleasure of the music, the lure of the song, but meant it to be performed in a manner that helped reveal the hollowness of bourgeois society (1993: 33-4).

But is this, however, really possible to achieve on stage, or do the performative qualities of song and music counteract this idea to a degree, so that it remains only a theoretical possibility? These are some of the questions up for discussion.

BRECHT, WEILL AND THE AVANT GARDE

The following will reflect upon the theoretical and ideological framework to which *The Threepenny Opera* belongs. This framework is part of what Peter Bürger has labelled the "historical avant-garde", and is reflected in Brecht's ideas; but it also has relations to the composer Kurt Weill's connection to the German *Zeit Oper* movement in the early part of the twentieth century (Bürger 1982: 15ff.).

In many ways what Bertolt Brecht wanted with his ideas for a renewed theatre was to focus on performativity. In order to do so, the question of the spectator's attitude towards the performance's elements obviously becomes crucial. Brecht uses a symbolic figure for this, when he compares the mode in which a person in the audience can be understood with a man smoking a cigarette (1993: 31). The smoker is already occupied with his own act of smoking, and is not necessarily interested in being spellbound by the actions in the theatre. Thus, Brecht argues, the spectator must be engaged in the events on stage for other reasons. But here a very important point may be made: when song and music is part of the performance, is this rather laid back attitude actually very often possible? Or is it more likely, given the impact of music on human beings, that the audience exactly at that point—both physically and mentally—leaves the cigarette in the ashtray and becomes involved? Not because they get politically aroused, but simply because music theatre appeals so directly to us, that it is really hard to remain unaffected.

The basic idea of Brecht's epic theatre was the separation of the elements. This is very clear in his music theatre works, where the performing of songs became an essential part of the performance, not by way of furthering the understanding of the singing character (in a "classical" operatic way), but by pointing to the performing itself, and separating it to some extent from the other parts of the performance. The smoker's attitude was not to be challenged by sentiments as in the traditional opera, but through reason and reflection on the musical actions on stage.

Whether this really does happen in a specific performance is part of what can be explored through an elaboration of the use of the concept of performativity. I am going to suggest that we as audience members are often so committed to the pull of narrative and Aristotelian dramatic conventions that it is difficult not to psychologise characters in order that we can relate to them, asking—for instance—what kind of motivation the young Polly Peachum in *The Threepenny Opera* actually has, or how she feels, when on her wedding night with the villain Macheath she sings a song about a pirate girl killing men.

The techniques of epic music theatre were intended to make content an independent component to which text, music and scenery might "relate" by giving up the idea of illusion and focusing instead on what Brecht called *der Diskutierbarheit* "the discussability" (1993: 23). The spectator was encouraged to "give his vote to" the performance rather than experience it; to be aware of it rather than be thrown into it (Bürger 1982: 23); and the ultimate reason for this was of course the transformation of the social function of theatre, which was Brecht's goal.

This idea Brecht also spelled out in his theoretically-based notion of three levels of vocal communication which are available in the epic theatre (Brecht 1993: 32-33). Here, according to Brecht, we must distinguish between speech, enhanced speech, and song. These three are not in a hierarchal order, but supplementary to each other and thus they are juxtaposed, possible modes of expression. In Brecht's opinion there is not, as we have been conditioned to think, a progression towards ever-more-elaborate expression from speech to song. As he says, "it is never the case that song appears where the excess of emotion makes words insufficient".[5] So what is song's function?—we may ask. One answer is given in a typical Brechtian paradox: music should be "meditative and moralising".[6]

Theoretically then, we are able through the techniques of epic theatre to distinguish not the way the musical elements enhance the emotions involved in the actual, fictional events portrayed on stage, but rather how all the theatrical elements discuss the issues brought forward. Theatre's social function should in that movement be shifted from providing pleasure (or fear, sadness, joy or anger) to showcasing important issues in need of a debate. Again paradoxically, Brecht somehow realises that music—and certainly the kind used in *The Threepenny Opera*—possesses qualities that allow it to reach beyond a theatrical poetics of reflection to engage spectators, through its performativity, in the very act of its performance. This "problem" is handled by theoretically arguing that, because the 'songs' are representing a parallel universe (i.e., showing that criminals can have similar emotional lives to bourgeois people), the satirical distance thus created counterpoints the narcotic and potentially "culinary" qualities of the music (Brecht 1993: 240-41ff.). However, the events of the opening night offer an interesting window through which Brecht's theoretical claims can be put to the test.

CONCEPTS AND THEORIES

The specificity of the concept of performativity is elaborated by contemporary theoreticians such as Erika Fischer-Lichte, and it appears that many of these insights are actually very well suited to music theatre (see Fischer-Lichte 2004: 31ff.). The idea here, so to speak, is to test Brecht's ideas through the use of methods developed from the theories of theatricality and performativity.

First the performative viewpoint. The argument is that the concept of performativity is not primarily interested in the performance as a work of art; it is not hermeneutic aesthetics that we should apply. The aim is not to understand the performance as a closed entity, a work; it is to experience it. And the project in question here will then also be to investigate how we can work with these matters of experience in historical performances (Fischer-Lichte 2004: 17).

The focus of the theories is—as already mentioned—to experience the process of establishing a new reality. Not to interpret it, but to *live it*, or at least to *live through it*, and thereby experience a certain kind of new reality. The argument is that the audience does not tend to think during a performance what it is about; they try to sense what kind of experience it offers, and they reflect on their own experience rather than on the significance of specific elements.

A music theatre performance will provoke both bodily and emotional reactions as well as intellectual reflection. But I will try to argue that in the actual situation—right there in the theatre—you will perhaps focus more on the quality of the experience, the pleasure or anxiety of the moment, than on understanding or interpreting meaning. That does not mean that reflection is not possible, simply that during the specific performance, the sensory and emotional experience are foregrounded. It is for the most part an active participation—bodily as well as emotional—that drives music theatre, rather than physically passive, intellectual reflection. This may be true even if the theatrical strategies used to create a performance, as with the performance in question, are meant to stimulate intellectual activities.

You might say that in music theatre the phenomenological body never gets hidden behind the semiotic body. The bodily presence of the singer and the sound of the voice will be as important a part of the experience as the fictional character that is presented through it (see Fischer-Lichte *et al* 2005: 14ff.). This does not mean that we do not reflect on what we see in a music theatre performance. But according to Fischer-Lichte, our reflection is more concerned with why certain performative actions on stage trigger certain reactions, than in trying to understand the meaning of the actions (2004: 17-18).

This way of interpreting the concept of performativity has led Fischer-Lichte (in an article co-written with Jens Roselt) to a useful specification of it, when it comes to the understanding of the closely related concept of performance (Fischer-Lichte and Roselt 2001) .[7] A division into four parts is the basic idea of how we can work with an understanding of performance: materiality, mediality, aestheticity and semioticity are the elements that constitute what goes into the strategies for the construction of performances on a theoretical level. And given the framework provided by Brecht, we may take a look at these elements in *The Threepenny Opera*.

First, materiality. According to Fischer-Lichte and Roselt, this is constituted through space, body and sound, but not only through the mere *presence* of these elements; also through the *use* of them. The materiality of theatre in the basically conventional set up Brecht worked with and which the strategies of the epic theatre pinpoint, for instance, trades off the distinction between private and public space. Given this, one important feature of the mediality of Brechtian theatre is rooted in the fact that the spectator is a collaborative agent in the event moving between the private phenomenological state and the public role they inhabit. The techniques of *Verfremdung* are designed to constantly challenge the rules that normally would govern the relationships between stage and auditorium.

In Fischer-Lichte and Roselt's view a very crucial feature about theatre as art must be observed in order to grasp it analytically: the experience will often drown out the event's function as work of art. This is due to the fact that the performance as a work of art is constituted by the experience of it. It is, again according to Fischer-Lichte and Roselt's idea, the process of constituting the experience of the work of art, rather than the theatre event as a closed entity of art, with a meaning to understand, that makes up the specificity of the aesthetic part of performance. The experience of the aesthetics involved in theatre as art is realised according to the experience of body, space and objects. Here the theatrical strategies Brecht relies upon instil an element of doubt: is it an aesthetic experience we are having, or—for instance—an ethical one? That is to say, the strategies involved in *The Threepenny Opera* leave us with a question and a choice: should we experience the actions and elements of the performance to understand the meaning of them (and of the play) or should we ask ourselves what we think of the performance as such as a statement?

Finally the element of semioticity in performance: here again Brecht offers a choice. The techniques of epic theatre are intended on the one hand to realise a drama, presenting characters that are meaningful even when part of the play (in *The Threepenny Opera*) is absurd (in its carnivalesque upside-down idea of villains acting as noblemen). On the other hand, as already mentioned, these techniques are based on an urge to reduce semioticity, to use songs as signs and *Gests* as iconic indicators of specific social relations.

The performativity in the strategies that underlies *The Threepenny Opera* is thus one that opens up a number of possible attitudes towards the events on stage, which are actually not necessarily the ones we normally assign to Brecht. And a closer look at the opening night of *The Threepenny Opera* in 1928 may pinpoint elements of another approach to Brechtian theatre than the one we usually take.

A NIGHT IN THE THEATRE
I will start with a brief look at the opening sequence of *The Threepenny Opera* as outlined by Brecht and Weill in the libretto and score, then compare it to a look at the actual performance and its circumstances,[8] thereby trying to link the theatricality of the performance to the play's use of a specific performative mode.

As the lights go down the overture begins, we read in the libretto; as they go up again during the overture, we see a small curtain opening with the title of the play written across it, and two huge screens with the projection of a text on them. Then the curtain closes again, and when it opens for the second time, actors have taken their positions and the title of the *Vorspiel*, "Die Morität von Mackie Messer", is projected on screens. The scenery comes to life, depicting a fairground in Soho, London, and a marketplace singer sings the song accompanied at first by a barrel organ and later—as the song's six verses progress—by the orchestra in a steady crescendo. Immediately after the song, Macheath quickly leaves the stage as everybody anxiously gives way to him and Jenny points out: "Das war Mackie Messer" ("That was Mack the Knife").

The opening scene is thus operating both with the aesthetic roughness of the content of the song and of its delivery, the narcotic pleasure of the tune and the accompaniment, and the narrative excitement of the potential in the scenes to come. The basic elements constituting the play are the curtains, the screens and projections, the visible orchestra, and of course the actors/singers. The following two scenes—in Brecht's terms, "pictures"[9]—take place in Mr Peachum's shop in which he equips professional beggars, and in a barn which forms the background for his daughter Polly's wedding party where her husband Macheath, his six associates, a priest, and later the Chief of Police, Tiger Brown, celebrate the occasion.

The now famous Theater am Schiffbauerdamm was in 1928 not as iconic as today. In her memoirs, leading actress and the original Jenny, Lotte Lenya, describes it as

> a wonderful old house, all red and white and gold, with plaster nymphs, Tritons and Cherubs, adorably kitsch. Located in the principal theatre district, [...] it had somehow been bypassed, obscured by big buildings on all sides, vaguely jinxed by repute. (Bentley 1964: ix)

The theatre had been closed for a while, but in January 1928 it was taken over by a young actor, Ernst Josef Aufricht, who had ambitions as a producer and wanted to open his first season with a new play which, as Lenya puts it, "would re-open his theatre in a blaze of glory" (Bentley 1964: ix). Aufricht was part of the left-wing milieu in Berlin at the time, albeit not a radical. Actually, he later recalls with quite a bit of irony how he and the people surrounding him in hindsight must have appeared:

> We had the customary political left tendency. [...] When we thought we'd discovered just a spark of the old tradition, we would stamp blindly with both feet on the already cold ashes of the past and thereby overlook the glimmer of a new fire.[10] (Aufricht 1966: 47)

In that atmosphere, Aufricht looked around for something in the style of the new theatre presented at that time in Germany by Erwin Piscator and others. He would ask around among theatre people and look up playwrights and producers in their workplaces or in cafés. In one of the latter a contact was made with Brecht, whose consort Elisabeth Hauptmann was working on a translation of John Gay's 1728 mock-opera *The Beggar's Opera* into German. By then he had begun re-writing and working new elements into her text. At the point when he met Aufricht, six scenes of the "new" play had been finished. Brecht gave them to Aufricht to read, according to Lenya and others, without mentioning Kurt Weill's music (Bentley 1964: x).

Having read the fragments of the manuscript, Aufricht decided to commission Brecht to finish it. When he then discovered that Weill was to write the music his reaction was to get acquainted with some of Weill's work, and consequently to ask the young Theo Mackeben (who would later conduct the orchestra on the opening night) to dig out J. C. Pepusch's original music for Gay's opera, to have a back-up should the strange atonal music which Weill and other *Zeitoper* composers wrote have to be abandoned (Aufricht 1966: 48). As time has shown, this did not turn out to be necessary after all.

Brecht and Weill produced the remainder of the play during the spring and summer of 1928, barely meeting the deadline for the opening on 28 August, and still re-writing and changing all the way up to the night before the premiere.[11] A number of things which today seem inevitably part of *The Threepenny Opera* (the barrel organ song, the curtain etc.), and iconic elements of epic theatre, were last-minute changes (often due to practical circumstances) in both text, music and performance.

Aufricht cast the show carefully, mirroring the prevailing (avant garde) idea of juxtaposing actors from various parts of the theatre landscape. As Macheath, he engaged Harald Paulsen, a very well known operetta star of the time, and a daring choice since he was not at all part of the new theatre, but on the other hand someone who perhaps appealed to an audience that would otherwise not have attended the Theater am Schiffbauerdamm. The role of Mrs. Peachum was played by Rosa Valetti, "the grand-dame of the Berlin Cabaret with a wrinkled face, vulgar voice and Berlin audacity", as Aufricht later put it (Aufricht 1966: 49).[12] Despite this, Valetti, who had been singing quite daring songs in cabaret, refused during rehearsals to sing such "filth" (Bentley 1964: ix). As the Chief of Police, Tiger Brown, Aufricht cast the beloved, voluptuous cabaret comedian Kurt Gerron, and since his role was considered too small for his popularity, the "Morität" that opens the play was specifically composed for him. Four days before opening night, Roma Bahn substituted Carola Neher as Polly. Bahn was also a well known actor of the modern stage, and in Aufricht's words, perfect because "this gracious, blonde, blue-eyed lady was bitter and unsentimental" (1966: 57).[13] As mentioned, Jenny was played by Kurt Weill's wife Lotte Lenya, who in her own words "couldn't read a note—exactly why I was chosen" (Bentley 1964: vii). She was introduced by Weill to Aufricht with the wish of having her as one of the prostitutes. Aufricht was a bit reluctant since he didn't know her, but later writes: "she looked intelligent, had beautiful movements and she pleased me" (1966: 58). This was the line-up of leading actors with which *The Threepenny Opera* went into rehearsals.

REHEARSAL AND SCENIC SET-UP
The rehearsal period was close to chaotic. The libretto underwent a number of changes, and the feeling in the cast as well as with Ernst Josef Aufricht was that nobody (except perhaps Brecht) was at all certain that there would be a striking new performance to present to the quite fastidious and pampered Berlin audience.

The rehearsals began in the theatre on 10 August; in other words, there was a total period of twenty-one days on stage to get the very raw material to work. This process is well documented elsewhere, so here are just a few examples of elements of specific performative importance that came into being during the last hectic days before opening.[14] At this time the production was in principle in the hands of director Erich Engel, with whom Brecht had numerous discussions, often about the position of the songs, and the extent of their separation from the rest of the action on stage. The discussions continued to the point that Engel proposed simply to strike the songs (Aufricht 1966: 55). However, anecdotal details relating to the production reveal interesting causes behind the inclusion of the music and the striking dissonances it effected with the show's aesthetic.

Harald Paulsen, the successful operetta and light theatre actor, was a handsome and also apparently somewhat vain man, who cared much about his physical appearance. The costumes for the play—due to the fact that it is set among poor people—were deliberately shabby, recycled costumes from the theatre store rooms. But Paulsen had his costume for Macheath tailor-made to the highest fashion of the time by one of the finest Berlin tailors.[15] Macheath was thereby dressed exactly as the wealthy upper middle class audience in the auditorium.

In spite of this fashionable presentation of the character, Paulsen during rehearsals began to insist on wearing a huge, light blue silk bow tie in the style of traditional nineteenth-century operetta heroes. He declared close to opening night, when asked to lose it, that he would rather lose the role (Aufricht 1966: 55). Typically, Brecht had an inventive idea, and stated: "Weill and I will introduce him through a Morität which sings of his terrible, infamous deeds, and he will seem even scarier then with a light blue bow" (*Ibid*.).[16] This is an effect on the audience that Aufricht had actually already foreseen when casting Paulsen, of whom he later wrote: "He was nice and indulgent. In excitement he had something uncontrolled and appeared uncanny" (*Ibid*.: 49). So the performative presence of the combination of Paulsen's temperament and a light blue bow was perhaps what really made the character Macheath affect the audience. The British correspondent A. Ebbutt for *The Times* commented on the costumes:

> It is vaguely about the end of the nineteenth century, a period which provides picturesque and convincing costumes and make-ups for Peachum and his beggars, though it has led to a temptation to present Macheath's "street bandits" as music-hall tramps of the present day. (Hinton 1990: 102)

Brecht's idea of introducing Macheath through a new song, a theatrical strategy almost synonymous with epic theatre, was as shown something that actually sprang from Paulsen's weird bow tie. However, Kurt Weill had already, earlier in the summer, been to the Berlin organ manufacturer Bacigalupo to order a barrel organ for the show. The manufacturer did not think his new organs were able to play enough half notes [sic], so they agreed on re-building an existing one (Fleck 2008: 24). The idea of the organ, therefore, must have predated Paulsen's choice of bow tie. Nevertheless, when the idea was accepted, Weill and Brecht wrote the song in one night (Bentley 1964:

xi) and had the music sent to Bacigalupo the next day to have a roll made so that the barrel organ could accompany Kurt Gerron, who was to sing the song. As we shall see shortly, that was a hazardous performative element to introduce.

The large, traditionally red curtain of the Theater am Schiffbauerdamm was only meant to be drawn for the intermissions between the acts of the performance. But because of the division of the show into eight scenes, a second, smaller curtain was established, behind which the stage workers would be able to re-arrange the setting (wearing felt shoes to mute their steps, so that the action could be hidden under the incidental music: so much for open, epic shifts and no culinary surprises).

The scenographer Caspar Neher had designed a curtain in heavy, green silk with parrots on it, but Aufricht recalls that he found it strange, and labelled it "the hearse cloth of the opening night" (Aufricht 1966: 58). Finally—apparently on the day of the opening— Neher gave in, and removed the curtain. Brecht however, wanted the changes to be masked, so in the basement of the theatre a large roll of sack cloth was found, and Neher—having to abandon the parrots— simply painted the title of the play directly on it in large quirky letters. The paint was still wet and smelling as the audience entered the theatre (Aufricht 1966: 59). In *The Times*, Ebbutt noted:

> The production of the piece is deliberately crude. Adopting the idea that it should be a "Threepenny Opera", which fits well with tendencies now in the dramatic air, the producers have provided a dirty cream-coloured curtain about 10 ft high, worked by a primitive arrangement of strings, such as might be used in amateur theatricals. Across the curtain is painted in crooked, badly formed letters "Die Dreigroschenoper". [...] There is an occasional expressionistic touch, such as the sudden letting-down of a placard by ropes from above. (Hinton 1990: 103)

Directly above this curtain, photographs from the original set show us that three big lamps, almost in the style of huge, round modern steel-work or photo lamps were hanging.[17] These were lowered and lit to provide the essential part of what Brecht in the libretto labels "Song Light":[18] when a song was introduced, the rest of the lighting was dimmed and the singing character would be placed in these three cones of light. Behind the line of the small curtain, on both sides, rather large projection screens are seen: about five square metres in size, oblique, with five or six metres between them, creating a sort of gateway. The centre of the stage is occupied—almost dominated—by a huge organ, with majestic pipes stretching high up, and flanked by large, chubby cherubs with trumpets also pointing upwards. On both sides of the organ and clearly visible for the audience—but behind the singing actors—the orchestra is situated. No borders block the view to the rigging loft but the back wall of the stage is covered by small curtains. All in all it was a rather complex and almost messy visual impression that met people when they took their seats on 31 August 1928 to see what the relatively unknown playwright and composer had put together.

SILENCE AND STANDING OVATIONS

As the audience filled the theatre, many would have been reading the so-called *Programm-Zettel*,[19] which has since been mentioned many times because of the lack of Lotte Lenya's name in it. Somehow her role had been left out in the printing process, causing a furious Weill to threaten Aufricht in the first intermission that she would leave the performance instantly—though Lenya herself was quite relaxed about it. This, however, has meant that later reproductions of the programme have focussed on the list of participants. But when studied in its entirety, the programme actually tells us much more about the context of *The Threepenny Opera*, rather than just its significance as a one-off production.[20] Almost two-thirds of the space in the publication is occupied by advertisements, and the nature of these gives a hint as to the type of audience that might have been in the theatre that night—since the goods and services advertised must to some extent have been what were thought might interest them.

The main impression is that what might appeal to the audience of the Theater am Schiffbauerdamm was luxury and expensive pastimes. On the cover a large advertisement states: "The Elegant Lady only wears corsets and brassieres from G. Neuman";[21] nice to know, although an interesting—almost daring—choice for a play about hustlers and prostitutes. Elsewhere in the programme, alongside short, factual details about the performance, are scattered various other ads, for instance for the German-Russian Restaurant Angeno-Casino in the same street as the theatre, "a meeting point for Berlin artists";[22] or for fur shops, expensive hairdressers, more restaurants, Steinway and Blüthner grand pianos, more fur, more hairdressers, and finally, towards the end, an ad for a jeweller, J. Pich, who announces that he is "Buying (for America) diamonds, pearls and coloured stones (mainly large objects)"!²³ Even having spare diamonds was an option for the people waiting to be provoked to change society by the radical theatrical experience of *The Threepenny Opera*.

Now—finally—we arrive at the event, presenting the result of all these elements for an impatient audience.²⁴ As the curtain rises, we see the huge Kurt Gerron standing centre stage with his hand on the barrel organ. Around him, members of the cast as people in the marketplace. The overture has died down while the curtain was raised, and there is silence. Gerron starts to turn the handle on the organ and begins to sing. But the organ is numb. It does not work. We in the audience, of course, do not know whether this is deliberate or not, but the experience is surprising. At the beginning of the second verse the orchestra starts to accompany the Morität, and the music and song rises to a crescendo ending on a loud chord, but strangely undecided. No reaction from the audience. In the silence, Harald Paulsen puts his walking stick under his arm, and elegantly crosses the stage with a spring in his step. The prostitutes follow him with their eyes, and Lenya, in her deep, hoarse voice, utters: "*That* was Mack the Knife". The curtain falls—no reaction. But reflection? Well, probably. The question is: would the audience be reflecting on the social criticism or on the experience they are in the middle of? If we accept Brecht's point from the beginning of this article, that in the provocative actions we see realities re-established, then the question is really: what realities are at stake here? Perhaps this silence reflects the pleasure of attending something fashionably radical. And the hesitant reaction may also stem from a reluctance to be the first to admit that this is also just great theatre.

The curtain rises for the second scene. We are in Peachum's shop. Sharp wit, satirical cynicism and comic elements alternate as he demonstrates how he has made a business out of systematically cheating people into believing that his beggars are actually sick, blind or kicked by a horse. Mr. and Mrs. Peachum end the scene in front of the small curtain singing a short, quick and witty song about how young girls of today—as opposed to their own generation—are subject to modern, sentimental ideas of love, derived from romantic ballads with "Can you feel my heart beat?" lyrics. Still no reaction. Still an expectant silence.

The third scene takes place in a barn. On the projection screens large images of horses almost in the style of nineteenth-century genre paintings appear. The young Polly Peachum is dressed in the bridal fashion of the 1920s with a turban and myrtles, the symbols of innocence; Macheath is dressed in his tailor-made suit and the bow tie. The dialogue again is quick and witty, and more songs feature: the deliberately boring "Wedding Song" performed slowly and without energy by the gang of thieves; and shortly afterwards Polly's subsequently famous song "Pirate Jenny". Still no reaction.

Then Kurt Gerron enters again, now in his role as the chief of police, Tiger Brown. He and Macheath are old comrades of war, and he is a guest of honour at the villain's wedding. The two men engage in talk about the old days, and then burst into the "Army Song", a pastiche on soldiers' songs, with a marching drum combining a swung theme and heavy off-beats. As the song comes to an end there is a short silence. And then all hell lets loose. People stamp, yell, applaud and whistle. It will not stop. Gerron and Paulsen try to continue with the dialogue, but their voices are drowned out by the raving audience. Before the performance, Aufricht had forbidden encores, since he "found them un-serious" (Aufricht 1966: 66)[25]—a point on which he and Brecht fully agreed. Now, through the noise, Gerron and Paulsen look appealingly at Aufricht in his private box.

After a while, Aufricht gave in, nodded, and the orchestra repeated the prelude to the "Army Song". People stood and cheered the pair on stage singing about how they killed and fornicated their way through a colonial war, a brutal and unsentimental echo of Kipling's *Road to Mandalay*. Epic theatre, the strategies of *Verfremdung* and cool intellectual reflection were all instantly over-ruled by the pleasure of a great, sharp, catchy song, and the audience's desire to give in to the experience of enjoying the moment—together.

FINALE

The concept of performativity and close performance analysis as tools for investigating historical performances and for discussing Brechtian ideas have been the guiding principles for this chapter. These reveal the complex and problematic issues of the audience maintaining a Brechtian theoretical standpoint when experiencing music theatre. The intention of keeping the audience in a certain double position of both engaging in the event and keeping a part of their conscience alert to the structural and social statements underlying the specific actions on stage is easily compromised.

Perhaps *The Threepenny Opera* has been placed in a context where it does not really belong, merely because Brecht later became who he did—and because he and others wanted to make it an important part of a specific kind of (political) theatre. But actually already in its own time, this was questionable. Monty Jacobs wrote in his review of the opening night, that: "Yesterday everything flashed of venture, temper, aggression without noisily turning the leaves of the Party Membership book" (Wyss 1977: 52). Aufricht also recalls that at the time, *The Threepenny Opera* was not intended to be a radical piece of theatre:

> We saw the play as it was written as a gay, literary operetta with some flashes of social criticism. The only aggressive song we took seriously was "First comes the eating, then comes the moral". We had not yet learnt that, without morality, there is no eating. Brecht and Weill were not yet key figures. The profound interpretations of the socio-political statements in *The Threepenny Opera*, which Brecht also later shared, have in hindsight given the piece a false importance. (Aufricht 1966: 48)[26]

This is a harsh judgement of an event that Aufricht himself played a substantial part in organising, and it is probably also an unjust one. The importance of a phenomenon like *The Threepenny Opera* for the development of twentieth-century music theatre can hardly be underestimated. But perhaps Jacobs' and Aufricht's comments pinpoint something which in the aftermath of the 1920s golden era of political theatre has to some extent been put aside: the question of whether that which the playwrights, composers, scenographers, directors, actors and producers wanted (both theoretically and in practice) was—and indeed *is*—at all possible.

Perhaps it was—and is—an impossible task Brecht and his companions set themselves: making people (wearing their fur coats, filled with the delicious food and the atmosphere of the restaurants, rattling their jewellery) reflect upon the unjust organisation of society during the performance. And perhaps the performative presence of great actors, singers, musicians, sound and action in the astonishingly strange and exciting scenery did overtake the audiences' minds and bodies to a degree where the experience itself became the main issue. History, however, shows that reflection *is* an important part of theatre no matter what kind. But perhaps it is asking too much for that reflection to take place right there, right in the middle of everything— while the music is playing and the show is going on.

NOTES

[1] "Leuten, die an chronischen Schlaflosigkeit leiden, empfehle ich zur Zeit dringend einen Besuch des Theater am Schiffbauerdamm" (quoted in Wyss 1977: 50) (all translations from German in this chapter are by the author). The newspaper was strongly conservative and was written under the motto: "Gott mit uns" (God is with us).

[2] "So zwanglos in die Groschenoper eingestreut sind, [und] entscheident den Triumph des Abends. Ihre Einfügung in das Spiel ist eine der Verdienste der ausgezeichneten Inszenierung Erich Engels" (Wyss 1977: 52). *Vossische Zeitung* was in that period comparable to *The Times* or *Le Monde*. Founded in the eighteenth century it had been edited by, among others, Gotthold Ephraim Lessing and later by Kurt Tucholsky. During the early years of the twentieth century it went from being *königlich privilegiert* ("with royal privilege") to being a liberal advocate for a republic. Monty Jacobs was a well-known theatre critic and writer, among whose books were *Ibsens Bühnentechnik* (*Ibsen's Stage Technique*) from 1920.

[3] "Von moderner sozialer oder politischer Satire keine Spur" (Wyss 1977: 83).

[4] "Im Provokatorischen sehen wir die Realität wiederhergestellt" (Brecht 1993: 18-9).

[5] "Keinesfalls also stellt sich, wo Worte infolge des Übermasses der Gefühle fehlen, der Gesang ein" (Brecht 1993: 32).

[6] "Die Musikstücke [...] waren meditierender und moralisierender Art" (Brecht 1993: 240).

[7] The notion of performance in the article is closely linked to the German concept of *Aufführung*, which is difficult to translate because it implies both the actual events on stage and the fact that they may be the product of different things, most commonly a written text.

[8] This section is based on the critical edition of *Die Dreigroschenoper* by Joachim Luchesi (Brecht 2004: 131ff.).

[9] In the libretto the German term is *Bild*; the play is divided into eight of these pictures or scenes, each with a title describing the actions. The play also includes a total of twenty songs (Brecht 2004).

[10] "Wir hatten die übliche politische Linkstendenz. [...] Wenn wir nur einen Funken der alten tradition zu entdecken glaubten, trampelten wir blindwütig mit beiden füssen auf der bereits kalten Asche der Vergangenheit herum und übersahen das Glimmer eines neuen Brandes" (Aufricht 1966: 47).

[11] Text-wise, John Fuegi attributes more than eighty per cent of the libretto to Elisabeth Hauptmann, based on his investigations into the first drafts that formed the basis of the copyright claim. In addition, he detects work by the middle-aged poet Villon, as well as by contemporary writers Karl Kraus and Rudyard Kipling (Fuegi 1994: 1996).

[12] "Die grosse Frau des Berliner Kabaretts mit dem zerfurchten Gesicht, der vulgären stimme_under der Berliner Kodderschnauze" (Aufricht 1966: 49).

[13] "Diese grazile, blonde blauäugige Frau war herb und unsentimental" (Aufricht 1966: 58).

[14] These events have been described by the already quoted Lenya, Aufricht, Bentley and Fuegi, and also in an interview with dramaturg Robert Vambery made sixty years after the production (Zeitung 1998: 47-48).

[15] See Fuegi 1994: 202; Aufricht 1966: 55.

[16] "Weill und ich führe ihn durch eine Moritat ein, die seine grausigen schandtaten besingt, um so unheimlicher wirkt er mit seiner hellblauen schleife". A Morität was a "Murder Deed" song often sung at fairs and markets, depicting horrible, bloody stories of killers and crimes (Aufricht 1966: 55).

[17] The following observations stem from research in the three files labelled "Die Dreigroschenoper, Uraufführung 1928" 1, 2, and 3, which are in the Brecht Archiv, Brecht Haus, Berlin. They contain photographs from the original production, some of which were official ones probably made for PR purposes, and others taken during a performance, with an audience present. These are undated and the photographer is not credited. It is known, however, that Ruth Berlau, one of the many female co-workers with whom Brecht engaged, was a skilled photographer, and a number of stage photos credited to her exist.

[18] "Song-Beleuchtung".

[19] Programme note.

[20] A number of these *Programm Zettel* are in File 1 of the Brecht Archiv, Berlin.

[21] "Die elegante Dame trägt Korsetts u. Büstenhalter nur von G. Neumann".

[22] "Treffpunkt der Berliner Künstler".

[23] "Kaufe (für Amerika) Brillianten, Perlen u. Farbsteine (Besonders grosse Objekte)".

[24] The following "reconstruction" is based on information combined from reports by Lenya and Aufricht (*op. cit.*), the theatre's dramaturg Heinrich Fischer (Fassmann 1958: 55ff.) and the reviews (Wyss 1977).

[25] "Ich hatte vor der Vorstellung jede Wiederholung von Songs als unseriös verboten" (Aufricht 1966: 66).

[26] "Wir sahen das Stück so, wie es geschrieben ist, als lustige literarischer Operette mit einigen sozialkritischen Blinklichten. Den einzigen aggressiven Song 'Erst kommt das Fressen, dann kommt die Moral' nahmen wir ernst. Die politische Realität hatte noch nicht drastisch bewiesen, dass, wenn die Moral verschwindet, das Fressen auch verschwunden ist. Brecht und Weill waren kein Klassiker. Die Tiefsinnigen Auslegungen über die sozialpolitische Aussage der 'Dreigroschenoper', an denen sich später auch Brecht geteiligte, haben dem Stück rückwirkend eine falsche Bedeutung gegeben" (Aufricht 1966: 48).

CHAPTER 8

THE *ACOUSMÊTRE* ON STAGE AND SCREEN:
THE POWER OF THE BODILESS VOICE[1]

JEONGWON JOE

Since the emergence of motion picture, opera and cinema have been
mutually attracted to each other and each has influenced the other. As
early as 1904, George Méliès produced *La Damnation du Docteur
Faust*, based on Gounod's opera *Faust*, and many other silent films
were based on operas: Bizet's *Carmen* alone inspired more than thirty
silent films, including Cecil B. DeMille's *Carmen* (1915) and Charlie
Chaplin's *Burlesque on Carmen* (1915). Also, many of the Vitaphone
shorts, which were popular around cinema's conversion period (1926-
1931), were "opera shorts", as they are video recordings of single
arias.[2]

Figure 8.1: Giovanni Martinelli (1885-1969) as Canio in *Vesti La
Giubba* (1926), Vitaphone No. 198 directed by Edwin B. DuPar.[3]

Opera's attraction to cinema, too, has a century-long history. As early as 1928, Franz Ludwig Hörth and Emil Pirchan used a film screen in their Berlin production of the *Ring* cycle for the entry of the gods into Valhalla at the end of *Das Rheingold*. Cinematic idioms and techniques were employed not only at the level of production as stage directors' choice but also intended by the composers. One of the earliest examples is Alban Berg's *Lulu* (1935), in which the silent images have double functions: they provide a narrative gap between Lulu's arrest after she accidentally kills Dr. Schöne and her escape from the prison, and they also function as a visual analogy of the structure of the music—a palindrome—that accompanies the silent images.[4] Sometimes, cinematic techniques are used to bring multiple and synchronic temporalities and to enhance onstage actions, as in Libby Larson's *Frankenstein, The Modern Prometheus* (1990), in which video screens were employed to provide flashbacks, visualise characters' unspoken inner thoughts, or show the close-ups of the onstage action. There are many other effects that cinematic idioms and techniques can bring to opera's live theatre. In this essay, I explore how cinematic elements change the voice-body relationship in opera performance with particular attention to how the mediatised unity between voice and body of the cinematic apparatus has changed the "embodied-ness" of the operatic voice in live theatre.

Charles Ludlam's 1983 play about Maria Callas, *Galas: A Modern Tragedy*, is a dramatisation of the (in)famous "Rome walkout", Callas's cancellation of the performance of *Norma* after the first act at the Rome Opera in 1958.[5]

Mercanteggini:	But you must finish the performance!
Galas:	I can't! I wish to God I could. But I can't. The voice... the voice is slipping.
Mercanteggini:	Slipping?
Galas:	Yes, slipping! Slipping! The voice will not obey.
Mercanteggini:	*(Growing more and more alarmed)* How can that be?
Galas:	I told you, sometimes the voice obeys and sometimes it will not. Tonight it will not!
Mercanteggini:	You're speaking of your voice as though it had a will of its own.
Galas:	*(With horror)* It has! It does! Tonight it will not obey.
Mercanteggini:	You've got to get hold of yourself. It's your voice. You must command it.
Galas:	*(In a hoarse whisper)*: It's no use.

(Act 1, Sc. 5) (Ludlam 1983: 88-89)

The endowment of the voice with its own will in this scene addresses the central issue my essay explores: an uncanny autonomisation of the voice in opera and film. I focus on a recent trend in operatic theatre, which explores what is known as cinema's "castration anxiety", that is, the separation of voice and body, for in cinema, voice and image are separated on physically different tracks. In psychoanalytically-oriented film theories, cinema's castration anxiety is interpreted as the origin of its envy of a live medium where the voice is naturally embodied.[6] Given these theories, the voice-body separation in recent operatic theatre—in other words, a contemporary tendency for live operatic theatre to separate voice and body through multi-casting roles, using dancers and/or masks, or other means—can be read as opera's "reversed envy": reversed in the sense that it is *opera's envy* of the cinematic separation of voice and body instead of *cinema's envy* of a live medium. In my essay, I trace opera's envy of cinema's anxiety to cinema's ironic privileging of the voice/sound in spite of the seeming dominance of the visual in the cinematic medium, as Slavoj Žižek argues. I support my argument by demonstrating a parallelism between what Žižek calls an "uncanny autonomization of the voice" in sound film (1996: 92) and "the uncanny aspects" of operatic performance: namely, the notion of the performer as a lifeless musical instrument, an automaton, animated by the force of music, as Carolyn Abbate argues in her book *In Search of Opera* (2001: 5-7). By contextualizing film theories developed by Kaja Silverman, Žižek, and other related scholars in Abbate's recent discourse on opera performance, I intend to show how those theories can provide a methodological perspective, from which the re-negotiated relationship between voice and body in live operatic theatre can be analysed, and in so doing, how they can expand and enrich the hermeneutic scope for analysing the opera-cinema encounter. I cannot over-emphasise that what I argue in this essay is *one possible interpretation* that may not have much, if anything, to do with the intentionality of the composer, the stage director, or the film director. The voice-body split in operatic theatre can be found at the level of production: in other words, such a split was not intended by the composer but added by stage directors. Julie Taymor's Saito Kinen Festival production of Stravinsky's *Oedipus Rex* in 1992 is an example, in which Oedipus is portrayed by a dancer-mime and a masked singer. In this essay, I focus on the works in which such a split is employed at the compositional level. Three examples I analyse in detail are two pieces from Alexander Goehr's *Triptych* (1968-71)—*Naboth's Vineyard* (1968) and *Sonata About Jerusalem* (1971)—Harrison Birtwistle's *The Mask of Orpheus* (1986), and Philip Glass's *La Belle et la Bête* (1994).

Figure 8.2: Oedipus represented by the singer (Philip Langridge) with an extended mask above his head and the dancer-mime (Min Tanaka) in Julie Taymor's Saito Kinen Festival production of Stravinsky's *Oedipus Rex* in 1992. This still image is right before Oedipus pierces his eyes.

THE CASTRATION ANXIETY OF THE CINEMATIC APPARATUS
Sam Abel contends that in live theatre, performing bodies are the primary condition for emotional and psychological communications between performers and the audience, whose bodies occupy the same space at the same time of performance (1996: 164-5). In cinema, direct communication between performers and the audience through their bodies disappears. Film theorist Christian Metz defines this difference between live theatre and cinema in terms of *absence*:

> During the screening of the film, the audience is present and aware of the actor, but the actor is absent and unaware of the audience; and during the shooting, when the actor was present, it was the audience which was absent [....]. The exchange of seeing and being-seen will be fractured at its center. (Quoted in Tambling 1977: 266)

Metz notes that in theatre, reality is "physically present in the same space as the spectator", while cinema gives reality in a "primordial *elsewhere*" (*ibid.*, my emphasis). Unlike live theatre, in which real actors depict fictional characters, film is the representation of a representation in that the screen image creates another level of representation—the two dimensional representation of the real actors who represent fictional characters. Other film scholars, such as André Bazin and Jean-Louis Comolli, also argue that given the absence of the real object in cinema, the cinematic apparatus is characterised by a "fundamental" *lack*. Metz uses the term "castration" to describe cinema's "structuring" lack, the ontological condition of the cinematic text that exists in "perfect isolation" from the viewer, which is analogous to a baby's withdrawal from his/her mother's body—i.e., the loss of the object, and the entry into language.[7] Freudian theory explains the concept of castration as follows:

> It has been urged that every time his mother's breast is withdrawn from a baby he is bound to feel it as a castration (that is to say, as the loss of what he regards as an important part of his own body); that further, he cannot fail to be similarly affected by the regular loss of his faeces; and finally that the act of birth itself (consisting as it does in the separation of the child from his mother, with whom he has hitherto been united) is the prototype of all castration. (Quoted in Silverman 1988: 15)

This Freudian concept of castration has been applied to another dimension of absence in the cinematic apparatus, namely, the absence of the natural unity between voice and body. Unlike traditional live theatre in which the voice is embodied, in cinema, voice and body—sound and image—are separated in the process of recording, and they are preserved on, and reproduced from, physically separated tracks. Thus, a "technologically mediated unity" between voice and body is the "primordial" condition of the cinematic apparatus. For Michel Chion, the lip-synch—"assiduous but never perfect"—represents the ontological condition of the cinematic medium, that is, "the impossible unity" of voice and body (1982: 125). Because of cinema's castration anxiety about its irretrievable loss of the natural unity between voice and body, mainstream cinema, especially Hollywood classical cinema, has tried to disavow its anxiety by synchronising voice and body—that is, the soundtrack and image track—as tightly as possible. This is where cinema's simulation of live theatre, cinema's envy of opera, can be traced.

As a reaction to the mainstream tradition, some film directors, mostly non-Hollywood directors, have shown different approaches in dealing with voice and body. Marguerite Duras is one such director. Her films are distinguished by the radical dissociation between sound and image and the destruction of the "reality effect" of synchronisation. For instance, in the script of *La Femme du Gange* (1973), Duras literally enunciates the split between the soundtrack and the image track as constituting two separate films, as "the film of the voice" and "the film of the image" (Günther 2002: 25). In general, Duras uses voice-off in very unusual ways, creating a strong sense of the separation between voice and body. In the opening scene of *Nathalie Granger* (1972), for example, Isabella (Lucia Bosé) and her husband are having a meal with their two children and the parents' voices are heard as voice-off during the entire sequence. After their children leave the dining table, the parents' conversation continues as voice-off while the camera shows the empty chairs on which the children had been sitting. A piano lesson sequence later in the film is fascinating for the way it expresses the separation between sound and image. It begins with Nathalie practising a simple tune, the sound of which is heard synchronised with her fingers. Later, the camera pans to the desk nearby, which is covered with music scores, including one of Bach (figure 8.3). The camera pans back to the piano keyboard and shows in close-up Nathalie's hands and those of her piano teacher, guiding the student's hand position. Nathalie is now playing different music from that in the opening scene. What is striking in this scene is the superimposition of the music from the opening scene over the piece she is currently playing; in other words, two different tunes are heard simultaneously, and the current tune is gradually eclipsed by the previous one, resulting in a complete dissonance between sight and sound, between what is seen and what is heard (figure 8.4).

Hans-Jürgen Syberberg, one of the New German Cinema directors, is another director who has explored non-synchronous sounds against the mainstream cinema's (especially Hollywood's) general practice of using embodied voice as a fetish to disavow cinema's castration anxiety. In his cinematic production of *Parsifal* (1982), Syberberg intentionally employs inaccurate (i.e., asynchronous) lip-synching in order to demystify the seeming unity between voice and body in the cinematic medium—a kind of Brechtian aesthetic strategy.[8] Chion describes the wide disparity between Amfortas's voice (sung by Wolfgang Schöne) and his body (performed by the conductor of the recording, Armin Jordan) as follows:

Figure 8.3: Music scores on the table near the piano, in the piano lesson sequence from Marguerite Duras' *Nathalie Granger* (1972).

Figure 8.4: Nathalie's hands and her piano teacher's, in the piano lesson sequence from Marguerite Duras' *Nathalie Granger* (1972).

Figure 8.5: Armin Jordan as Amfortas lip-synching Wolfgang Schöne in Hans-Jürgen Syberberg's *Parsifal* (1982).

> Here Syberberg focuses his camera, as nobody has ever done or ever would
> again, on the bewildering face of Armin Jordan, who is miming the voice of
> Wolfgang Schöne for the character of Amfortas, and one sees the black
> abyss of the mouth, the monstrosity of the lips in action, the strange beast of
> the tongue coming forward from the bottom of the throat, all of which
> attempt to seize the voice—and one is completely moved. (Chion 1982:
> 126)

Duras' films and Syberberg's, however, represent an exception and reaction to the dominant politics of body and voice in mainstream cinema. As many psychoanalytically oriented film scholars have indicated, it has been a common aesthetic strategy of the mainstream cinema to tightly synchronise the voice with the body as a "fetish" to disavow the castration anxiety of the cinematic apparatus. Freud describes a fetish as something that a man, who is incapable of accepting a woman's lack of the penis, substitutes for the missing penis—something that was part of what he originally saw, such as another part of the female anatomy or something attached to it, such as a shoe or a garment—in order to disavow the anxiety of the fear for his own castration. In short, Freud anchors fetishism to female lack— "to establish fetishism as a male defense against the female condition to castration", and what he disavows is the possibility of his own insufficiency (Silverman 13-18). Feminist film scholars such as Kaja Silverman, Laura Mulvey, and Amy Lawrence, argue that female characters have been employed for the purpose of this strategic synchronisation with their voices presented in an "emphatically embodied form", solidly anchored to their bodies. In other words, the embodied female voice functions as cinema's fetish to conceal its primordial lack of the natural unity between voice and body (Lawrence 1991: 149).[9]

THE SEPARATION OF VOICE AND BODY IN OPERA

If a tightly synchronised sound and image, voice and body, characterises dominant practices in cinema and represents its aspiration to simulate the condition of live theatre, isn't the separation of voice and body in operatic theatre an interesting phenomenon?

Conventional operas are not devoid of the disembodied voice—for instance, voices from dead characters, such as Titurel in Wagner's *Parsifal* and Antonia's mother in Jacques Offenbach's *Tales of Hoffmann*—but it is in recent music theatre that the separation of voice and body is noticeably increased.[10] The first and the last works of Alexander Goehr's *Triptych*—*Naboth's Vineyard* (1968) and *Sonata About Jerusalem* (1971)—are among the works characterised by the intriguing use of the voice-body split.[11] *Naboth's Vineyard* is described as a "dramatic madrigal" and *Sonata About Jerusalem* "a cantata". In these works, characters' bodily presence is represented by mimes, while their voices are provided by onstage singers. In both works, Goehr creates stylised forms of separation between a silent performer physically representing a given character and the sung text associated with that character. The story of *Sonata About Jerusalem* is based on a twelfth-century chronicle about how the Jews of Baghdad came to believe in the Messiah and returned to Jerusalem. In this work, the Jewish women are split into three dimensions of representation: the female chorus represents the aural dimension, that is the voice; the narrator provides a verbal description of the visual element; and the mimes offer the bodily dimension of the Jewish women. The story of *Naboth's Vineyard* is taken from Chapter 21 of the first book of *Kings* from the Hebrew/Old Testament Bible. King Achab longs for Naboth's vineyard and suggests a favourable trade, but Naboth declines Achab's offer for the trade because God did not permit him to give away his property. Queen Jezebel makes a false charge for Naboth's blasphemy and Achab takes the ownership of Naboth's vineyard. God sends Elijah to reproach Achab; Achab repents and God decides not to punish Achab. In Goehr's setting of this tale, two mimes represent the various characters by using multiple masks while the voices of those characters are provided by the singers.

John Cox, the producer of the premiere of this piece, describes his staging as follows, which is included in the published score:

> In the original production of *Naboth's Vineyard* the action was presented by two mimes wearing identical costumes. They put on or carried masks to represent the characters in the drama, exchanging them as the exigencies of the action required. Every attempt was made to keep the mimes indistinguishable from one another, so that the masks were the only "characters". (Cox in Goehr 1973)

The indistinguishableness among the characters, except for their masks, creates the "lifeless-ness" of the bodies, and in so doing, intensifies the separation of the voice from the body—or the disembodied-ness of the voice—rendering the voice as if it were from "elsewhere". Goehr's intention for the original staging, as described by Cox as follows, further supports my argument, as it minimises the performers' bodily action.

> The composer insisted at the outset that the mime should not be choreographed, or even musical in feeling. [...] Nor is continuous mime required. Certain sections of the work are purely musical and need no action; at other points stillness is the most effective action.[...] In the ideal performance, instrumentalists, singers and mimes should all be visible and equal in visual importance, there being constant and close dramatic rapport amongst all the component parts of the work. An orchestra pit and all the other conventions of "opera" must be avoided at all costs. (*Ibid.*)

Goehr's separation between voice and body, then, is quite Brechtian in the sense that the highly illusionistic operatic theatre of the Wagnerian *Gesamtkunstwerk* is avoided. The following is how Bertolt Brecht described his epic theatre, which was intended to be an aesthetic antidote to the Wagnerian theatre:

> When the epic theatre's methods begin to penetrate the opera the first result is a radical *separation of the elements*. [...] So long as the expression "Gesamtkunstwerk" (or "integrated work of art") means that the integration is a muddle, so long as the arts are supposed to be "fused" together, the various elements will all be equally degraded, and each will act as a mere "feed" to the rest. (Brecht 1964: 37)

In my interview with Goehr on 4 July 2007, he did acknowledge a Brechtian element in his *Naboth's Vineyard*. He even mentioned that the subject of the work for him is "Brechtian" in itself and that Kurt Weill once considered setting Naboth's story as an opera. During the interview, Goehr also revealed Charlie Chaplin as another influential source for his operatic *oeuvre* in general and indicated the aesthetic connection between Brecht and Chaplin: the latter's work, especially *The Gold Rush* (1925), significantly influenced the former. In silent film generally, there is no such thing as an embodied representation of the voice simply because of the absence of the voice. As another motivation for his separation between voice and body in *Triptych*, Goehr mentioned that he wanted to let the singers "act through their voice", not through their bodily gestures, which is opera's fundamental condition for him.[12] It is perhaps in this respect that Goehr's *Triptych* has been regarded as having a strong kinship with the Japanese Nōh theatre, in which a singer only represents the vocal dimension of a character, while his/her bodily representation is enacted by a dancer (see Daiken 1980).[13]

Philip Glass's *La Belle et la Bête* (1994) is another example of the split representation of a character's body and voice. Over the past few decades, Philip Glass has shown a strong interest in the operatic exploration of cinema. *Orfeé* (1993), *La Belle et la Bête* (1994), and *Les Enfants Terribles* (1996) form the "Cocteau Trilogy" and each employ cinematic approaches in different ways. Each work in Glass's trilogy adapts Cocteau's three corresponding cinematic works. *Orfée* is a straightforward operatic setting of the film, using a condensed version of the film's screenplay as the libretto. The last work, *Les Enfants Terribles*, is a dance opera in which dance participates in the expression of the drama as an equal partner with music. Most of its characters are portrayed by one singer and one or two dancers. Lies, the heroine, for instance, is sung by a singer and also portrayed by three dancers. By doubling or tripling characters, Glass and the choreographer Susan Marshall intended to amplify single emotions or express the characters' conflicting and divided emotions. *La Belle et la Bête* is the most intriguing fusion of opera and cinema especially in terms of the renewed relationship between voice and body. This work is an operatic adaptation of Jean Cocteau's 1946 film. In this opera, Cocteau's cinematic images serve as the visual content of the opera, while Glass's operatic music replaces the original soundtrack.[14]

During the performance of Glass's *Belle*, there is no mimetic or staged acting. Singers perform the opera standing on-stage below a gigantic film screen on which Cocteau's images are mutely projected (because Cocteau's *Belle* is a sound film, Glass had to silence its original soundtrack, composed by George Auric, in order to replace it with his live music). Using Cocteau's original scenario as the libretto, Glass designed his music so as to ensure a reasonable synchronisation between the singing and the projected images. Glass wanted to keep the original Cocteau scenario intact when it was converted to the libretto for this opera. A consequent technical problem was the synchronisation of singing with the on-screen characters' lip movements. Glass originally planned to time the dialogue with a stopwatch and to compose music to match it. But this method was too crude, and he finally ended up using a digital time code—a black bar showing elapsed minutes, seconds, and fractions of seconds—added to a print of the film.

Unlike traditional operatic theatre, in which live bodies are an essential part of opera's spectacle, Glass's opera makes singers' live bodies superfluous to the visual and representational points of view, because acting and the visual content of the opera are provided by Cocteau's cinematic images. While in traditional operatic performance the singer's body becomes a physical manifestation of the voice, in Glass's *Belle*, singers' voices are re-embodied in cinematic images, destroying the traditional unity between voice and body. When Cocteau's cinematic images replace the opera's visuality, the singers' bodies lose a signifying function. By simply standing on stage, fixed and immobile, impotent to act, Glass's singers—more precisely, their bodies—no longer function as a tool to represent the emotions and psychology of the opera's characters.[15]

Harrison Birtwistle's *The Mask of Orpheus* (1986) is another example of the voice-body split. It tells multiple narratives about the Orpheus myth from different characters' perspectives, as there are various versions of the myth itself, and the stage is divided into different areas to show different narratives. Each of the major characters—Orpheus, Euridice, and Aristaeus—is represented in three forms: a singer, a mime, and a puppet. All of the singers are requested to wear masks, following the tradition of Greek tragedy. Masks, as Robert Wilson notes, engender "a distance between the sound and image", voice and body, and in so doing, contribute to the disruption of hearing and viewing senses (quoted in Birringer 1991: 224). The use of puppets creates an additional degree of separation and distancing between voice and body. Unlike his earlier opera, *Punch and Judy* (1967), in which singers pretend to be puppets, Birtwistle uses actual puppets in *The Mask of Orpheus* and their voices are provided by off-stage singers. The separation of voice and body then is more radical than in Glass's opera: in *La Belle et la Bête*, the surrogate body is still a human body although it is a two-dimensional cinematic image; in Birtwistle's work, the human body is replaced by an inanimate puppet, which further enhances the sense of disembodied-ness of the singing voice.

THE POWER OF THE BODILESS VOICE: THE VOICE FROM ELSEWHERE IN FILM AND OPERA

How can we explain a recent operatic trend that shows an extreme fascination with the separation of voice and body? Of course, the influence of some Asian theatres, such as Japanese Nōh theatre, as mentioned above, has been a motivation. But considering a century-long history of the mutual attraction between cinema and opera, the voice-body split in operatic theatre can be contextualised against the "castration anxiety" of the cinematic apparatus. Why does opera embrace what has been an "anxiety" to cinema? Why does opera relinquish cinema's aspiration to simulate opera's embodied voice? I trace a *possible* answer to cinema's ironic privileging of the voice in spite of the seeming dominance of the visual. When the voice is isolated from the body that produces it, the voice acquires a more autonomous power. In fact, this phenomenon of the autonomous voice is inherent, although hidden and elusive from our perception, in the cinematic apparatus. Slavoj Žižek's argument is illuminating in this context. He contends that to the contrary of people's expectation, the effect of adding a soundtrack to silent film is the exact opposite of being a more realistic imitation of life. This is because the separation of the image track and the soundtrack in talkie films promotes an "uncanny autonomization of the voice":

> What took place from the very beginning of the sound film was an uncanny autonomization of the voice, baptized "acousmatisation" by Chion: the emergence of a voice, that is neither attached to an object (a person) within diegetic reality nor simply the voice of an external commentator, but a spectral voice, which floats freely in a mysterious intermediate domain. [...] The voice acquires a spectral autonomy, it never quite belongs to the body we see, so that even when we see a living person talking, there is always some degree of ventriloquism at work: it is as if the speaker's own voice hollows him out and in a sense speaks "by itself", through him. (Žižek 1996: 92)

The autonomous and uncanny power of voice in the cinematic and televisual media can easily be experienced when the image track is out of synchronisation with the soundtrack. Even a split-second discrepancy in synch yields a fatal destruction of what Roland Barthes calls the "reality effect", as images transform into a shadow play of the flat images, losing their flesh, whose illusion is created by synchronised sound. This is the moment that unveils the intrinsic authorial power of the soundtrack, of the voice, in the cinematic medium. This unveiling is visualised in the most exaggerated way in the *"Teatro Silencio"* scene in David Lynch's *Mulholland Drive* (2001). In this scene, a female singer (Rebekah Del Rio) is lip-synching her recording of Roy Orbison's "Crying" in a Spanish rendition ("*Llorando*"), and her recorded singing voice continues after the singer collapses on stage while singing (figure 8.6).

Figure 8.6: the "*Teatro Silencio*" scene from David Lynch's *Mulholland Drive* (2001).

This is the moment Žižek describes as the autonomisation of the voice as "a pure spectral apparition of a bodiless 'undead' voice" (2004: 169).[16] I argue that the "uncanny autonomization of the voice" in film can be regarded as a reason for opera's natural and unconscious attraction to cinema. This is because in opera performance, too, voice acquires autonomous power, separated from the singer's body, in spite of the embodied performance.

At the beginning of her book *In Search of Opera*, Carolyn Abbate discusses Orpheus's last song emanating from his decapitated and floating head as a "master symbol" for the central issues her book addresses: "the complications of the performance network" (2001: 5). Orpheus's post-mortem singing, she argues, is also a literal embodiment of the music that comes not from the human body but from *elsewhere*—just like cinema's reality resides in a "primordial elsewhere", according to Christian Metz as discussed above—which she regards as the uncanny aspect of musical performance in general and operatic performance in particular. For Abbate, "a powerful metaphysics of absence" (*ibid.*: 6), of elsewhere, in spite of the visible presence of the singing body, characterises the state of voice in opera performance. In her theory, the dead (musical) instrument and live performer are collapsed because both are inanimate objects given life by music (*ibid.*: 5-9). In light of Abbate's theories, the voice-body split in the three examples analysed above can be regarded as the visualisation of the intrinsic condition of operatic voice and performers. The mimes in Goehr's *Triptych*, the fleshless on-screen cinematic images in Glass's *La Belle et la Bête*, the puppets in Birtwistle's *The Mask of Orpheus*, and the collapsed singer in Lynch's *Mulholland Drive* all represent the lifelessness of the performers, whose voices have emanated from "elsewhere". This is the voice having "a will of its own" as in the case of Ludlam's Callas, quoted above—the voice whose autonomisation, whose power, comes from its bodiless-ness.

NOTES

[1] This essay was evolved from the conference paper I presented at the annual conference of the International Federation of Theatre Research (FIRT) held in St. Petersburg in May, 2004. An earlier version of this paper is included in my monograph *Opera as Soundtrack*, published by Ashgate in 2013 (ISBN 978-0-7546-6718-6).

[2] Vitaphone was one of the sound-on-disc processes, which does not print the soundtrack on the actual film but issues it separately on phonograph discs that were played while the film (the image track) was being projected. Many early talkies, including the first talkie, Alan Crosland's *The Jazz Singer* (1927), used the Vitaphone process. For a comprehensive study of Vitaphone opera shorts, see Fleeger 2009.

[3] Martinelli is famous for his refusal to wear Pagliacci's hat. "No hat!", he has declared. This short is available as a Youtube clip online at:
http://www.youtube.com/watch?v=ad3fWkTJU_E&feature=related (consulted 15.2.2013).

[4] This is a visual palindrome in the sense that the last half of the silent images correspond to those in the first half only as an analogy: for instance, five people in the court in the first half correspond to five people who help Lulu's escape from the hospital in the second half, and the automobile (a police van) in the first half corresponds to the automobile (an ambulance) in the second half.

[5] Callas was cast for the title role of *Norma*, which was the opening piece of the 1958 season of the Rome Opera House. The day before the opening night, Callas was not feeling well and she suggested to the Rome Opera's management that there should be a standby. But she was told that, "No one can double Callas". After the first act of the opening night, Callas did not feel strong enough to continue to sing and cancelled the performance, whose audience included the then president of Italy, Giovanni Gronchi. Callas was accused of walking out on the president of Italy in a fit of temperament,

and the press coverage aggravated the situation. Callas brought a lawsuit against the Rome Opera House and she won, although it took thirteen years to settle the case.

[6] For instance, Silverman 1988. Psychoanalytically-oriented film theories have been criticised by such scholars as David Bordwell and Noël Carroll (1996) in part because such theories do not consider the audience and the spectatorship. But those theories are cogent for my argument in this essay, as I focus on "the apparatus" of cinema rather than its audience.

[7] Silverman explains that "to admit that the loss of the object is also a castration would be to acknowledge that the male subject is already structured by absence prior to the moment at which he registers woman's anatomical difference—to concede that he, like the female subject, has already been deprived of being, and already been marked by the language and desires of the Other" (Silverman 1988: 15).

[8] For Brechtian elements of Syberberg's *Parsifal*, see my article, "Hans-Jürgen Syberberg's *Parsifal*: The Staging of Dissonance in the Fusion of Opera and Film" (Joe 1998).

[9] For a critical challenge to the feminist theories developed by Lawrence, Mulvey, and Silverman, see Sjogren 2006.

[10] In the preface of her book *In Search of Opera*, Abbate calls disembodied singing an "operatic cliché" (2001: xv), but I think it is an exaggerated statement to support her argument for the ontological autonomy of voice in opera performance.

[11] The second work of the *Triptych* is *Shadowplay* (1970).

[12] My interview with Alexander Goehr was conducted in Cambridge, UK, on 4 July 2007. He also mentioned to me that he was invited to score for a film that was supposed to be directed by Michael Powell featuring Bing Crosby, but it did not materialise.

[13] Anthony Sheppard noted that in a telephone conversation with him, Goehr informed him that his early interest in the films and theories of Eisenstein had aroused his interest in Japanese theatre (Eisenstein had repeatedly acknowledged the influence of Japanese theatre on this work.). Following the composition of *Naboth's Vineyard*, Goehr planned to set two of Yukio Mishima's modernized Nōh plays and traveled to Japan to meet with the writer and to study Nōh. Mishima committed ritual suicide before this meeting could occur. However, Goehr has recently composed music for these plays (see Sheppard 2001: 297-98).

[14] For a detailed discussion of Glass's *La Belle et la Bête*, see my essay in *Between Opera and Cinema* (Joe and Theresa 2002: 59-73).

[15] There are a couple of places in the opera in which the singers imitate the position of Cocteau's cinematic images: for instance, the dinner sequence, in which the Beast is standing behind Belle. But the operatic singers are mostly immobile on stage throughout the opera.

[16] Žižek compares Lynch's scene of the undead voice to the opening of Sergio Leone's *Once Upon a Time in America*, in which a phone is ringing loudly and when a hand picks up the receiver, the ringing still continues.

CHAPTER 9

DANCING IN THE TWILIGHT:
ON THE BORDERS OF MUSIC AND THE SCENIC

DAVID ROESNER

MUSIC, SCENE, INTERMEDIALITY

Musical and scenic performances normally meet on well-established grounds: genres and conventions have in most cases answered all open questions about their hierarchy, the chronology of the artistic creation processes, and the kinds of expectations about their form and function. No one is surprised if a character bursts into a song in a musical, if music fills the "gaps" between acts in a theatre production, underscores the scenes of a film or play, or if the orchestra conveys the subtexts and psychologies of Verdi's or Wagner's heroes.

My interest begins within the wide fields of music(al) film and music theatre,[1] or, even more widely, with the interplay of music and performative arts or formats (including installations, television, performance art, video games) where the well-established grounds are abandoned. My chapter focuses on production processes and performative phenomena that render the clear distinctions between "music" and "theatre" or "music" and "film" problematic if not obsolete.

If we take two current theories and approaches towards music theatre as an example, we find that they investigate theatre as a synthetic vision, as a *Gesamtkunstwerk* (Hiß 2005) or as "musical multimedia" (Cook 1998) but these ideas still talk, for the most part, about performances with clearly distinguishable components and how to read them historically and analytically. Both approaches earn merit by challenging the idea that forms of interaction between music and theatre could be dealt with simply by comparing their expressive contents on a scale of concurrence, complementarity or contrast. Hiß unfolds the different historical manifestations of the synthesis of music, movement, image and text on the stage and their philosophical backgrounds and visions. Cook questions the notion of independent meaning-making processes for musical multimedia works, and demonstrates how musical multimedia enables the "construction of meaning that does not inhere in one medium or another, but emerges from the interaction between media and subject" (Cook 1998: viii), so that meaning is "the product of an interaction between sound structure and the circumstances of its reception" (*ibid.*: 23).

I would, however, like to challenge the assumption that music theatre, music(al) film and its related formats have to be *additive* phenomena in their production and analysis.[2] Historically speaking, we seem tempted to consider music theatre for example as being based on the division of labour, with a process of "sedimentation" creating a layering of successive aesthetic strata (libretto/book, lyrics, music/score, set and lighting design, musical and scenic direction, interpretation by the performers). Consequently, we also consider analysis to be the reverse process—an "excavation", as it were. In a chronological order, the elements uncovered would be the libretto, the score, the set design, the direction, the concretisation through the singers and performers and the theatrical apparatus. In film, the ingredients and their order of appearance are perhaps slightly different but they are often similarly separated, both temporally and spatially. So for both music(al) film and music theatre all these layers may be interlinked and blended into each other, but remain clearly distinguishable, comparable and attributable.

In contrast, I am interested in forms of music(al) film and music theatre where those stages (and thus also the participating "arts", or "media") become almost or even completely indistinguishable, where they are not additive, but "fusional" phenomena: where authorship is often collective and blurred, where combined terms like "music film", "film musical" or "music theatre" are challenged, because it becomes increasingly difficult to clearly distinguish the two parts of the respective term.[3]

There are some theoretical and methodological considerations that underpin this focus. The discourse about intermediality provides a series of insights and differentiations that inform my investigation: Christopher Balme, for example, describes one particular category of intermediality, which is most relevant to my line of enquiry, as "the attempt to realize in one medium the aesthetic conventions and habits of seeing and hearing in another medium". He elaborates: "The key term here is conventionality. This means that media are regarded as a set of historically contingent conventions, which may or may not be predicated on their technical devices" (Balme 2004: 7). The theatre works of Robert Lepage, which Balme analyses in this context, are a very good example: works for the theatre, which employ many "conventions and habits of seeing and hearing" in cinema, such as short narrative sequences, lighting that works like film editing or the use of intimate voice qualities due to radio microphones, etc.

Irina Rajewsky also highlights the system reference (*Systemreferenz*) that one medium (e.g., theatre) makes to another (e.g., music, or vice versa), in a "process of meaning making of a medial product with reference to the semiotic system of a medium conventionally perceived as distinct within the means of an enabling medium" (Rajewsky 2002: 5).[4] Both notions raise questions about the materiality of media, the inseparable connection of medium and form,[5] and the nature of meaning making and representation.

In addition, Jens Schröter proposes the necessity or at least possibility of a *tertium comparationis* that serves as a transmedial reference point within or during the processes of what he calls "transmedial intermediality" (Schröter n.d.: 6). He quotes Joachim Paech who remarks that "one could say, there is no intermediality between literature and film, but only between the media of literary and filmic narrative" (*ibid.*).[6] Here, as Schröter argues, narrative can be such a reference point, connecting the two media without being exclusively attributable to either of them. With regards to music and the scenic, I am also thinking of rhythm, timbre, repetition, or *Darstellung,* "[re]presentation", as possible points of comparison and/or encounter and will come back to the latter in the analyses of Lars von Trier's and Heiner Goebbels' works.

When thinking of the particular types of cohesion and amalgamation that music, film and theatre (and their different medial elements and aspects) undergo in the cases of transmedial intermediality as described above, I would like to distinguish between three different types or processes of this cohesion using three visual metaphors. The first could be described as a kind of picture puzzle, *Suchbild*: an image within an image that you may see or may not, but whose emergence does not prevent you from seeing the whole. The consequent process is the emerging of something. For example, people tend to see hidden faces in images, as exemplified in Wiseman 2011, in which a man's face emerges from a forest floor.[7]

Secondly, music-scenic events may present themselves as *Kippfiguren* (reversible ambiguous figures), images, sounds or actions that can seem to be perceived alternately as one or the other, but never both at the same time.[8] The central process or movement is the tilting of the eye's focus, an effect achieved in the classic visual pun of Charles Allan Gilbert's "All is Vanity" (1892) (figure 9.1), in which you can either see a woman in front of a mirror or a skull, but not both at the same time.

A third condition that music(al) film or music theatre may find itself in is the stage of liminality: being on a threshold, "betwixt and between" (Turner 1986: 93).[9] Distinguishing itself from Victor Turner's theory of liminal phenomena in social rites, liminality in music theatre or film, as I would describe it, may not necessarily be a temporary passage between the two, e.g., between music and theatre as two conventionally identified arts, or media, or dispositions of perception, but it could be a sustained position between them. I would suggest a process of "hovering" as the movement that symbolises this state.[10] Fittingly, in M. C. Escher's picture "Day and Night" (1938)[11] he keeps his black and white birds hovering over and out of a tiled ground. In the middle of the picture the birds are in a liminal state: not square fields anymore, not yet black or white birds.

I will now exemplify and challenge these methodological considerations by looking at a musical film which is highly reflexive of its theatricality, and a music theatre production which makes extensive use of live video and explores a wide range of interplays between music, theatre and film.

1. DANCER IN THE DARK (2000)

First though, I will look at the musical film that deals quite uniquely with the transmedial intermedialities of music, theatre and film and with a liminality of process and product: Lars von Trier's *Dancer in the Dark* (2000). I will try to show how the transitions between the film and its musical "numbers" may exemplify and reflect the different stages and qualities of the transmedial relationship between the components described above. I will also argue that Selma, the film's main character, played by Björk (the avant-garde singer-songwriter Björk Guðmundsdóttir)—who was also the composer and vocal performer of the film score—can be seen as an embodiment of the new devising and perception processes that are connected with contemporary forms of scenic music, that abandon or at least question

Figure 9.1: "All is Vanity" by C. Allan Gilbert (1892).[12]

preconceived hierarchies and methods. I approach the film via the three aspects I introduced earlier: the picture puzzle (here also a sound puzzle), the tilting and reversible ambiguity of cinematography and character, and the liminal status of the performance space.

1.1. THE PICTURE/SOUND PUZZLE

When watching *Dancer in the Dark* it would be difficult not to notice that music is one of the driving forces of the film and its appearance. Its main character, Selma, escapes her grim reality by transforming her miserable existence into glossy musical daydreams. This shift between two fictional realities coincides with the alternation of two filmic genres, which I will come to in more detail, and extends the techniques of musicalisation from the performances (the represented) to the mode of presentation (i.e., the filmic and theatrical means). Within the musical numbers of the film it becomes especially and increasingly difficult to draw lines between music and the scenic: in many instances musical performance is embedded or hidden in the theatrical performance, which again is filmed in a highly rhythmitised montage, that ignores narrative coherence or continuity or even the most basic filmic principles—like the 180° degree rule—[13] completely. The filmic puzzle that von Trier creates hides acoustic and visual elements in each shot, which constantly transform and change their classification: a dancer emerges from a factory worker, a beat from the sound of a machine, a musical caesura from editing, a full blown film score from a sound ambience (see figure 9.2).[14]

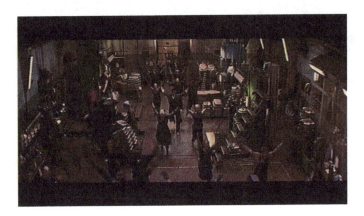

Figure 9.2: Dancing in the factory in *Dancer in the Dark* (2000).

In this example, it is the simultaneity and cohesion of media, of song, stage and screen that is striking. The elements cannot be separated in a meaningful way any longer. This is astonishing since the way these sequences were produced was much more divided, even more than would usually be the case in filmmaking. Rather than controlling the amalgamation of elements at the level of pre-production through the use of detailed storyboards, etc., von Trier decided to place more emphasis on post-production with regard to the filmic composition: first, Björk wrote and produced the music that was then theatrically staged, choreographed and performed in the factory space, then it was filmed by Lars von Trier and Robby Müller, his cinematographer, with the infamous one hundred digital cameras (Matthews 2000) that were positioned at every possible spot on the location, capturing fixed and random images of whatever happened to occur in front of them. The editing then, obviously, became the main compositional process: the creation of an audiovisual score, which both accompanies and subsists within the musical and choreographic score.

At the level of the audience's perception, however, the different media and their respective materialities—at least in the way that we would conventionally classify them—become blurred: the music is at the same time diegetic and non-diegetic, the movements oscillate between being representational (actors playing factory workers) and presentational (dancers dancing), non-fictional, fictional and super-fictional (that is: daydream fiction inside a fictional character's imagination), and the filming and editing at the same time follows an almost documentary approach but then transforms the gained footage into a rhythmical and highly stylised montage. Music, film and theatre and their respective materials and aesthetic strategies emerge from and out of each other in an intermedial dance.

1.2. THE TILTING IMAGE

While some elements of this particular scene can be two things at the same time—such as the sound of a machine and the beat of a song, I would propose that the cinematography follows a different logic in this intermedial setting.

I would argue that the idea of the *Kippfigur*,[15] where one thing presents itself in two or more different and mutually exclusive ways—the transition being either temporal or spatial—applies to the shifts undertaken by the different modes of filming/shooting with which

Lars von Trier chose to distinguish the fictional reality and Selma's imaginary musical world.

Within all the scenes that host the musical numbers, there is a tilt, quite often literally, between the documentary/Dogma-style handheld camerawork[16] and the static, more colourful shots by hundreds of stable cameras, from much more unlikely, and often superhuman perspectives (see figures 9.3 and 9.4).[17] This shift occurs in synchrony with the music, but it is also part of the music: the rhythm of the montage contributes largely to our perception of the musical score, as does the sound and movement portrayed in those shots.[18] Within the narrative or psychology of the film, this tilting symbolises Selma's

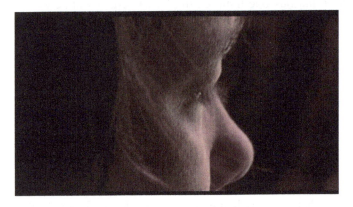

Figure 9.3: Level hand camera shot in *Dancer in the Dark* (2000).

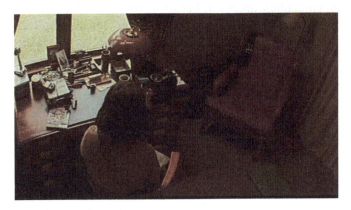

Figure 9.4: Fixed camera shot in *Dancer in the Dark* (2000).

escape into another daydream, which is triggered by an external acoustic motivation: the machines, a record player's needle tripping at the end of a record, a courtroom journalist's pencil drawing, a train passing by. Some of these transitions are just new emerging perspectives, new contextualisations—the scratching needle additionally becomes the pulse of the song—others are properly tilting and mutually exclusive, particularly the performances: David Morse's character Bill, in the following example, is dead one moment, and alive the next (see figures 9.5 and 9.6). He tilts between his fictional character, and Selma's dream version of it; and as he then starts to sing, the tilt is as much contributing to the music, as the music is to the

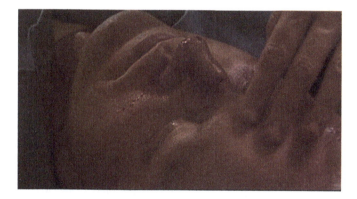

Figure 9.5: Bill (David Morse) having died...

Figure 9.6: ...and having been resurrected, *Dancer in the Dark* (2000).

tilt. And finally, Selma herself, and the situations she dreams herself into, are lost in transformation; they remain on a threshold, betwixt and between. This is most evident in the final rehearsal scene of the film, when Selma sings about her love for musicals while the director of the amateur musical society notifies the police, who want Selma for murder.[19]

1.3. THE LIMINAL SPACE

Kathleen Murray writes in her article "Beyond Genre. Towards a Playful Grammar of Musicals" (2003), which analyses *Dancer in the Dark* against (or with) Deleuze and Bakhtin:

> When a number begins in a musical, the film creates a new space. This space exists within, and on top of, the narrative world. The music sweeps the regular world out of its path and ushers in an alternative: a dream world that is simultaneous with the narrative world, but distinct (2003: 14).

I agree with her argument, but would locate the "new space" *in between*, rather than *on top of* and *within* the narrative world. In the case of Selma (and this may well be valid for many other performances in contemporary music theatre or music film) this liminal state extends to the position of the character/performer.[20] In the rehearsal scene just mentioned, Selma and the space she finds herself in are stuck halfway between the unglamorous rehearsal of the amateur musical club, invaded by a harsher reality (personified by the police, see figure 9.7), and a musical dreamland in which every animate and inanimate object is part of a song, a dance. Within a single shot viewers can see elements of both worlds and watch performers acting exclusively according to one of them: some join in, some watch in disbelief (see figure 9.8). Only Selma synthesises both worlds: she is dancing *and* being arrested at the same time, she is the threshold that connects both worlds.

The liminality of this intermedial setting also applies to her performance: in the musical scenes Selma transgresses her character and hovers between her fictional self, her imaginary self and the professional and private selves of Björk, who, allegedly, had a nervous breakdown in real life while shooting the film.[21]

The processual nature of this emerging, tilting and hovering is captured clearly in the musical sequences: you can practically watch Selma *and* Björk, as they amalgamate reality and fiction, day-to-day

Figure 9.7: The police enter in a scene from *Dancer in the Dark* (2000).

Figure 9.8: Jeff watches the super-fictional dance in *Dancer in the Dark* (2000).

movement and dance, sound and music, and different layers of character, without finalising the process. As Murray writes, using Bakhtin's notions of "unfinalizabilty" and "noncoincidence":

> Nothing is completed. No one is ever finished. There is no done. Everything and everyone is in a state of becoming. [...] "Noncoincidence" with oneself

takes on epic proportions because of the layers of performance that musicals
demand. The performer is playing on many layers simultaneously. (Murray
2003: 5)

This concept of simultaneous layers, which we can see with
Björk/Selma, is characteristic of the kinds of interplay between the
music(al) and the scenic which I am discussing. Elsewhere are further
examples—the musicians of the Ensemble Modern in Heiner
Goebbels' *Black on White* (1997), for example; the carefully
composed and notated theatrical actions of Mauricio Kagel or Manos
Tsangaris; the singing actors of Christoph Marthaler; the editing
rhythms of Thomas Riedelsheimer's films[22]— all play on those non-
coinciding and unfinalisable layers, and like many contemporary
forms of music theatre and music film point at the gaps and cracks in
the conventions of their related genres.

Heiner Goebbels' *Eraritjaritjaka* (2004), which I will address in more
detail in the second part of this chapter, is a performance of string
quartets and essayist texts by Elias Canetti that hovers somewhere
between concert, recitation, music theatre, music film, etc., and
challenges the audience to investigate exactly how the constant
crossing of genre and media borders takes place and succeeds. The
distinction of different intermedial tiltings, emergences or liminalities
would be interesting not only for the performance analysis (when does
the audience realise the strict musical organisation of the live film,
which shows actor André Wilms in a seemingly private apartment?
What happens to Bach's *Contrapunctus No. 9* from *Die Kunst der
Fuge* when enriched by a fifth voice, namely Wilms' recitation of
Canetti?), but is also a strong issue in the devising and composition
process, which, as Goebbels reports (see e.g., Goebbels 2002, 2007,
2012 and Sandner 2004), is frequently determined by intermedial
collective processes, where institutionally-requested distinctions
between costume, light, film design and composition become
questionable or even obsolete.

Looking back at Lars von Trier's/Björk's Selma we could see a
personification of these transformative, translational, sometimes
transgressive artistic activities that contemporary music theatre evokes
in its agents; agents which are often collective, sometimes operational
and who often create works or processes that are co-authored or co-
composed in some way by the audience. Selma also bridges these
gaps between observing and participating, between character

representation and musical performance, between different artistic materials and means of expression. The gaps continue to be there, but their course has become more fluid. Selma thus overcomes the additive notion of music and film, music and theatre, etc., but equally defies the notion of a *Gesamtkunstwerk* (total work of art), in which all the arts unite and contribute to a higher end. Instead, *Dancer in the Dark* evokes a piece of art, the beauty of which consists in its paradoxical nature, in its contradictions, and the primary dissolution of conventionally fixed artistic disciplines.

By discussing a second example, I would like to consolidate the notion of intermediality discussed above, but also to challenge the operability of the three analytical categories that I have suggested. Rather than trying to identify them individually however, I will now indicate their co-existence and amalgamation within several key moments of Heiner Goebbels' music theatre production *Eraritjaritjaka* (2004).

2. *ERARITJARITJAKA* (2004)
2.1. THE BEGINNING (SHOSTAKOVICH)

Eraritjaritjaka almost begins like a conventional chamber music concert; the theatre venue, however, with its black stage and curtains, the particularly focussed lighting and—unusual for classical concerts—the amplification of the Mondriaan Quartett, suggest theatrical things to come. The quartet plays the first two movements of Shostakovich's *Eighth String Quartet* at the end of which Goebbels (and sound designer Willi Bopp) surprise the audience by electronically extending the final chord far beyond its natural duration. The echo is sampled, looped and becomes electronically modified: the evolving sound becomes increasingly distanced from its source. First, it just breaks free of its producers acoustically (the quartet has visibly finished playing and gets up from its seats), but then, over the course of about one minute the sound also becomes altered to the degree that it does not resemble a chord from a string quartet anymore. It tilts into a crackling noise and thus "deteriorates" into pure sound with the qualities of white noise and electronic malfunctioning.[23] As the sound negates what it was and where it came from, it also seems to adopt a new function within the performance as a piece of incidental music: it initiates a theatrical and even rudimentarily narrative interplay of the string quartet with the stage, and, subsequently, with actor André Wilms and the lighting and video settings with which he is engaged. The sound that took a life of its own sets the scene for the dense and complex varieties of intermedial oscillations that Goebbels plays with in *Eraritjaritjaka*. Where music can become electronic sound, no longer traceable to its acoustic source, it becomes a versatile performative partner, ready to adopt various functions as incidental music, installation, film music, ballet music, etc., ready to underscore, accompany, contrast, lead, follow, interject and merge with the theatrical action.

After the string quartet has repositioned its seating arrangement during the one-minute cloud of "noise", they begin to play Alexeij Mossolov's *String Quartet No. 1, op. 24*. The new staging of the quartet—seated end-on to the audience in one line, facing a white rectangle of lit cloth in front of them—renders the musical performance theatrical.[24] The act of performing music is no longer self-referential but seems to be directed at something and to anticipate someone's appearance on the empty stage, which looks like an empty sheet of paper in want of a pen. As actor André Wilms enters from the left, he recites the following passage:

> I have no sounds that could serve to soothe me, no violoncello like him, no lament that anyone would recognise as a lament because it sounds subdued, in an inexpressibly tender language. I have only these lines on the yellowish paper and words that are never new, for they keep saying the same thing through an entire life. (Goebbels 2004b: 1)

From this new music-theatrical setting that introduces an actor and spoken words to the scene, another function or attribute of the music emerges. Mossolov's composition is now both a painting over and underscoring of the text, as well as being its subject matter: the text seems to directly refer to the music. Because of the way Goebbels has staged the first encounter of actor, text and music in *Eraritjaritjaka*, the text becomes quickly joined crosswise with the music, creating a sense of dialogue or "call and response". Thus text and music—and actor and musicians—become intertwined in a way that renders both liminal in terms of their medial affiliation. The text becomes part of the score; the music and the act of playing it become part of the theatrical event.

The medial oscillation becomes further enhanced and extended when the brightly-lit square upon which Wilms stands narrows down to a beam of light extending from his feet towards the audience. It begins to circle around Wilms according to musical impulses, with the performer turning as the centre of this circle. The beam of light becomes a choreographic part of the scene, if not its driving force. The interdependence of the music, the text, and the movement of the actor and the light are obvious, but their causal relationship remains mysterious and open: does the light follow the actor as an inverted shadow? Does the music follow the light as an imaginary conductor? Does the text attribute a semantic meaning to the light?[25] Does the music dramatise the text? The involved media in this short scene hover between those possible connections and conventional medial functions and acquire and mimic each other's characteristics in a truly transmedial form of intermediality: paraphrasing Balme (2004: 7) one could say that the light seeks to realise some of the aesthetic conventions of "seeing" in the medium of dance; the spoken prose seeks to realise some of the aesthetic conventions of "hearing" in the medium of chamber music, and so on.

Due to the precise *compositional* connections that Goebbels establishes between the scenic elements, their interaction oscillates between being abstract, illustrative, explanatory, narrative, voluntarily confusing, etc. They constantly defy a simple or straightforward allocation to being either conflicting or congruent; the intermedial connection remains productively ambiguous (see Goebbels 2007).

2.2. TRANSITION (TAXI RIDE)

Almost exactly midway through the performance there is another significant medial transformation. André Wilms is suddenly being filmed as he puts on his coat and leaves the theatre. The video-feed is projected live onto the façade of a tall white house-front with four dark double windows. Wilms leaves the building and gets into a taxi, accompanied by the cameraman, Bruno Deville. While Wilms moves through the city reciting Canetti, the Mondriaan Quartett plays Ravel's *String Quartet in F.* The theatre performance has tilted somehow into a cinema matrix, and the music serves as film music and resembles the live accompaniment of silent films. But Goebbels manages to irritate and question this new genre again: as the black windows of the façade perforate the film image we are constantly reminded of our theatrical setting and, as the quartet's cellist sits in front of the "screen", he becomes part of the projected image, a visible source of the music, and a live presence within the broadcast of a larger-than-life close-up. Additionally, two scanners[26] roll onto the empty white stage-cloth and begin to move to the music. Relieving the scanners of their technical and medial purpose to light something, a resemblance of two dancers emerges from this *pas de deux* with its elegant and synchronous movements.

2.3. THE ENDING (BACH)

The ending of *Eraritjaritjaka* quite literally solves part of the puzzle that is caused by the enigmatic interplay between presence and absence in this performance. For quite a while the audience is under the impression that they have witnessed André Wilms travel to an apartment somewhere in the city. However, there are several indicators during the performance, that somehow this apartment is actually located in the house on stage (the façade of which we have seen). While the performance does not give away how Wilms secretly got back onto the stage despite being filmed constantly, the topography of the apartment, which we have only seen through the fragmented view of the hand-camera, reveals itself. The performance finishes with Wilms visibly sitting behind the bottom left window of this house and writing and reciting aphorisms by Canetti, which Goebbels has collocated into a piece of serial poetry that he then carefully inserted into Bach's *Contrapunctus 9* from the *Art of Fugue*. During this, a new projection very slowly fades in across the façade. It shows the interior of the apartment in exact scale, shot from the front with the fourth wall missing.[27] We simultaneously look *onto* and *through* the house front and see the interior emerging from the exterior. Again, Goebbels provides us with a "presence that is held in a constant state of suspense" (Goebbels 2002: 136).[28] We witness a liminal stage with a kind of Heisenbergian uncertainty principle to it, as the *décor* is also a screen, the text also a subject in Bach's fugue, the actor also a musician, the exterior also the interior and the live also the mediated, and it is equally impossible to isolate one from the other analytically without profoundly changing the observed, as it is impossible to determine and study both simultaneously.

CONCLUSION

I have offered three major points in this chapter: 1. Experimental forms of music and scenic media can be a fusional phenomenon that does not necessarily add and mix music, words, gestures, narrative, and so on, but helps them overstep their respective medial boundaries; 2. The resulting intermediality is transformational; 3. The transformation can take different forms in process and perception that I associate with three types of images that facilitate the (a) emergence, (b) abrupt change or (c) co-existence of two or more perspectives.

While my argument is based on the experience and observation of contemporary music theatre and music(al) film practices and experiments that evade more traditional analytical concepts, like the alignment of corresponding or conflicting meanings in music/scene arrangements, I think it applies more widely. Any attempt to draw clear lines that would separate contemporary practices from more traditional forms of music theatre is problematic: however separated the development processes of libretto, music, *mise en scène* may be, in the actual moment of the performance *any* kind of music theatre or music film will contain transformational qualities and instances in which singing becomes acting, acting becomes dance, words become music, etc., despite the still influential paradigm of the separation of the arts that has left such a strong mark on Western culture. I would also argue that these instances create not only what we could call particularly memorable aesthetic experiences, but also a great methodological challenge for the music theatre scholar, because they slip so easily through our analytical fingers. By trying to acknowledge and investigate their intermedial evasiveness and the strategies and consequences of the afore-mentioned transformations, I hope to have offered a valid first step.

NOTES

---

[1] I am referring to the wide definition of music theatre as it is distinguished by Andrew Clements from the particular manifestations and counter concepts of opera presented in the 1960s up until today. See Clements 2001: 534-35. With "music(al) film" I mean films, for which music plays a significant if not central role, be it dramaturgically or structurally. Where "musical film" points at the more established and conventional end of the spectrum of films that include diegetic musical numbers, often even through-composed scenes and choreography, "music film" refers to a more experimental development in film making, where musical structures and principles become instrumental in the formal aspects of film, such as the editing and montage. Famous examples are Dziga Vertov's *Man with a Movie Camera* (1929) and Walter Ruttman's *Berlin—Die Sinfonie der Großstadt* (1927), but also, more recently Thomas Riedelsheimer's *Touch the Sound* (2004).

[2] Recent scholarship in film music, for example, also still follows this basic assumption, see for example Goldmark *et al* 2007, Gorbman 1987 or Cooke 2008.

[3] Matthias Rebstock and I have recently explored these developments in more detail in our edited book *Composed Theatre* (Rebstock and Roesner 2012).

[4] "[...] Verfahren der Bedeutungskonstitution eines medialen Produkts durch Bezugnahme auf [...] das semiotische System [...] eines konventionell distinkt wahrgenommenen Mediums mit den dem kontaktnehmenden Medium eigenen Mitteln" (all translations in this chapter are mine).

[5] Schröter underlines Niklas Luhmann's insistence on the inseparability of medium and form, as "Formen [...] immer nur in einem Medium erscheinen, Medien selbst immer nur in Formen aktualisiert erscheinen" ("forms only appear within a medium, media themselves only exist when actualised in forms") (Schröter 2002: 5). In addition, Sybille Krämer emphasises the performative nature of Luhmann's coupling of medium and form, claiming that it becomes the "temporal, instable, ephemeral, contingent concretisation of one of the potentials for creation of form, to offer which is the task of the medium" ("Die Medium/Form Kopplung wird zur "temporalisierten, instabilen, flüchtigen, kontingenten Konkretisierung eines jener Potentiale zur Formbildung, die bereitzustellen die Aufgabe des Mediums ausmacht") (Krämer 1998: 565ff., cited in Schröter 2002: 8).

[6] "Man kann auch sagen, daß es keine Intermedialität zwischen Literatur und Film gibt, sondern nur zwischen Medien literarischen und filmischen Erzählens" (cited in Schröter n.d.: 6; originally from Paech 1997: 335, reference 7).

[7] Wiseman, Richard. 2011. "Can you spot the hidden face?". Online at: http://richardwiseman.wordpress.com/2011/12/13/can-you-spot-the-hidden-face/ (consulted 15.01.2013).

[8] "Eine Kippfigur zeichnet sich [...] dadurch aus, daß sie immer zwei Sichtweisen eines Phänomens oder eines Gegenstandes erlaubt, die jedoch niemals gemeinsam miteinander auftreten können" (Flaßpöhler, Rausch and Wald 2007: 8).

[9] See also Broadhurst 1999.

[10] In this sense, music theatre can be liminal theatre in Susan Broadhurst's sense; that is, experimental, hybrid, marginal, intersemiotic, disquieting, playful, etc. (Broadhurst 1999: 1 and 69). In this chapter I am just using the term "liminal" when referring to singular performative events that are situated in an intermedial no-man's land, which does not necessarily characterise the entire performance as liminal.

[11] Online at: http://www.artchive.com/artchive/E/escher/escher_day_night.jpg.html (consulted 15.01.2013)

[12] A wide range of similar illusions can be found online at: http://www.illusionen.biz/blog/?page_id=57 (consulted 15.01.2013).

[13] This rule specifies that when filming a dialogue between two people, the camera should not cross an imaginary line between the two so that the relative location of the two people left and right is not reversed. See also Mackendrick 2004: 235-250.

[14] Examples of these effects can be seen in *Dancer in the Dark* between 36'36—41'36.

[15] You can for example see a dice from different sides and it will reveal different numbers, but it's impossible to see more than three sides at once.

[16] Rule 3, for example, states: "The camera must be a hand-held camera. Any movement or immobility attainable in the hand is permitted. The film must not take place where the camera is standing; filming must take place where the action takes place" (see http://en.wikipedia.org/wiki/Dogme_95 (consulted 12.07.2011), which

lists all ten Dogma rules). For an academic discussion of these rules see Schepelem 2005.

[17] Examples of these effects can be seen in *Dancer in the Dark* between 1'08'52—1'09'10.

[18] Murray's concept of the intransitive nature of the musical is actually subverted in what I perceive in *Dancer in the Dark* (and consequently in potentially all music theatre and film): singing and dancing as intransitive action is altered—things/devices, etc., can be "sung" or "danced", etc., due to the translational capacities of spectator and or creator.

[19] See *Dancer in the Dark*, 1'21'18—1'25'42.

[20] It is worth noting that the relationship between Selma and Björk is itself a phenomenon. Björk's lack of acting technique and her strong performativity as a music celebrity provides several examples of all three proposed categories. I restrict my investigation to this particular example, simply because of its being most visibly connected or induced by music.

[21] Ann Powers writes in the *New York Times* of 17 September 2000 about the blurred lines between the character's and the actor's pain: "She [Björk] immersed herself in the part, to the point where it sometimes worried her friends". Powers quotes Björk saying, "'I would come home after fourteen hours of crying and nervous breakdowns" (Powers 2000). *The New Zealand Herald* of 5 May 2004 reports that "in *Dancer in the Dark*, his [Lars von Trier's] Palme d'Or-winning musical, he subjected Björk to such intense pressure that she went AWOL from the shoot" (Anon. 2004); she was, according to the *Observer*, "rumoured to have been so unhappy while filming a role in Lars von Trier's *Dancer In The Dark* that she ate her own cardigan" (Vernon 2007).

[22] For example *Touch the Sound* (Riedelsheimer 2004).

[23] See Hegarty 2003 on the notion of noise as the "other" of music.

[24] See production images online at:
http://www.heinergoebbels.com/en/archive/works/complete/view/11/photos (consulted 18.01.2013).

[25] "More than anything we resemble bowling pins. They set us up in families, approximately nine. Squat and wooden, we stand there not knowing what to do with our fellow pins" (Canetti in Goebbels 2004b: 1).

[26] Remotely controllable lights, which in this performance were mounted on equally controllable wheels.

[27] See images online at: http://www.klausgruenberg.de/eraritjaritjaka.htm (consulted 18.01.2013).

[28] "Einem kontinuierlichen Schwebezustand gehaltenen Präsenz".

CHAPTER 10

TURKISH POST-MIGRANT "OPERA" IN EUROPE:
A SOCIO-HISTORICAL PERSPECTIVE ON AURALITY

PIETER VERSTRAETE

In European countries with a high level of urbanised multiculturalism and migration density, such as the Netherlands and Germany, new forms of music theatre are emerging that include different communities and social groups. One such development is opera and music theatre produced *for, by* and *with* people from communities with a Turkish migration background.[1]

Certainly, opera has a long tradition of representing "the Turk" (more precisely, the Ottoman) and other related Eastern identities on the stage, in the so-called *Türkenopern*[2] (or "Turkish" operas) mostly with exotic/Orientalist and racist undertones. The genre was often exercised to expose and, thereby, to reconfirm European values. Musically, the term *à la Turca* came to denote a "wrong-note-style", bending or breaking established rules in European classical music, thereby questioning those same values in the listening experience. With the presence of artists with an ethnically Turkish background in a second and third generation after the arrival of the "guest worker" generation, the genre of "Turkish opera" is taking new forms, meanings and expressions, as well as audiences. Remarkably, this newly emerging body of work—which I describe as "post-migrant" after a successful coining by Shermin Langhoff[3] in the Berlin scene— represents the first involvement that any of the European Turkish themselves have had with either the content of "Turkish opera" or its production process. This causes us to question the counteractive and, perhaps, self-orientalising tendencies of the operatic past, tendencies which need historicising.

Central to my argument is how music works as the point of access to and the vehicle of social history in these performances, negotiating socio-cultural issues, among others, of cultural memory, tradition and the experience of modern subjectivity as constitutive of the post-migrant identity in the twenty-first century. Through the adaptation of "traditional" music theatre conventions such as those of opera, with its specific history in Western Europe, these performances are also produced for local audience members with the help of more institutionalised music theatre ensembles and opera production houses. The production of these works often fulfil the demand to be pedagogical and reflective of cultural diversity as well as engender cultural and political education in the widest sense, involving larger audiences and generations. Therefore, the historical contextualisation of this new trend needs to encompass a heterogeneous group of listeners in the auditorium. This would need to take account of the current individual listening experiences within a larger framework of the emancipation processes of post-migration and multiculturality, which also necessitate a broader concept of aurality.

I will be referring to two productions as illustrations of this trend, both produced in 2010: *Lege Wieg / Boş Beşik*, produced by Korean composer Seung-Ah Oh and Dutch director Cilia Hogerzeil in the Netherlands, and *Tango Türk*, produced by Turkish composer Sinem Altan (from Ankara) and Dutch director Lotte De Beer in Germany. The former is a new opera production in the "post-Wagnerian" vein by a Dutch small-scale music theatre company in Dordrecht, Hollands Diep, in collaboration with VocaalLAB in Zaandam (both are production houses for experimental music theatre, subsidised by the Netherlands Fund for Performing Arts, also known as "NFPK+"). The production came about after a series of workshops with Turkish and Dutch women from the community in Dordrecht, who formed the chorus in the performance. The opera was staged at Het Energiehuis in Dordrecht, which is a former power plant on an old industrial site in the city. The latter, on the other hand, is a post-dramatic music (or even "musical") theatre piece staged in the Neuköllner Oper in Berlin, which is situated in the centre of a highly concentrated multicultural part of the city. Both performances blur the traditional boundaries between music theatre and opera today, whilst incorporating Turkish and "European" musical cultures.

The examples of works within this chapter are read for their internal meanings and processes as much as the acknowledgement of the dynamic and ever changing conditions, particularly the cultural policy climate, that enable the development of post-migrant theatre.

One should realise that most projects are not structurally funded but rather temporary events, supported by the national and international festival circuits in Europe and Turkey.[4]

Therefore an understanding of the development of Turkish post-migrant opera and music theatre in Europe can be gleaned, alongside external factors such as artistic networks and cultural policies, by looking at both the social and cultural-historic dynamics that are at work *within* these performances. However, the notion of a so-called "democratisation" of music theatre and particularly of opera also poses some questions about the hybrid aesthetics and the experience of these performances by a heterogeneous audience. This touches upon the very definition and self-legitimisation of music theatre and asks us to reflect on the social and aesthetic needs of its receivers. Therefore, this chapter proposes to look not only at the singularity of these music theatre projects, including the specific aesthetic strategies used to represent and communicate their individual (hi)stories. It also includes the history, the permanence and the points of convergence underpinning the socio-politics of this emerging art form in the wake of modernisation, democratisation and migration issues specific to the Turkish—and Kurdish—communities. This is eventually seen in relation to its contribution to the development of music theatre in Europe.

Since this art form addresses both social and aesthetic needs, this chapter tentatively tries to connect specific questions of the performances to culture, aesthetics and social life. I take as axiomatic the link between music theatre and *aurality*—that part of our cultural discourse that both enables and disciplines the values, norms, meanings and opinions related to listening, not just in our aesthetic encounters in the auditorium but also everywhere else in our daily lives. I take it as a given that in their arrangement of sound within the particular construct of representation, opera and music theatre can display the secret workings of aurality. This happens most when the music performance asks from the spectator-auditor a highly acute awareness of her listening attitudes and expectations, for instance regarding certain musical traditions that are reinterpreted in these culturally hybrid performances. Traditionalism plays a significant role in identity formation, so we need to ask if convergence between different musical traditions is at all possible and how it affects post-migrant identity. As such, these music theatre performances reveal aurality to be a discursive space that is continuously contested, not only in relation to the present day and its dominant, hegemonic cultural forces, but also to the ways we want to see ourselves.

Ultimately, this chapter demonstrates how music theatre responds to and helps to shape this invisible space of aurality in relation to its mixed audiences. I believe that it is in this shared space that music theatre and the individual audience member can create meaning in relation to one another. No matter whether it is "opera" or "music theatre", in their strictly distinguished sense, we need to ask ourselves how this type of community-based (and often, project-based) art makes meaning and is meaningful for a segment of society in the way these audiences respond to the music and the performances as a whole. The chapter aims then to disclose aurality as a social force, which, although it concerns *contemporary* listening cultures in the first place, is foremost tuned to social history. It is in this historically determined space of aurality, which constitutes music theatre or opera, that the listeners find each other in different aesthetic experiences giving access to different cultural memories that are as much about the modern individual today as about the collective.

PERFORMING MULTICULTURALITY

The emergence of opera and music theatre for Turkish post-migrant communities in Europe needs to be seen in relation to their shared socio-cultural developments, on the one hand, and within the more recent context of a migrating Europe, on the other. Both have to do with cultural policies and state-organised funding as much as with the aesthetic urges of individual artists who respond to the current cultural climate. Important influences we need to take into account are the culturally dominant modes of performance in Europe today: post-dramatic theatre and (New) Music Theatre in its third wave, both of which have developed since the 1980s.

Music theatre—as we know it today in its exclusive sense, according to Eric Salzman and Thomas Desi (2008)—was born out of a sense of necessity to renew music drama and small-scale opera after the late-modernist experiments with chamber opera in the 1910s, in a first wave, and with a plethora of experimental music theatre forms in the 1960s, in a second. Just as much as post-dramatic theatre has a complicated relation of resistance and continuity towards text-based drama and is a heterogeneous development comprising besides regular theatre also some performance art, dance theatre and "musicalised" theatre, music theatre has developed a heterogeneous response to its past. Some music theatre developed from theatre—where musicalisation became a potent tool to tell new stories or explore different ways of narrativity on the stage.[5] Other music theatre developed from chamber opera's attempts to free itself from stringent but outmoded aesthetic conventions, genre distinctions, disciplinary hierarchies and other limitations, and to search for a sense of theatricality in musical expression.

Parallel to this renewed interest in theatricality, music theatre—including new opera—developed post-dramatic traits alongside the theatre scene, which stemmed largely from the 1980s with earlier influences in the 1960s and the theatre avant-garde at the turn of the twentieth century, as discussed by Hans-Thies Lehmann (1999).[6] With often an implied artistic manifesto, the new generation of music theatre practitioners reacted vehemently against Wagnerian music drama in which music was a vehicle for drama but in a too rigid, "total" (or "totalitarian") constellation. They also responded to its immediate late-modernist predecessors recycling the outmoded *Gesamtkunstwerk* model, drawn to finding new syntheses between the different artistic disciplines.

Today, music theatre is a prolific tool for cultural negotiation and historical reflection that, due to its very successful legitimisation process during the last two decades, has created a heterogeneous landscape of forms. Although it has defined itself in opposition to pre-existing art forms in theatre and opera, music theatre is also part of the wider history of music drama and theatre from which it constantly borrows, deconstructs and recycles mechanisms. It is a historically loaded hyper-genre that, due to its constant re-invention and post-modern aesthetic, has become an effective means by which issues of multiculturalism and its fragmented history can be addressed.

The reasons why music theatre and opera are adopted for expressing the social concerns of history, identity and community in a multicultural environment are at least threefold. First and foremost, "small-scale" music theatre presents us with a highly flexible form that, compared to the large-scale opera industry, can re-organise artistic labour in such a way that it favours—or even necessitates—artistic collaboration between creative artists and executing practitioners with long rehearsal periods for devising. However, this has made it heavily dependent on State subsidy systems and co-production. Since the 1990s, there has been an increasing interest in supporting music theatre financially through the mechanisms of the

Arts Councils and cultural ministries of Flanders, the Netherlands and Germany. There has also been a growing potential for co-production and collaboration with opera houses since the boundaries between opera and music theatre are becoming porous.

A second reason is that music theatre initially found new audiences, which opera lost due to its high ticket prices, despite discount offers and subscription deals. Opera is generally seen as a bourgeois activity, whereas music theatre—due to its small-scale and thereby less costly set-up and touring conditions—was able to reach out to middle class and multicultural environments, as part of a democratising agenda. Again, cultural policies supporting socio-artistic work have shaped this development. It comes as no surprise that a lot of the new music theatre projects in Europe by the end of the 1980s and the beginning of the 1990s were engaging with other tonalities and rhythms, re-establishing ritual aspects of the musical experience. However, in its democratising stance towards musical composition, including popular music and non-classical vocalities, it has constantly been at odds with musical theatre in terms of legitimising itself as an autonomous art form. Music theatre, therefore, adopted similar aesthetic mechanisms to post-dramatic theatre as a way of anchoring itself to other developing post-modern art forms, including installation art, electroacoustic music and visual arts such as video montage, kinetic sculpture, telematic performance, etc. This has entitled it to be seen as a "hypermedium" (Chapple and Kattenbelt 2006), opening a space for heterogeneous experiences with flashes of self-reflexivity in the beholder. In turn, the beholder might be seen more as an "emancipated spectator" (Rancière 2009) than a "consumer", as one might term the spectators of popular mass and often spectacle-oriented entertainment.

Opera has undergone a comparable development in the adoption of post-dramatic principles in order to address new audiences. It also temporarily embraced the term "music theatre" in its all-inclusive sense as a way of rejuvenating its image and, thereby, its audience.[7] However, because of its openness to new styles, it has also increasingly produced more slippage in its very definition, giving rise to the awareness that opera history is as heterogeneous as music theatre is today. Because of such broad spectrum and slippage between opera and music theatre forms, to which music theatre's self-legitimisation has indirectly contributed, the operatic form today seems again open for reinvention, for thinking about anew. In this context, we can understand our case studies: Hollands Diep's music theatre production makes a democratised version of opera, whereas the established Neuköllner Oper, though on the fringe, sells its "Musiktheater" production as opera, despite stylistic influences from post-dramatic theatre, spoken drama, and even, musical theatre. As such, both performances yield the possibility for us to reflect on the nature of their respective forms as part of a shared history between music theatre and opera.

A third reason why music theatre and opera today seem appropriate for expressing post-migrant concerns can be found in their ability to address notions of identity through different musical—and thereby, listening—cultures. This is a point I will explore further in the rest of this chapter. Most central to this analysis is sociologist Simon Frith's processual understanding of identity through music, which starts from a double realisation:

> first that identity is mobile, a process not a thing, a becoming not a being; second, that our experience of music—of music making and music listening— is best understood as an experience of this *self-in-process*. Music, like identity, is both performance and story, describes the social in the individual and the individual in the social, [...]; identity, like music, is a matter of both ethics and aesthetics. (1996: 109, quoted in Şahin 2009: 12)

With music presenting an image of this "self-in-process", the multicultural basis for music theatre becomes self-evident. Music is that part of aurality that offers structures of listening that are culturally and historically determined but never absolute: they are constantly negotiated against the dominant, hegemonic norms and values. Within that discursive space of practices and roles of music and performance in a society, music theatre could be an adequate tool to express multicultural and post-migrant identities, as it is itself continuously negotiated against the past. We will see later, however, that this is a predominantly Western development. Suffice to say here that music theatre is a flexible medium through which to negotiate issues of identity and history as it defines itself as an emerging art form, renegotiating its identity in relation to the past, to its traditions and attitudes in listening. Post-migrant Turkish music theatre can, therefore, offer us a glimpse into the workings of aurality in different cultures.

Now, I call this newly developing music theatre form that is primarily focused on the Turkish communities in Europe "post-migrant", but I might as well have termed it "post-diasporic" or "intercultural" (terms which have already been proposed in different artistic and academic contexts). However, there is one more historical influence that should be taken into account: the Turkish theatre that developed in Europe concomitant to the immigration waves. Through its inherence in the history of migration, Turkish music theatre and opera seems to distinguish and emancipate itself from that migrant theatre history, which is a hybrid of traditional forms of Turkish theatre and amateur theatre within a larger process of the professionalisation (and partly, institutionalisation) of grassroots initiatives. Significantly, migrant theatre in the Netherlands and Germany went through a transformation at the end of the 1980s and the beginning of the 1990s, at the same time as music theatre received its most fertile boost thanks to the artistic developments of post-dramatic theatre and the support of government strategies. Migrant theatre grew successfully from the social needs of the first wave of economic immigrants (aka *Gästarbeiter*) following the labour treaties with the Turkish Ministry of Labour (*Çalışma Bakanlığı*) in 1964-65; it developed with the second immigration wave from 1974 (particularly after the 1980 coup d'état which made many leftist political dissidents flee the country), and started to disintegrate in the time of family reunion law (which would entitle Turkish families to emigrate to Europe if any member had been working in the Netherlands or Germany for at least a year). Its decline, by the 1990s, came along with the gradual breakdown of leftist associations, trade union movements and other social clubs and institutions for second generation German and Dutch Turks.[8] As a result, European Turkish theatre practitioners and composers with a second and third generation migration background felt the need to open up to more "universal" topics, incorporating post-modern mechanisms that would also address a wider audience.

Today, we can observe that these European Turks are gradually entering the art scene as a way of consolidating their social, predominantly middle class existence within the broader multicultural and urban society. Music theatre and opera, though perhaps not the most obvious art forms, constitute one way of voicing their social identity within this cultural network. This is occasionally supported by local, regional and national governments that see value in these emerging art forms as they could be beneficial to the larger migration and integration debates. Integration is today a social priority and a

State-funded undertaking focusing on interconnected communities and a need to make them claim ownership in society. Culture, art and legacy are often the canvas for such social concerns that colour the political agenda. As such, the "social artistic" objective of the 1990s has contributed to the emergence of the new cultural policy targets of "multiculturality" and "cultural diversity". The performances that I will briefly discuss here are singular projects within that particular political, social and cultural environment. However, I do wish to reveal some continuity in the thinking about cultural representation and adaptation by means of music and libretto between these performances.

NEW MUSIC THEATRE AS SOCIAL HISTORY
Now that the historical and social contexts of multiculturalism as integral to the recent developments of music theatre and opera have been elucidated, we should zoom in to the performances and the makers' points of view, including the particular histories and social concerns they try to capture. As such, we need to look at the specific performance histories, the people involved in the productions and their audiences. However, as this chapter only sets out to encapsulate the historical emergence of an art form, I am limiting this discussion to a comparison of two performances to the extent that they illustrate crucial aspects in the representation of migration and multiculturalism in Europe today: *Lege Wieg / Boş Beşik* (in English, "The Empty Cradle") by Hollands Diep in Dordrecht and *Tango Türk* by the Neuköllner Oper in Berlin, both produced in 2010.

A central idea that both performances share is that of music as a vehicle or catalyst for historical understanding. Different representations of history are implied here, namely individual vs. collective history, personal vs. cultural memory, and private and collective experiences of aural history through Turkish songs and music. The performances include diverse ways of representing these notions of history through different theatrical and narrative mechanisms. Concomitant to these aesthetic and discursive mechanisms, they also include diverse ways of representing post-migrant identity as a self-in-process through musical experience. Again, a sense of history in music and song proves to be the go-between.

Lege Wieg / Boş Beşik is based on a story from the area of the Taurus Mountains in Southern Anatolia, which presumably dates back to the sixteenth century, but is mostly known through its film adaptations, of which the 1969 version by Orhan Elmas, with Fatma Girik and Tugay Toksöz in the leading roles, is the most well known. The story recounts the tragic destiny of a village woman, Fadime (portrayed simultaneously by soprano Jennifer Claire van der Harst and "alter ego" Caroline Cartens), who falls in love and marries a city citizen, Nomad (tenor Gunnar Brandt-Sigurdsson), outside her class and much against the will of the latter's in-laws. When she cannot produce a child for years, the family's rejection increases. By a mysterious force, however, she does produce a son, which is later unfortunately snatched away from her by a vulture.

History is presented here as myth and its spectre in popular cultural memory: although the tradition has been kept through the oral tradition of *aşik*, or nomadic storytelling, as well as a network of traditional songs associated with the story, most Turkish people remember the story as a bedtime story or from secondary, popular forms such as the movie adaptation. Dutch librettist and author of young people's literature, Anne Vegter[9], has reinterpreted the myth once more by adding dramatic elements for the sake of suspense. For instance, a mythological figure called "Derman" (performed by Dutch baritone Arnout Lems) replaces the vulture, taking the child away on his seventh birthday. This adds or highlights a Rumpelstiltskin motif, making the tale a more "universal" story about motherhood from a Western point of view. The name is a contraction of "Derwish" and "Sjaman" and the figure represents a Hodja (master) or a Gin (spirit, like a sater) in Turkish folk culture. Coincidentally, *derman* also means "power" or "medicine" in Turkish. Throughout the piece, Fadime and Nomad, take on a journey as migrants since they become outcasts to their families and homeland. By the end, as they walk slowly downstage and underneath the platform housing the audience, Fadime carries a wooden bird—which obviously symbolises the child's soul—away from the dark stage and into the light, offering a more hopeful gesture towards the audience.

Whereas *Lege Wieg / Boş Beşik* produces some distance to the past through the imaginative retelling of a popular mythical story about migration, *Tango Türk* creates a closer proximity to its audience, as it is based on the politically and socially volatile history of migration since the political coup d'état of the 1980s. History is represented in the first place through a family story starting with the death of a mother,

Figure 10.1: Poster for *Lege Wieg / Boş Beşik* (2010). Graphic design and photo by Maarten Mooren. Muziektheater Hollands Diep, 2010. Courtesy of Cilia Hogerzeil.

Nur (Sesede Terziyan), who, as a spectre of the past, is constantly present on the stage. We relive her history through her son Cihan (Kerem Can, who is the dramatist of the play and plays his own biological father on the stage as well). He is a typical child of his time: a cosmopolitan, relatively successful entrepreneur with no interest in the past. He has no time to visit his mother but when she dies, he is suddenly thrown back into a family history, which is so connected to the political events of the 1980s. Snippets of this past are told by four senior men, immigrants who were mostly (leftist) political refugees after the coup d'état and appear as guests at the coffeehouse of Cihan's stepfather in Germany. They recount their experiences of the political events in the streets of Turkey and the reasons for their departure.

Both performances present us with different representations of social history, either "universalised" through myth or individualised through documentary eyewitness accounts. Most central to these histories is the question of migration to which the Dutch and German Turkish communities of Dordrecht and the Neukölln area in South-East Berlin could relate in various ways. A common denominator between the two community projects, however, is that the family is used as the nucleus of historical forces of migration defining one's identity, through contrasting feelings of belonging and denial. As much as Cihan journeys from a denial of his past to finding his place within family ties that are rooted in the history of migration, Fadime and Nomad each have to deny their pasts and family ties and emigrate in order to build a future of their own. Through the prism of the family, individual and collective experiences of history are interconnected. Although the story of *Boş Beşik*, on the one hand, belongs to the collective memory of many Turks of a certain generation, the operatic retelling may give rise to completely new and individualised experiences in which one could recognise aspects of one's own family life. *Tango Türk*, on the other hand, straightforwardly places a dramatised fictional—but possible—history at the heart of political, historical events that many German Turks still remember vividly. For the new generation, however, these stories and histories are becoming vague or are unknown. For them, in an autobiographical sense, these music theatre and opera projects give secondary access to collective roots that are already subject to forgetting.

Figure 10.2: Poster for *Tango Türk* (2010). Photo by Matthias Heyde. Neuköllner Oper, 2010. Courtesy of Bernhard Glocksin.

Hence, this is another important reason why post-migrant forms of music theatre and opera are emerging today in these multicultural urban environments: they help European Turks to reconnect individual, local needs for identity and representation of Turkish culture to a historical understanding of one's collective past and hybrid identity in a migrating Europe. A significant mechanism at work here is narrative discourse. Not just *what* but *how* the different histories are constructed on the stage is significant for the way the audience members experience and relate to them. In opera and music theatre, music takes a leading part in the discursive construction of the narrative. As Frith commented earlier, music sustains the connection between individual and collective histories by helping to describe "the social in the individual and the individual in the social" (109).

In the following section, the question addressed is how music—and thereby, aurality—participates in the construction and awareness of identity, particularly on this axis between the individual and the social. This will give us a more detailed understanding of the cultural necessity of post-migrant music theatre and opera in relation to present issues of cultural integration, adaptation and translation.

NEGOTIATING MUSICAL CULTURES

Lege Wieg / Boş Beşik and *Tango Türk* each combine music from different traditions. Different musical cultures are negotiated, or even reinvented. As such, they follow Frith's general idea that musical traditions only survive through constant innovation (2000: 311). The blend of these cultures and traditions as much as the reasons for a synthesis, however, needs to be looked at more carefully in order to understand what these post-migrant opera and music theatre productions actually aim to do with regard to their audiences. Traditionalism is closely knit together with the formation and confirmation of identity. Opera as an institutionalised, State-supported apparatus has a long history of homogenising national identities as well as questioning "other", particularly Eastern identities. Equally, listeners identify themselves through their musical tastes and the musical circles they wish to *belong* to. So by negotiating musical cultures in these forms of music theatre that are open for reinvention, one also negotiates identities. It is as such that music theatre and opera can contest the discursive space of aurality against which identities are also constantly negotiated.

The negotiation between musical cultures, however, necessitates a democratisation of production processes as well as reception modalities in order to include different communities that are not very familiar with opera. Melek Kömbe, a 38 year old Turkish participant in *Lege Wieg / Boş Beşik* who was born in Dordrecht and works at the Public Prosecution Bureau in Utrecht, summarises it very well when asked in an interview why this project is so important:

> For the Turkish people [...] I think they should come and watch because a Dutch ensemble takes the time to put a Turkish story on the stage. Out of respect for this, one should definitely come. For Turkish people, opera is not really known and I hope that they come to watch it so that they will discover a new world. With opera I always had the idea that it was all very nice but nothing for me. However, now that I see it myself, it is really quite fun.[10]

From the quote (and the success of the project according to the producers), we can deduce that there is a social demand amongst Turkish communities to appropriate this Western art form. The reason why opera is not so well known to European Turks is comparable to the reason why other European citizens within a similar social class find it unfamiliar: they simply have no or limited access to this art form. To have an established Dutch music theatre ensemble produce an opera based on an old Turkish story in collaboration with women from the Turkish-Dutch community—no matter if the content of the opera is (self-) orientalising—has great social value for a community that can "discover a new world". As such, opera re-establishes its social function in society and aural culture.

Historically in Turkish culture, opera played a vital part in Mustafa Kemal Atatürk's modernisation project after the Kemalist War of Liberation in 1923. The governmental support for staging and even producing operas was very much in line with the paradigm of "national economy" which already started under the Young Turk regime of 1908-1918. Already in the nineteenth century, opera was being staged and produced at the palace theatres of the sultan by Italian troupes in Istanbul as it supported the increasing involvement of foreign capital. The act of "modernisation", however, in most eastern countries meant largely a "westernisation" which became a tool for power negotiation, resulting in internal socio-political oppositions in economic development and external cultural imperialism. The westernisation of the new Republic, combined with cultural values defined by an ideology of class, to some extent discriminated against the taste of the Turkish commoner. This new culture demonstrated superiority and elite aesthetic values, and positioned the elite at a centre of power. The "good taste" standard was then all of a sudden measured by western and elite values, and resulted in a corresponding belief in the lack of such good taste among the common people.[11] Apart from the more global processes of modernisation, the westernisation also served a particular national campaign propagating a homogenising, pan-Turkish identity against the many ethnic groups living in the Turkish Republic.

Therefore, it does not come as a surprise that opera is now seen in urban areas of Turkey as a somewhat disheartening art form that is part of a culture that attempted to alienate the Turkish people from their native listening cultures and traditions. From the point of view of Turkey today, the democratising nature of an opera such as *Lege Wieg / Boş Beşik* could be understood as coming to terms with an incomplete modernisation project that is so entangled with *Turkishness* today.

However, the Turkish women involved in this project—some born in the Netherlands, others recently migrated[12]—seem not to have such socio-political aspirations, as this is more a historical process in Turkey than a real present-day concern for Turks in Europe. Rather, the democratisation of opera through such projects as *Lege Wieg / Boş Beşik* aims at coming to terms with cultural integration in the Netherlands, making opera accessible and thereby developing a new audience for it. However, despite its underlying strategy of taking opera out of the opera house and bringing it to the public, the specific politics of location of using "het Energiehuis" at a post-industrial site gives the project a fringe aura, attracting an appreciative audience but one that again excludes certain members of the community for whom this venue might pose a social threshold.

Moreover, although the music in *Lege Wieg / Boş Beşik* was greatly inspired by Turkish songs and their distinctive tonal scales, it differed most distinctly from Turkish traditional and classical music. The latter is as heterogeneous as Western musical traditions, but the Korean composer Seung-Ah Oh, who studied composition in the United States and The Netherlands, chose neither a traditional ensemble with Turkish instruments nor an opera orchestra. Rather, it is a small combo more common to Western European music theatre, including flute, accordion, cello, double bass and percussion. Interestingly, the Korean composer did try to learn about Turkish semi- and microtones, as part of the *makam* system of compositional modes and musical structures, which is central to a lot of Middle Eastern music, but the end result is stripped of any particular Turkish musical characteristics. What is more, the traditional Turkish songs have been reinterpreted and made more complex by adding polyvocality, which is so central to Western music drama. The vocal parts of the soloists are also highly stylised with expressive glissandos and leitmotivs supporting the content—and the drama—of their speech.

In this way, this project fulfils a double social function with regard to aurality that is most common in theories of Orientalism: on the one hand, through Western music drama conventions another culture is appropriated, do I dare say "colonised", to such an extent that it is alienated from its original contexts of production and reception. This is reinforced by the fact that most second and third generation Dutch-Turkish listeners may already be separated from their own musical traditions, as they are underrepresented in mainstream broadcasting and education. The participants' oral-based memories of Turkish songs, although a powerful tool for claiming collective identity, were already fragmented. On the other hand, it is through Western musical standards that one East—represented by the young Korean composer trained in the West—learns about the other East, in this case the Turkish traditional music that Nurhan Uyar, also schooled in the West, selected for this project. The result is an interesting mixture of music and listening cultures that reflects the collaborative artistic process as much as the multicultural reality in Europe today, but not without the help of the hegemonic, dominant culture.

Surprisingly perhaps for uninformed Western ears, *Tango Türk* takes as its departure point a tango song (sung by soprano Begüm Tüzemen[13]), which is based on the first instrumental composition in this genre in Turkey, composed by Muhlis Sabahattin Bey and released by "His Master's Voice" in 1928. Though the musical structure and metre are commonly perceived as "Western" (actually developed among European immigrants in Argentina and Uruguay near the end of the nineteenth century with influences from African dances), this hybrid genre easily opened up to Turkish tonalities and topics by the beginning of the twentieth century under the same modernisation and westernisation processes as opera in Turkey. Tango became part of what historians have identified as Atatürk's "ballroom diplomacy", derived from his numerous diplomatic receptions with balls at the Ankara Palace Hotel. Tango music was mostly sung in these elitist social settings by operetta singers, supporting the new Turkish identity.

One would expect similar feelings of resentment towards tango as to opera in a Turkish context. However, most recently tango is becoming increasingly popular again among young Turks as it both addresses gender issues and the *hüzün* culture in Turkish aurality, musical tradition and collective identity. The latter denotes a sense of nostalgia or melancholy but in a different way from which the Westerner would experience it. In fact, according to Turkish poet and novelist Orhan Pamuk in his fictionalised autobiography *Istanbul*, the *hüzün* feeling is quite distinctive from the European equivalents, as they would encompass the Romantic sorrows of a solitary person. Rather, *hüzün* comes closer to the *tristesse* of Claude Lévi-Strauss: "*Tristesse* is not a pain that affects a solitary individual; *hüzün* and *tristesse* both suggest a communal feeling, an atmosphere, and a culture shared by millions" (Pamuk 2005: 90). He further describes how classical Ottoman music, Turkish popular music, and particularly the arabesque music that became popular during the 1980s, are expressions of this powerful emotion but he adds that it "is not just the mood evoked by its music and its poetry, it is a way of looking at life that implicates us all, not only a spiritual state, but a state of mind that is ultimately as life affirming as it is negating" (Pamuk 2005: 82).

By pulling a similar emotional string, tango has become a significant subculture for a new generation of Turks in both Turkey and Europe, claiming their identity today in relation to the transnational influences in their social lives. Whereas Turkish tango played a significant role in the identity construction of Turkishness as dictated by Atatürk's nationalist campaign in the 1920s, it seems now to be re-adopted as a phenomenon of burgeoning popular taste, partly as a neo-traditionalist response to the ongoing westernisation of a global market and its cultural adaptation processes. In this way, the tango music in *Tango Türk* can be understood to address current identity issues for Turks in Germany who have only partial access to the musical traditions and histories of the mother country. Through its melancholic chords and lyrics, the Tango Türk song supports the historicised events surrounding Cihan's family in the diegesis of the play, whilst addressing a fundamental feeling central to the Turkish post-migrant existence in Europe:

That is why I could not embrace you, could not live your longing.
A bitter adventure it is, they have taken him from me.
He is the lover of someone else, who is now happy.
My soul has again become a land in ruins.[14]

The last phrase in particular is very telling of the new identity that is part and parcel of a fragmented post-migrant existence. The tango music, partly in the modern tradition, partly reinvented, draws on a post-migrant subjectivity that is marked by a split, as between two lovers separated from each other. The tango—and its *hüzün*—exists by means of this split awareness of belonging to two worlds, two sites in which Turkish identity is contested and negotiated as a self-in-process.

By using tango music as the central voice telling the story of *Tango Türk*, the performance carries contested experiences of identity and belonging. The lyrics of the song connect the individual with the social, in Frith's sense, thereby contributing to an experience of *hüzün* that can be understood by the audience on both levels. In its literal biographical sense, the lyrics could be understood on an individual level of Cihan's personal family story and history. The diegesis recounts through flashbacks how Cihan's biological father—played by the same actor—had to flee to Germany under the 80s coup d'état without giving notice to his mother who remained in Turkey. On his return years later, he finds out that the mother has already (re)married. The lyrics of the final song could then refer to how Cihan's identity as a German Turk—and his denial of his individual past in his rejection of the mother—is entrenched by the separation of his parents under the pressure of the political events in the democratisation processes of Turkey. The continuous exchange of past and present temporalities in Kerem Can's portrayal of both father and son is, therefore, a conscious narrative device that aims to remap the son's identity onto a collective past that Cihan tries to forget.

In this context, the song also addresses a coming to terms with history on a social level. The lyrics could then be understood to describe a relationship of displacement between German Turks and the loved but lost homeland. Its sorrowful tone displays a most common feature of the experience of this displacement in *hüzün* as described by Pamuk, namely not as a pain for which there is no cure, but rather as a choice that gives the artist "poetic licence" to be paralysed by the past:

Likewise, the *hüzün* in Turkish poetry after the foundation of the Republic, as it, too, expresses the same grief that no one can or would wish to escape, an ache that finally saves our souls and also gives them depth. For the poet, *hüzün* is the smoky window between him and the world. The screen he projects over life is painful because life itself is painful. (Pamuk 2005: 93)

Equally, the tango song in *Tango Türk* offers its audience a window through which they can read and understand the fictionalised history in relation to their own situation. Through the identification with Cihan's point of view (as focaliser), the spectator shares a wilfully forgetful memory about the political and historical forces that might linger as spectres of the past in the background of one's own post-migrant existence and identity in Germany. The performance, therefore, provides a perspective on a history that is becoming less accessible to most German citizens with a Turkish migration background and which helps Germans of a non-migration background to understand the complex implications of cultural integration.

As such, by addressing the individual in the social and the social in the individual through music and song, *Tango Türk* draws on the awareness that "belonging" depends on the experience of a fundamental split in one's identity and one's own recollections of individual and collective histories, which are intrinsically connected. As such, music production and perception can represent a hybrid post-migrant identity as a self-in-process, constantly renegotiating the splits between traditions and the contemporary dominant culture that are in themselves both subject to change.

CONCLUSION
My main concerns in this chapter have been to historically contextualise and describe the emergence of Turkish post-migrant music theatre and opera against the background of multiculturality in Europe by means of two recent productions. The Neuköllner Oper plays a unique role in this as it continues to dialogue with its direct multicultural environment. But equally, Muziektheater Hollands Diep took the opportunity to include an exchange of ideas and traditions with the Turkish community through workshops prior to the production.

A striking difference that would need more detailed historical research into the particular labour laws and cultural policies of the Netherlands and Germany, however, is that most of the producing artists involved in *Tango Türk*—besides its Dutch director—are second-generation German Turks who have studied music in Germany, whereas the artistic process of *Lege Wieg / Boş Beşik*—besides the artistic influence and guidance of the Turkish-Dutch choir by Turkish-born folk singer Nurhan Uyar—was mostly in the hands of experts of Dutch, English and Korean origin. Besides, the leading Turkish tenor was born and had studied classical singing in Germany. As such, these projects seem to indicate that there is a problem with universalising the issue of integration in Europe. Germany and more specifically Berlin, moreover, seem to play a pioneering role in the cultural education and support of post-migrant Turkish communities. Whereas *Lege Wieg / Boş Beşik* assisted in the cultural meeting point between different Easts through such a Western art form as opera, *Tango Türk* demonstrated the development of a "third culture" in Turkish music by German Turks influenced by transnational conditions that were already at work in the constitution of modern Turkey.

Despite their differences in organisation, aims and style, I discussed a similarity central to both projects in that they *perform* history as a way to inform hybrid audiences who are part of a cultural anamnesis of their own musical traditions and history. Through the reinterpretation of traditions, post-migrant music theatre and opera offer points of access to issues of identity, belonging, distance and cultural representation that are most relevant to the integration debates but equally to people who have had little previous access to traditional opera and music theatre. In doing this, I hope to have unveiled some of the key factors in the historical relevance and urgency of these newly developing art forms in relation to the people who through either artistic expression or aesthetic experience participate in understanding a migrating, multicultural Europe today.

NOTES

[1] This chapter is part of a larger research project that has received funding from the Turkish Scientific and Technological Research Council—Tübitak—at Ankara University and from the Mercator Foundation in Germany, in 2012, as part of the Mercator-IPC Fellowship Programme at Sabancı University in Istanbul. Earlier results have been presented at the IFTR Conference *Cultures of Modernity* at the Ludwigs-

Maximilians-Universität Munich, 25-31 July 2010, the PSi Conference #17 at the University of Utrecht, 25-29 May 2011 and during an invited talk at the *Òpera i Llibret Simposi Internacional*, organised by the Òpera de Butxaca i Nova Creació in Barcelona, 26-27 June 2011. I am grateful to all participants at these venues who have commented on my papers as well as Dietrich Grosse (Director of Mondigromax— Cultivos de Cultura) who invited me to speak about this project. I wholeheartedly thank my partner, Görkem Akgöz for her immense support, critical inquiry and careful re-reading of my work. I also want to thank Onur Suzan Kömürcü Nobrega for her invaluable intellectual contributions to this research project.

[2] Lully's *Le Bourgeois Gentilhomme* (1670), Handel's *Tamerlano* (1719), Rameau's *Les Indes Galantes* (1735), Gluck's *La Rencontre imprévue ou Les Pèlerins de la Mecque* (1764), Mozart's *Entführung aus dem Serail* (1782), Weber's *Abu Hasresan* (1811), Rossini's *Il Turco in Italia* (1814) Spohr's *Zemire und Azor* (1819) and Lortzing's *Ali Pasha von Janina* (1828) are but a few so-called "Turkish" operas. For a more exhaustive list, see for instance Christoph Yew's MA thesis "The Turk on the Opera Stage: A History of a Musical Cliché" submitted at the Musicology Department of the University of Osnabrück and published with Grin Verlag (2009).

[3] Shermin Langhoff helped to develop the term "post-migrant theatre", which she related to an Anglophone literary tradition alongside the coining of the term by Germany's most celebrated German-Turkish author Feridun Zaimoğlu, whose usage of the term is noted at a symposium more than ten years ago (Dell 2012).

[4] It is essential to note the far-reaching impact of the cultural (policy) climate with respect to the national and international settings of production houses as well as the international network of similarly minded venues growing in Europe. Many examples are beyond the precise scope of this chapter but it is vital to this mode of enquiry that they are mentioned. Recent and relevant theatre work in this respect is produced in Germany at Ballhaus Naunynstrasse, Heimathafen Neukölln, the Werkstatt der Kulturen, Haus der Kulturen der Welt, Uelum Theater and also Manheim National Theatre and recently, Rimini Protokoll (in collaboration with Garajistanbul in Turkey). These theatres may use musical aspects in their performances, but are not primarily concerned with music theatre. The festival "beyond belonging: migration" at the Hebbel am Ufer Theater played a significant role in Langhoff's development of the idea of "post-migrant theatre". There is also an explicitly Turkish-German theatre, Tiyatrom, which lost its subsidy after the arrival of Ballhaus Naunynstrasse in 2008 (see Kömürcü Nobrega 2011: 96). In the Netherlands post-migrant theatre can be found at Holland Opera (previously called Xynix Opera) and the Dutch-Kurdish RAST Theatre, although there the terms "community" or "intercultural" theatre are used. The Rotterdam-based Ro Theatre also supports collaborations with Turkey and Turkish artists. Singular theatre projects with Turkish artists or communities are often realised in Belgium under the "socio-artistic" label or the broader "interculturality" policy remit within the Arts Decree. Music theatre LOD's founding performance *Allons les gars* (1991) was a multicultural performance including Turkish-Belgian children as well as Turkish instruments and musical modalities. More structural support can be found in the intercultural centre De Centrale and the festival 0090 which will become an international workplace for artists, art processes and collaborations. In the United Kingdom, the centre for this type of work is the Arcola Fringe Theatre in London (particularly its associated "Ala-Turca" programme). The latter has direct ties with Yeni Kusak Theatre and Talimhane Tiyatrosu in Istanbul.

The existence of the 476 Players Theatre Co. is also noted here but its activities seem to have ceased due to a lack of funding.

[5] Based on a lecture by Helene Varopoulou (1998), the idea of musicalisation gives way to the metaphor of "theatre as music". In musicalisation, Hans-Thies Lehmann finds a different way of structuring theatrical communication that breaks free from the confinements of "logocentrism" (the word as centre of attention), causality and *telos* (purposefulness), as constitutive for dramatic theatre.

[6] In fact, because of its ambiguity, Lehmann regards music as an integral part of a larger project to break with the confinements of an obvious, linear, goal-oriented or teleological structure. In what he terms "postdramatic" theatre—a term that has now been generally accepted in theatre studies—Lehmann discusses musicalisation as a strategy in this project, which could expand to other elements in the performance, or to its whole organisation or way of structuring the communication of ideas and material.

[7] It was the counter-reaction by the Dutch Opera that (re-)claimed the catch-all definition in 1986 when it renamed itself "Het Muziektheater" with its opening of the new opera house next to the Amstel and the town hall in Amsterdam. Equally, despite the widespread usage of "Musiktheater" in its exclusive sense, more recent catalogues of music theatre in Germany—for instance *Praxis Musiktheater: Ein Handbuch* (2002) edited by Arnold Jacobshagen—include lists of both established opera and music theatre ensembles.

[8] With the military coup d'état in 1980, the migration of leftist Turkish people and an opening up of higher education to second generation Dutch and German Turks gave a boost to the social and cultural activities in The Netherlands and Germany. The Dutch government even implemented theatre in their cultural policy as a strategy to support the integration of the Turkish immigrants into Dutch society. An important figure was Vasıf Öngören, who not surprisingly was trained in Theatre Studies in Berlin and was invited in 1982 by OCW—the Dutch Arts Council at the time—to come and teach on an independent two-year theatre course to Turkish migrants, initiated by HTIB (the Turkish Workers Union in the Netherlands) and STIPT (the Foundation for Intercultural Projects concerning Theatre). Today, many Turkish classical singers are schooled in Germany, such as the leading tenor in *Lege Wieg / Boş Beşik*, Gunnar Brandt-Sigurdsson, who was born in Hamburg and studied singing from 1996 till 2001 at the Hochschule für Kunste Bremen. Most central to the *Boş Beşik* project was mezzo-soprano Nurhan Uyar, who was born in Corlu but trained as a singer in Berlin. In 2001, she founded the *Imece* choir with Turkish immigrants in Germany.

[9] In January 2013, Anne Vegter was given the honorary title of Poet Laureate ("Dichter des Vaderlands") of The Netherlands for four years, an initiatve of the NRC Handelsblad, the NPS, the Poetry International foundation, the Dutch Royal Library and the Poëzieclub Foundation.

[10] Original quote from the interview by Loesje Clement: "Voor de Turkse mensen... ik vind dat zij moeten komen kijken omdat een Nederlandse groep de tijd neemt om een Turks verhaal op de planken te zetten. Uit respect daarvoor moet je zeker komen kijken. Voor de Turkse mensen is opera niet echt bekend en ik hoop dat ze komen kijken zodat ze ook een nieuwe wereld zullen ontdekken. Met opera had ik zoiets van 'oh leuk en aardig, maar niets voor mij'. Maar nu ik het eenmaal zie, is het best wel leuk" (*Lege Wieg / Boş Beşik, The Making Of*, 2008).

[11] Music especially was restricted to an acute auditory politics in Atatürk's regime, thereby controlling what people listened to. In his speech to parliament on 1 November 1934, Atatürk emphasised that folk music must be investigated and introduced with its cultural power according to scientific principles and rules, as such reinventing and improving it to the standard of the Western classical idiom.

[12] In fact, most of the Turks living in Dordrecht—more than 6000 today—originate from Kayapınar in the Turkish province of Diyarbakır, which actually lies in the Kurdish region. With only opera houses in Istanbul, Ankara, Antalya, Izmir and Mersin, it is clear that most Turkish migrants in Europe will have had no previous access to opera as they often come from small villages and rural areas. This also poses more than a critical footnote to the way the theatre makers of *Lege Wieg / Boş Beşik*—and I—rather unfortunately refer to the participants and communities as "Turkish" whereas the majority are actually Kurdish.

[13] Begüm Tüzemen has a career in Germany as a classical, musical theatre and soul singer. She appeared previously in the production *Türkisch für Liebhaber*, which was Sinem Altan's debut at the Neuköllner Oper. Sinem Altan was classically schooled in Germany. She is composer in residence of the Neuköllner Oper since 2008. Together with Özgür Ersoy they contributed to the development of "German-Turkish" music in their YeDo ensemble (which is an abbreviation for "Yeniliğe Doğru", meaning "something new on the way"). Most recently, they re-launched the trio with "Olivinn", opening up to wider, non-Turkish speaking audiences.

[14] The original lyrics are in German: "So konnte ich dich nicht umarmen, konnte diese Sehnsucht nicht leben. Ein bitteres Abenteuer ist es, sie haben ihn mir genommen. Er ist der Geliebte einer Anderen, diese ist nun glücklich. Meine Seele ist wieder ein Land in Ruinen geworden".

CHAPTER 11

"POWERFUL SPIRIT":
NOTES ON SOME PRACTICE AS RESEARCH

DOMINIC SYMONDS

By way of a prologue, I am going to frame this discussion within a narrative of meaning, reiterating a nagging question in discussions of music theatre: namely, *how* does it mean? I am not seeking to answer that question, though, and indeed would rather let its associated musings flow—that music theatre means because of its music, despite its music, as a *Gestalt*, as more than the sum of its parts, in performance, in the score, at the moment of creation, during reception or even in anticipation, remembrance or nostalgia.[1] These musings are ancillaries to the discussion, though in a sense meaning-less themselves. What they reflect, however, is an insistent drive to understand; to understand forms, domains, disciplines, practices and genres and how they become meaningful to us. And even though the post-structuralist dismantling of obvious systems and less visible mechanisms that guide thought, practice and behaviour (aesthetics, ideology, culture...) has challenged this insistent quest, it has seldom interrogated the object of music theatre—or, to be more specific, its putative predecessor, opera—which itself is constructed in paradigms of pre-post-structuralist thought and contemporary revisionings of these.

The field of opera is littered with works that bow to classical conventions of the narrative, the diatonic, the structured and the dramatic. Even latterly the ripping apart of these conventions has constructed new ideologies: of the body, the voice and the concrete, for example. The same is true of other areas: the dissolution of language that Jacques Derrida enables in his writings (cf., *Of Grammatology*, 1976) may *comment* on language, but that he does this through language itself both undermines his aims and consolidates the very power he seeks to challenge—the medium *literally* becomes the message, to paraphrase McLuhan, resulting in an interesting and paradoxical conundrum. Where does this leave us in finding the meaning of music theatre when we in the West generally think, speak, write and practice in paradigms of thought that are neither musical nor theatrical, and when even the concepts of music and theatre are burdened with a deeply-rooted classical legacy: the legacy of opera?

Nevertheless, the twentieth century has introduced new ways of thinking that are beginning to wash away at the old. What was enabled by Derrida's questioning of the *eidos* and the self—a challenge to the stable transcendental foundations of Western thought[2]—has been continued in the work of Gilles Deleuze and Félix Guattari and other post-structuralists,[3] and in the immediate area of music theatre, theories of the post-dramatic (Lehmann 2006), the ecological (Kershaw 2007) and the emergent (Roesner 2010a) have become valuable tools in exploring music theatre beyond its hermeneutics. For Kim Vines, the Deleuzian way of thinking is idiomatic of a "cultural moment" in which we have experienced a paradigm shift in "understandings of knowledge" (Vines in Barrett and Bolt 2007). The breaking down of thresholds and boundaries that is central to this paradigm shift begins to dissolve notions of discipline ("music", "theatre"), and the disciplinary block that latches onto (and between) these terms in discussions of music theatre. Ironically (or perhaps not), what is revealed is that practices stemming from a disciplinarily theatrical tendency manifest and embrace the musical, and that practices stemming from a musical tendency manifest and embrace the theatrical: nothing here that would surprise the Ancient Greeks, the Camerata, Wagnerians or contemporary practitioners. Perhaps the problem now is that the term "music theatre" seems to become a catch-all to describe any performance event or artefact that features the slightest element of musicality—a Pandora's Box of a situation if ever there was one. Still, David Roesner, himself a contributor to this volume, has offered a very useful manifesto which proposes "musicality in theatre" as a performative "catalyst" between music and theatre that "enables interaction without being consumed itself" by the dominant spectres of those disciplinary labels (Roesner 2010b). Roesner speaks of musicality as a form of praxis (following McCullough 1998), and his thesis shares several conceptual similarities with another recent development in arts-based scholarship, the championing of Practice as Research as an example of the paradigm shift in systems of understanding. Broadly speaking, this suggests that we learn as much from the practical exploration of our discipline as we do from its theoretical study.

PRACTICE AS RESEARCH

The notion of practice being a legitimate and accepted mode of academic enquiry has long been popular in arts-based scholarship, though it has taken some time to gain acceptance from legitimising institutions and funding bodies. This perhaps needs a bit of clarification, since in principle (and historically) there is no obvious distinction between the practice of scholarship and the practice of anything else (as the shared etymology of "theatre" and "theory" attest. Historically, we could relate this to the division between mind and body that has been central to power structures in Western ideology, but which has been entirely manufactured to serve those political ends. Practice as Research, the embodied observation of the world through a prism of experience and action, is a fundamental if undervalued human endeavour, and the "innovation" of Practice as Research in the academy is more accurately a reclamation of an inherent principle of enquiry. Since much of the momentum for Practice as Research has stemmed from performance-related areas, not least the Practice as Research in Performance initiative (PARIP, University of Bristol, 2000-2006), it is an apposite methodology to appropriate in music theatre. A recent slew of academic publications[4] has contributed substantially to discussion about Practice as Research, and in a way re-legitimised it as a viable methodology for performance research. During this period a whole host of institutions have validated courses of study even at PhD level which use as their principal methodology a practical exploration of an area, and which submit for examination a far shorter written thesis than usual accompanied by documented evidence of performance practice in various media. In the UK at least it seems that Practice as Research is becoming increasingly supported, though it remains to be seen whether the completion of the PARIP project, or indeed the weighting of results from the current REF assessment[5] may lead to a reduced visibility for Practice as Research and therefore a devaluing of practice as a scholarly methodology.

It is worth turning to an explanation—and in some ways a defence—of Practice as Research from the PARIP project's Simon Jones. He suggests that a scholarly paradigm shift has happened (since the early 1990s) which introduces "practice" as a research paradigm that is different from but not covered by existing modes of quantitative or qualitative research. This challenges the traditions of the academy and is therefore resisted by it because it confronts many of the academy's most cherished values: it celebrates interdisciplinarity rather than disciplinarity; it recognises and even calls for collaborative work rather than monographs; and it validates praxis (i.e., process) rather than outputs (i.e., products):

> Unlike the good experiment, which can be written up, then endlessly reproduced globally, performance as a play of weakness troubles the strong logics of so-called rigorous disciplines: its very here-nowness resists the ubiquity of the commodity and offers us a glimpse of another way of knowing. (Allegue *et al* 2009: 25).

In many ways the value of Practice as Research can also be seen as its limitation: the embodied, experiential and tacit knowledge that can be identified through practice is by its nature difficult to share or even explain. Another contributor to this debate, Robin Nelson, offers an example of embodied knowledge to which we can all relate, and which exemplifies the difficulty posed to the academy in sharing this sort of understanding. He gives the example of riding a bicycle, which depends on the rider experiencing and understanding the notion of balance (Allegue *et al* 2009: 118). For all the instruction we might receive in riding a bike, the only way to understand the concept of balance is to practice riding the bike oneself. In this example, the value of knowledge communicated in writing (or through instruction) is undermined, and the value of practicing—learning kinaesthetically through doing—is evident. The debate, though, has sometimes centred not on whether practice is a viable methodology of *enquiry* but on whether it is an acceptable mode of *articulation* and dissemination of knowledge to the academy. This is a key question, particularly when the findings of practical research are ephemeral, or guided by time- or site-specific enquiry.

Such a difficulty in sharing knowledge might be seen as a fundamental obstacle to stated academic aims: the agenda of sharing the findings of scholarly enquiry between people and for posterity. Likewise, the different and varied manifestations of practical artefacts (performance, artwork, score, etc.) offer a challenge to conventional expectations of the logocentric archiving of knowledge. For both of these reasons it remains a debated issue whether practice can or should constitute a legitimised articulation of academic findings.

In this chapter, I would like to explore Practice as Research in relation to music theatre, but I would like to approach the discussion from a slightly different direction. I would like to suggest that Practice as Research constitutes not only a legitimate methodological approach to performance enquiry, as has been well argued, but that it also offers a critical and theoretical framework that we can bring to performance scholarship. In other words, without necessarily engaging in practice, we can use the framework of Practice as Research to observe fields of study and objects of enquiry. Like Roesner, I will suggest that music theatre is particularly suited to this critical framework since it is interdisciplinary, collaborative and often self-conscious. This chapter is an example of what I call "critical impro", a term deriving from Baz Kershaw's idea of the "thought experiment", which he introduces throughout *Theatre Ecology* (see Kershaw 2007: 242-309). This is a useful dynamic concept that allows Kershaw to explore critical and conceptual ideas freely in his writing, offering playful discursive provocations on a theme. While I am taken with this idea, the term "experiment" evokes for me a scientific idiom with an attendant expectation of verifiable results. For this reason, my own similar playful strategy uses performance terminology in the notion of "improvisation".

I will draw on three specific aspects of Practice of Research: firstly, the idea that practitioners articulate thought in the creative language of their own discipline; secondly, the idea that research develops knowledge in cycles of shared and passed on understanding; and thirdly, the idea that a stable research question might not necessarily inform practical research. I will consider how this process-based framework can be mapped onto Monteverdi's *L'Orfeo* (1607), viewing it as an ongoing Practice as Research project that continues to offer new insights. Throughout the discussion I will locate Practice as Research as a critical theory situated within a paradigm of contemporary post-structural thinking.

"A WRITING PROPER TO MAKING"
In looking at the legacy of opera, at the way that opera's long history and pluralistic identity has influenced the contemporary landscape of music theatre, Monteverdi's *L'Orfeo* (1607) seems a highly appropriate "text" to use: not only is it commonly recognised as "the first fully-fledged opera" (Whenham 1986: 2); it is also appealingly self-reflexive.[6] History tells us that it follows focussed attempts by the

Florentine Camerata to reconstruct the performance style of Classical Greek theatre[7]—*dramma per musica*—drama in which music was a principal aesthetic element. To return to this seminal case study seems worthwhile, particularly if asking what our understanding of music theatre is and how that understanding might have changed or developed as the practice of opera has matured, personalities have stamped influence, voices have been fetishised, apparati have emerged, and the form has been popularised, commodified and remediatised for our post-millenial sensibility.

Using conventional modes of analysis to talk about opera, though, can encourage us to "read" the conventional sites of analysis (or the space *between* them in which conceptual or metaphysical transitions take place): text and context, authorship and reception, notation and performance, performance and reception, etc. Instead, an understanding of experiential and embodied acquisitions of knowledge through practice allows for complex readings of material that are difficult to articulate in traditional discursive forms, but which might be explored in their own language. To clarify what I mean by this, I should stress that I am not referring simply to the scholarship of performance practice, which analyses performative aspects of (music) theatre: the phenomenological experience, the materiality of the voice, the jouissance of the performance moment. Rather, I am suggesting that each of these acts and moments of performance are themselves instances of scholarship which are articulated in their own language of embodied knowledge, but which resist transcoding into a language that the academy acknowledges.

This, "a *writing proper to making*" (Jones in Allegue *et al* 2009: 30), is the first aspect of Practice as Research that I will suggest can valuably be used as part of a critical theory. As John Freeman suggests, "performance studies sees systems of writing as inadequate" (Freeman 2010: 154); Alison Richards expands on this in categorically denying "the legitimacy of the assumption that knowledge about performance, or the knowledges which come into being through performance, can adequately be represented within written or logo-verbal systems at all" (cited in Riley and Hunter 2009: 52). Instead, suggests Brad Haseman, research findings and arguments should be articulated in the appropriate "language" of their discipline (Barrett and Bolt 2007: 148). It is a familiar call: for Robin Nelson, "the case for such praxis (theory imbricated with practice) is not only that it effectively makes new arguments but that the arguments are better made in the praxis [...] than in writing" (Nelson in Allegue *et al* 2009: 119). Thus it has now become common for Practice as Research doctorates to be presented in a partly practical format.[8]

Not surprisingly, there are a number of potential problems with this move. Firstly, practical (and particularly artistic) expression does not present itself in definitive and unambiguous statements, or indeed, in statements at all. Where we have been led to believe that scholarly language can articulate precise and accurate "truths" about the world, the languages of creativity (music, performance, fine art) all resist such claims to authoritative truth. Secondly, the various forms of artistic expression are not themselves universally accessible forms of expression in which everyone is literate; in contrast to the language practice of scholarly discourse, with which we typically expect those exposed to literacy to be familiar, creative expression—a score, for example—may require discipline-specific training and expertise to be decoded and understood. Of course, our perspective on this relationship between scholarly language and other creative forms of expression has itself shifted in the post-structuralist turn to recognise that language itself has slippery patterns of meaning, and that the languages of creativity are only imprecise when pitted against the constructed parameters of hermeneutics that have become accepted by the academy. Furthermore, the ideology that recognises language as "unmarked" and creative expression as "marked" (to use semiotic jargon—see Hatten), can itself be discredited as a conceit of the elitism of the academy. We perform ourselves and our politics in and through the formalities of writing just as transparently as we perform our identities in our creativity; again, the distinction between one expression (creative) and another (scholarly) can be challenged, revealed as a hangover from the pseudo-scientific empiricism of post-enlightenment ideals. One post-structuralist approach has been not only to discredit language's unproblematic claim to meaning-making, but also to challenge any drive towards meaning, decoding or understanding at all—an enticing invitation, though one which perhaps pushes too far beyond the human urge to understand.

Against this backdrop, then, and using Practice as Research as a framework for critical analysis, I would like to see examples of music theatre as examples of "a *writing proper to making*"; *L'Orfeo* is precisely that: it is the exegesis of the Camerata's research, articulated in the idiom of music theatre and meta-theatrically staging the experience, performance and emergence of the operatic phenomenon.

That the Orpheus myth was so recurrent in the New Music is typically attributed to its diegetic reflection of the aesthetic agenda (Kerman 1956: 48): Orpheus journeys into the Underworld to rescue his wife Euridice when she is fatally bitten by a snake, and it is the power of his music-making that so charms his listeners Charon, Pluto and Proserpine that they agree to release their captive as long as she walks to freedom without looking back. Of course, she does, and that human frailty serves as her tragic undoing and the tragic denouement of the plot. The plot, then, turns on the power of music, and in this sense *L'Orfeo* is a self-conscious exemplar of the expressive form that Monteverdi is central in creating. And Monteverdi (along with librettist Striggio) is keen to hammer home the emotive potential of *dramma per musica*, as Whenham indicates: "the choice of Music as the singer of the prologue, rather than Ovid ([in Peri's opera] *Dafne*) or Tragedy ([in the Peri and Caccini operas] *Euridice*), indicates that one of the main themes of the opera is to be the power of music" (Whenham 1986: 49). Specifically, it is the power of music *in performance* and *on its listeners*, which are subtle though important nuances observed by Van Leeuwen:

> Melodies do not only "express tenderness", they also and at the same time *caress*, they do not only "express scorn", they also and at the same time *mock*, they do not only "express longing", they also and at the same time *plead*, to give just a few examples. They are also *sound acts*. (Van Leeuwen 1999: 97)

Žižek and Dolar also note this self-reflexivity as a feature of the musical stage: "Music, in opera, stands in a self-reflective relationship—it performs its own representation, it stages its own power and its effects" (Žižek and Dolar 2002: 10); so we can see that Monteverdi's thesis (that music acts as a "powerful spirit") is articulated in his "writing proper to making", the powerful expressive language that he is exploring through his own creative work.

The power of music is a central theme in the opera: Act 1's chorus invokes the spirit of the sun and encourages Orpheus to sing to express his happiness.[9] In Act 2, we hear of Pan's emotional outpourings, linked directly to the music of his pipes.[10] The link between Orpheus' music and his emotions is pronounced: we are told of a period of suffering during which he scorned Euridice and saddened the countryside with his singing;[11] however, his emotions have undergone a significant turnaround, and this calls for expression in song.[12] Throughout the exposition, emotion is *always* linked to music: when Sylvia enters with the news of Euridice's death, it is the *sound of sorrow* that is noticed.[13]

Conventional score analysis can also reveal musical devices used by Monteverdi: he connects the audience to the emotion of the piece by using recurring triple sequences implying emotional urgency. Most notable is Orpheus' response to the Messenger, with its strong rising bass and repeated motif.[14] Here several devices are used to represent symbolically Orpheus' deepening anguish: the sequence rises melodically in pitch, both in the vocal line and the bass; the vowel sound of the penultimate syllable in each line opens, placing the sound deeper inside the body and closer to the emotional core: / ɛ / ɑ / ɔ /; the expected regular meter of the sequence is upset as each line tumbles faster into the next. Thus melodic, phonetic and rhythmic aesthetics contribute to the semantic and mimetic discourse. This represents a canny understanding of how music, language and drama can work together, communicating to the audience that Orpheus' deepest emotional instincts are expressed in music theatre terms; shortly thereafter Monteverdi employs a perhaps even more heightened example of this, the only wholly silent bar in the entire opera (bar 239), in which Orpheus is likened to a mute stone.[15] As we so often are in moments of intense emotion, he is struck dumb, dumb-founded, gob-smacked. These introductory acts serve to prepare us for the real drama in Acts 3 and 4, when—famously—Orpheus' music charms the underworld to release Euridice from death, in the most potent example of his musical power (and the musical power of the New Music), "*Possente Spirto*". Here the "powerful spirit" of music is used and displayed by both Orpheus and Monteverdi, rhetorically heightening the emotive power of the New Music in comparison to traditional technical display.[16]

CYCLE OF ENQUIRY

A second element of Practice as Research that is useful to its operation as a critical theory is the idea that experienced knowledge can be cumulative and that enquiry develops in cycles of research. Brad Haseman talks of an "enquiry cycle", of what he calls "double loop learning", in which knowledge is fed back into and developed through continuing practical research (Barrett and Bolt 2007);[17] John Freeman explains this using the anology of the Italian painting technique of *pentimento*, of "an early draft being somehow made visible [...] half-thoughts and potential changes of mind being exposed rather than edited out [...] an act of seeing once and of seeing again" (Freeman 2010: xii); for him, "research is also always re-search: a drawing on one's previous experience and developing this into knowledge' (*ibid.*: 264); meanwhile, for Barrett and Bolt, "methodologies in artistic research are *necessarily* emergent and subject to repeated adjustment, rather than remaining fixed throughout the process of enquiry" (2007: 6). Smith and Dean (2010) present the idea of an

> iterative cyclic web, [which] combines the cycle (alternations between practice and research), the web (numerous points of entry, exit, cross-referencing and cross-transit within the practice-research cycle), and iteration (many sub-cycles in which creative practice or research processes are repeated with variation). (Smith and Dean 2010: 8)

Brown and Sorensen suggest that an "iterative process between expression and reflection is essential to all research and is integral to arts practice" (in Smith and Dean 2010: 163). Finally, Roesner's manifesto on music theatre as a practical research tool suggests that "everything is in motion, everything is repeated, but due to the fact that the work is collaborative, there are infinite changes and shifts in the constellations, which allow for continuous novelty" (Roesner 2010 2010b).

There are a number of ways in which we might see a research cycle stemming from and through the work of Monteverdi. Most obviously, his is simply one iteration in an ongoing cycle of exploration focussing the work of the Camerata. Several composers of the period were practicing with ways of making music theatre, and prior to Monteverdi, both Jacopo Peri and Giulio Caccini had explicitly sought to dramatise the Orpheus myth through music, using a pastorale by Ottavio Rinuccini as a libretto and called *Euridice*.[18] Thus here are two ways in which Monteverdi's work can be situated within research cycles: one exploring a development of the operatic form; one exploring retellings of the narrative of Orpheus and Euridice. Both of these are cycles that have continued in numerous other iterations, and each iteration has built on previous knowledge encountered in the Practice as Research forum of the creative field.

There are also a number of other important cycles of research that can be identified in the development of a piece of theatre, and here, the multiplicity of collaborative voices in music theatre makes this field particularly interesting. The collaborative research cycle is initiated and gestated by one artist (say, a librettist), before being passed on to another (the composer), then another (the director) and another (the performer). This is a theme taken up by Bruce Kirle in *Unfinished Show Business* (Kirle 2005), and one that is worth pursuing in more detail. Not only does each collaborator offer a different disciplinary articulation to the developing process—the different skills of a musical director, a choreographer and a lighting designer, for instance, but each also comes to the discussion with a different mind-set, trained in the vocabulary and internal perspectives of their own discipline. A musical pattern of thought will offer a different development in the research cycle than a performative pattern of thought; one is likely to bring metaphors of counterpoint and vocality to the laboratory, while the other may bring different metaphors of internalisation and truth. In some instances, the "triple threat"[19] ability of a contributor (composer-lyricist, director-designer) may present an approach to the enquiry that is multi-faceted and consistent in its exploration of certain dynamics. More often, the various creative voices working on the enquiry will be subtly distinct, conversant but engaged in creative discourse that itself generates new and unique insights. To illustrate how this affects collaborative practice, it is worth considering two different collaborators' contributions to a piece of music theatre—for example Striggio's libretto and Monteverdi's music—and conceptualising how they "fit" together: do we "hear" these individuals' creative "voices" harmonising in counterpoint; or do we imagine the relationship to be "cross-fading" between one mediatised medium and another?[20] These differences in conceptual approach are increasingly evident as ever more collaborative work develops between the live, the mediatised and the virtual.

We can also see how the cyclical re-search in this area has developed as new modes of thinking have emerged and as traditional aesthetics have been called into question. I would suggest that this happens in two main ways—firstly in new thinkers and practitioners articulating their new findings in different and challenging ways: Wagner, Cage, Berberian, etc.; secondly in new thinkers and practitioners revisiting existing theses and re-contextualising, re-phrasing or re-interpreting them. Such is the value, then, of contemporary re-workings of the canonic classics, whose re-stagings offer new articulations of Practice as Research that contribute to an ongoing debate. In so doing, these reveal and confront the problematic definitives (of authorship, the work, etc.) that post-structural critique has identified. Francesca Placanica discusses just such a case in relation to Cathy Berberian, who was perhaps surprisingly invited by Nikolaus Harnoncourt to collaborate on a number of Monteverdi recordings. Placinica reveals that not only did she see this dialogue with the composer as an opportunity to explore ways in which voice and music could lead to new interpretative possibilities, but also to explore expression through a different medium, stage design. Placinica picks up on Berberian's own comments about this ongoing, cyclical exploration, merging a respect for the musical past with an anticipation of musical futures (Karantonis and Verstraete *et al* 2013).[21] As a second example, we might also point to the further authorial "encodings" that informed the English National Opera's 2006 production of *L'Orfeo* (Cummings and Shi-Zheng 2006): a Chinese director's English-language production of this Italian opera of a Greek myth received through Latin texts and featuring a troupe of Javanese dancers. Production choices for this iteration of *Orfeo* used "authentic" instruments to reflect Monteverdi's "intention", transposed the piece up one whole tone "to recognise the high pitch of Monteverdi's time" (Cummings 2006),[22] and cast a black Eurydice (Ruby Philogene) in a striking gesture of "colourblind" casting. Does this gesture remain unmarked, or does it help construct a narrative of the white hero emancipating the black slave, implying that Monteverdi's "strikingly quiet" Eurydice (Abbate 2001: 46) is, in director Chen Shi-Zheng's perception, a comment on the twenty-first century silencing of black women? Or is it folly to conflate "authorial" decisions made 400 years apart and in extremely different cultural, political and social landscapes? Is it possible—or even desirable—to peel away these layers of and influences on authorship to reveal a definitive text?

The idea of practice being a constantly evolving and developing expression of understanding is one that appeals in an academy whose existing articulations of knowledge are often rationalised into universalising definitives and/or crystallised into static and always-outdated "truths". In this sense, the search—the quest for new understanding—always contains an act of historical inscription, in which each iteration of a cycle reifies a current process of thought. If this is what happens to the research output, there is all the more call for a process-based understanding of research which allows emergent understandings to be foregrounded.

This also has an impact on how we understand conventional performance practice, and particularly the re-enactment of historical or "authoritative" versions of a work (see for instance Harnoncourt and Ponnelle 1978, Savall and DeFlo 2002, Christie and Pizzi 2008). Is there call for re-iterating a thesis already stated? Does Jorgi Savall's iteration of *L'Orfeo* from 2002—using authentic instruments, period costumes and taking place in the historical Gran Teatre del Liceu in Barcelona—offer no more than a "reprint" of the original Monteverdi, or does this build on existing knowledge? Does *L'Orfeo* serve as such an important work that—like the writings of canonical theorists such as Marx or Freud—it bears a second edition? Or does such insistent reiteration of established thought simply perpetuate our commitment to classical discourse and conventional paradigms?

In many ways this points us to the context of the iteration, and reminds us that research does not develop in simple progressive pathways. Here the sort of rhizomatic understandings of knowledge that Deleuze and Guattari (and others) present are useful as conceptualisations, through which we can recognise (if not explicitly see) the fact that there will be multiple threads of influence contributing to each subsequent iteration of practice. Through more rhizomatic understandings, the snapshot of context that cultural materialism offers in its periodising approach can be extrapolated to read influences from several "directions" and "dimensions". Thus the specific contextualisation that made John Cage's "4'33'''" resonate in its original performance (1952) becomes utterly transformed in later iterations such as the choice of this record by poet Ian McMillan on Desert Island Discs and its (partial) broadcast on BBC Radio 4 (Young 2010), or the British Cage Against the Machine campaign to undermine the reality television show *X Factor*'s claim to the Christmas Number One pop music chart spot (both 2010).[23]

RESEARCH QUESTION
Finally, the third characteristic of Practice as Research that I will turn to as a useful element of critical thought is its interrogation of the research question. As Smith and Dean explain, it is conventional for research to begin with "an initial plan and a clear idea of an ultimate objective or target outcome" (2010: 23). By contrast, Practice as Research projects typically confound this expectation:

> to be process-driven is to have no particular starting point in mind and no pre-conceived end. Such an approach can be directed towards emergence, that is the generation of ideas which were unforeseen at the beginning of the project. (*Ibid.*)

Indeed, in the same book, Baz Kershaw suggests that, paradoxically, the more rigorous the research question, the more likely the practitioner is to obscure any learning being made, and as Graeme Sullivan puts it,

> what is of interest to practice-led researchers [...] is the possibility of new knowledge that may be generated by moving [...] from the "unknown to the known" whereby imaginative leaps are made into what we don't know as this can lead to critical insights that can change what we do know. (*Ibid.*: 48)

The notion that the research question might be eschewed in favour of a more exploratory, non-anticipatory approach to knowledge-finding, has a direct correlation with Derridean thought in which he challenges the notion of the *eidos* or idea as an unquestionable guiding principle. If, along with post-structuralists, we are going to unpack the conventional tenets of knowledge and their contingent goals of meaning, understanding and enlightenment, the adoption of systems in which there is no pre-determined expectation seems a step in the right direction.

Monteverdi's research was clearly based on a hypothesis of sorts (a research question), though to identify that hypothesis will bring us close to discussions of authorial intention and is not really the point; Practice as Research is not interested in what is *intended* but what is *learnt*, and as we have seen, there is even a danger that a rigorous research question may obscure the scope for learning through practice. After all, a research question can only be conceived from within existing pools of knowledge, prior to enquiry and the emergence of new knowledges. For all its sophistication and complexity, *L'Orfeo* is the pidgin utterance of a new expressive form still in its infancy and voiced in existing paradigms; Monteverdi himself was (inevitably) a neophyte practitioner of his particular idiom, putting together his articulated exegesis in component parts from existing sign-systems with which he was familiar. To add further complexity, this immature expression has served as an exemplar from which subsequent practitioners have modelled their understanding of and expression in the idiom. Over several centuries a knowledge of opera and music theatre has developed, but all of this has been predicated on the Platonic assumption that we (already) collectively know the idiom we use, an embodied virtuosity that comes from primitive examples of that idiom, and an intellectual understanding of it that translates this embodied knowledge into the "inadequate" system of language. Research findings have themselves been obscured by a rhetoric of success that accompanies the narrative of the Camerata and supports the development of opera (in the form that it developed) as progressive, validated by its apparent return to Classical roots and championed by generations of subsequent practitioners, musicologists and teachers. This is also rhetoricised directly within the narratives of *L'Orfeo* and other operatic works. Monteverdi's conceit, then, is to *demonstrate* his thesis (that the spirit of music can be powerful), a thesis restated by, for example, Richard Wagner, and re-enacted in countless subsequent music theatre works from *The Magic Flute* (1791) to *The Soldier's Tale* (1918) to *The Phantom of the Opera* (1986) to *Rent* (1996).

SO WHAT?

For all that *L'Orfeo* might be considered a "writing proper to making", a practical exegesis of Monteverdi's thoughts, it nevertheless only ever remains a persuasive, rhetorical insistence that music theatre is powerful and that this power is borne out of abstraction and expression, the musicalisation of human utterance. In this sense, its irony is that it adopts similar strategies to the logocentric academy in instituting the practice of rhetoric as a tool of intellectual-political determinism. In the narrative of *L'Orfeo*'s metaphor, the music theatre of the sympathetic hero has its triumphant effect over the antagonist characters; but for the audience it is this narrative and the dialectic between characters that causes the drama. Monteverdi and his collaborators, to be sure, call into use an impressively sophisticated arsenal of music theatre techniques for such an early piece: we have already noted the use of musical and linguistic imagery, and as Calcagno notes in the use of deixis in both script and score, this is a text "no longer destined *in primis* to reader [...] but to audiences" (Calcagno 2002: 384). However, the "*possente spirto*", that magical effect of music theatre's alchemy is in crucial respects nothing more than a reported, conceptual premise internal to the narrative. And it is interesting that the bold statement of music's performative power remains endlessly qualified in music theatre by the fact that the music is forever wedded to a descriptive linguistic explanation telling us (in case or because we hadn't noticed?) that the music is, indeed, powerful: the *"possente spirto"*, "the power of the music that I write".[24] In a similar bluff, the legacy of political leaders such as Barack Obama and Tony Blair may in part be determined by their rhetorical manoeuvres ("Yes we can!" / "Education, education, education!").[25] Whether their practice matches their statements is a contestable issue, though unquestionably the valuable legacy of all of these scenarios is that we have *learnt* through experiencing them in practice far more than has been gained through the weight of rhetorical demonstration.

On the other hand, there is in Monteverdi's work a tension between what is being demonstrated and what is in the process of being learnt. Several important lessons are learnt, cumulatively, through the ongoing Practice as Research project initiated by the Camerata, and many of these challenge the dogma that has been constructed. One of the research discoveries from this project seems to be that music is not as powerful as the *"possente spirto"* hypothesis suggests: Monteverdi shrewdly avoids the ultimate voicing of the "powerful spirit" so that we do not actually hear how Orpheus charms the Underworld; and in a self-deprecatingly ironic gesture, the most explicit voicing of Orpheus's music ("Possente Spirto") lulls Charon to sleep! This and subsequent explorations of the power of music have conceded its impossibility: where Orpheus' musicality is the unexplained talent of a demi-God, Tamino's (in *The Magic Flute*) is explicitly a *magic* gift, and the Phantom of the Opera's an *other-worldly* expression by the "angel of music", balancing his demonic deformity. Indeed, one of the overwhelming findings of the operatic project may have been voiced by Nietzsche (1968) (even if his work may be riddled with overtones of nationalism and condescension): operatic expression is not a natural or obvious form of human expression, particularly at moments of heightened emotional intensity, and there is little to be gained in trying to integrate incompatible expressive forms such as words and music.

By and large, Nietzsche's criticisms of opera have been overwhelmed by a rhetoric that has enshrined the development of the form for over 400 years. Nevertheless, for all the claims that the music is the drama and that the composer is the dramatist (Wagner, Weill, Kerman), we see repeatedly (at least until the twentieth century) that the form has been forever beholden to the exigencies not of music but of dramatic narrative. Monteverdi's initial naivety allowed him to slip into an easy and misleading subterfuge that his *story* about powerful music was being told in the *language* of powerful music. In fact, music theatre from the time of the Camerata has used music to illustrate and accompany dramatic narratives whose power is in the interplay of characters and the development of dramatic scenes.

IF AT FIRST...

Having said this, a number of important and positive discoveries have been made in the "laboratory"—and this is testament both to the necessity and importance of music theatre as a Practice as Research model and to the fact that unexpected research outcomes ("ideas which were unforeseen at the beginning of the project" (Smith and Dean 2010: 23)) may be borne out of practical research. The fact that *L'Orfeo* is (only) a story about the power of music theatre does not mean that the power of music theatre itself is a fiction. This is clear from the attraction of the singing voice—not least the castrato—which, though tangled within issues of cultural capital, the aristocracy of culture (Bourdieu 1986) and the fascination with celebrity, is an attraction that indicates the "embodied cultural capital" (Barrett and Bolt 2007: 8) of the performative experience. It has taken a number of twentieth-century shifts in thinking and vocabulary to elucidate this—first the developments of psychoanalysis and phenomenology; then the dismantling strategies of post-structuralism; now the embracing of emergent and embodied knowledge—though discussions of *jouissance* (see Poizat 1986) and the "grain of the voice" (Barthes 1984) do rationalise the sort of "magical" experience that is possible in music theatre and that *L'Orfeo* stages. In the wake of these paradigm shifts it has become acceptable for subsequent composers to reconsider music theatre in their own experiments, and examples of more contemporary music theatre are the practical exegeses of these thoughts—the latest cycles in the ongoing Practice as Research project of the Camerata.[26]

Nevertheless, it is to Monteverdi's credit that he not only stepped into the unknown with a naïve understanding of what could be achieved and a practical enthusiasm to explore that, but also that he was able, with his contemporaries, to develop symbolic structurings that enabled the subsequent exploration of music theatre's magical alchemy.

NOTES

---

[1] The adage that the whole is greater than the sum of its parts has become a familiar assertion, though one with the problematic implication that some sort of alchemical expansion take place *between* the parts: in a threshold space that for all its liminal potential nevertheless remains complicit in separating the elements. The wholeness of the *Gesamtkunstwerk*, or as Weber puts it, an "interdependent network of relationships in which no one instance can be said to dominate the others, or even to function without them" (Weber in Levin 1994: 119), articulates a conception of an holistic music theatre form, though one which has also been problematised. Similarly, the Broadway musical's own *Gesamtkunstwerk* project of integration has recently been interrogated (McMillin 2006, Rebellato 2009, Taylor 2009).

[2] The foundations of Derrida's whole life-work stem from his earliest musings on "transcendental reduction" in *The Problem of Genesis in Husserl's Philosophy* (Derrida 2003). Specific references to the *eidos* and the self appear later in relation to Plato's pharmacy (see Derrida 1981); though simplistically the concept of *eidos* can be seen as linked to any habitual energy that grounds its reason in a notion of origin, idea or genesis.

[3] Deleuze and Guattari also predicate much of their writing on the problematic of the transcendental, a theme that runs throughout *A Thousand Plateaus* (1987).

[4] Smith and Dean (2010), Freeman (2010), Allegue *et al* (2009), Barrett and Bolt (2007), Riley and Hunter (2009).

[5] The Research Excellence Framework is the UK Higher Education sector's national assessment of research quality, currently monitoring the outputs, impact and environment of research institutions and individuals for the period 2008-2014. Practice as Research, currently an accepted mode of enquiry for this assessment, has been welcomed by performance-based assessment panels, though a general hesitancy amongst Higher Education institutions to offer Practice as Research projects for evaluation has been detected (see "REF Expert Advisory Groups" 2010: 20-21).

[6] "Music, in opera, stands in a self-reflective relationship—it performs its own representation, it stages its own power and its effects" (Žižek and Dolar 2002: 10).

[7] Rolland's succinct report of this in Whenham (1986: 119-125) is brief; for more detailed discussions see Kerman (1953) or Pirrotta (1982). Note the emphasis on *performance* in this agenda, in relation to the quest to find authenticity in the *score*.

[8] Elsewhere, new technologies have proven to some extent useful in offering new platforms for the presentation and dissemination of practical work (if not the replication of performance experiences), and have begun to be welcomed alongside more conventional outputs such as written books and journal articles.

[9] "Sia testimon del core qualche lieta canzon che detti Amore", bars 121-126 (Monteverdi 1968).

[10] Bars 91-99 (Monteverdi 1968).

[11] "S'a tuoi lamenti già festi lagrimar queste campagne", Act 1, bars 113-116 (Monteverdi 1968).

[12] "In questo lieto e fortunate giorno / ch'ha posto fine a gli amorosi affanni / del nostro semideo, / cantiam, pastori, / in sì soavi accenti, / che sian degni d'Orfeo nostri concerti. / Oggi fatta è pietosa / l'alma già sì sdegnosa / de la bell'Euridice", Act 1, bars 13-16 (Monteverdi 1968).

[13] "Qual suon dolente il lieto dì perturba?", bars 183-5 (Monteverdi 1968).

[14] "D'onde vieni? / Ove vai? / Ninfa, che porti?", Act 2, bars 221-225 (Monteverdi 1968).

[15] "Un muto sasso", bars 299-300 (Monteverdi 1968).

[16] Accounts of this section of *L'Orfeo* are numerous: see for example Whenham (1986). An interesting deconstructive take on the meta-textuality of *L'Orfeo* is found in Abbate (2001).

[17] See also McKechnie and Stevens' concept of a practice-research-practice cycle in Smith and Dean 2010.

[18] See Sternfeld in Whenham 1986.

[19] I borrow the term "triple threat" from the jargon of performer training, where musical theatre performers are required to hone virtuoso discipline skills in singing, acting and dancing. The technical demand for multiple performative skills that this represents is complexified by a juggling of idiomatically different behavioural processes, something akin to patting one's head whilst rubbing one's belly. Parallels to such a multiplicity of processes are also significant for Practice as Research enquirers whose own work requires a juggling that is not quite a *transliteration* between embodied knowledge, intellectual reasoning and scholarly expression.

[20] Here I am indebted to Karen Savage's insights on intermediality and the fade (Savage 2010), which helped inform our own collaborative experiences—and our awareness of different approaches—on the Practice as Research project *Sweet FA* (2009) (Savage and Symonds 2010).

[21] Placanica cites Berberian 1966.

[22] Arnold and Fortune would validate this decision (1985: 325).

[23] The *X Factor*'s monopoly of the UK charts over successive Christmas periods (2005-2008) led to a campaign in 2009 for the rock band Rage Against the Machine's single "Killing in the Name" to be strategically re-released. Public animosity against the *X Factor*'s perceived commodification of the charts (!) led to an unprecedented number of sales for the alternative single, which trumped *X Factor* winner Joe McElderry's "The Climb" and took the Christmas Number One slot. A similar campaign in 2010, wittily titled "Cage Against the Machine", re-recorded John Cage's "4'33'"" and attempted to trump the *X Factor* again, this time with "silence". Ultimately the campaign was unsuccessful, with "4'33'"" placed at number 21 and *X Factor* winner Matt Cardle taking the top slot with his single "When we collide". See Michaels 2010.

[24] "The Music of the Night" from *The Phantom of the Opera* (Lloyd Webber and Hart 1987).

[25] Tony Blair's famous soundbite appeared in his 1996 speech at the Labour Party conference in Blackpool, UK: "Ask me my three main priorities for government and I tell you: education, education and education" (Blair 1996). Some eight months later the Labour Party was elected to government in a landslide victory, with Blair as Prime Minister. Barack Obama's famous "Yes, we can" speech was delivered at the New Hampshire primaries in the run-up to the 2008 presidential election (Obama 2008). At the start of 2009, he was sworn in as the first black President of the United States.

[26] There have been many subsequent explorations, and perhaps only the most obvious are the work of Berio, Bussotti and Berberian in the Studio Fonografie during the 1950s; the work of Peter Brook with his *Orghast* experiments in the 1970s; and contemporary practice by groups such as Gardzienice. It is also worth noting that much of the legacy of opera that is encountered in this domain is concentrated in

Western practices (of thought and creativity); other cultures present many different approaches to music theatre and to paradigms of thought. A useful overview of music theatre's development (particularly through the twentieth century) is provided by Salzman and Desi (2008).

ABSTRACTS

1. IS THIS STILL OPERA?
MEDIA OPERAS AS PRODUCTIVE PROVOCATIONS

BIANCA MICHAELS

Many contemporary operas not only cross the boundaries of different media but make the problematic question of what the term "opera" actually means even more complicated. Relying fundamentally on audiovisual media, these works establish new conditions of communication between production and reception process thus creating new "operatic experiences". The aim of this chapter is two-fold: to introduce contemporary opera forms that are widely neglected within the academic discourse on opera and—based on these forms— to focus on mediality as a productive area for opera research. Whereas technological inventions in the past have mostly affected individual elements of the performance, the technological influences that are enabled by electronic media led to developments that can fundamentally change our conceptions of opera as a form of music theatre. Works such as Robert Ashley's *Perfect Lives* (1978-1983) and Steve Reich's *Three Tales* (1998-2002) challenge our common understanding of this art form and at the same time oblige us to reconsider some of our familiar propositions. A closer look at their particular characteristics demonstrates that opera is not inextricably bound to the theatrical stage. Based on audiovisual and digital media, "media operas"—as they are called by the author of this chapter— serve as productive provocations of our common understanding of what opera can look like. Furthermore, media operas remind us that a theoretical discourse of opera should not limit itself to opera as an art form but must also incorporate the varied perspectives on opera as an institution and as a social and cultural practice. Thus, media operas cause a productive provocation for us to take a closer look at our "blind spot", at our underlying, often barely reflected premises and expectations concerning opera and music theatre.

2. A NEW GLIMMER OF LIGHT :
OPERA, METAPHYSICS AND MIMESIS

NICHOLAS TILL

In this chapter I will argue that throughout the 400 years of its existence, opera has served to inscribe and endorse some very fundamental metaphysical tropes of western thought, that this metaphysics is both ideologically overdetermined and ignores the predominately anti-metaphysical tendencies of modern western thought from Nietzsche, phenomenology and positivism to structuralism and post-structuralism. The implicit metaphysics of opera, which still haunt the form, are therefore maintained within a culture whose structures and thought systems no longer sustain this kind of metaphysical thinking. Charting the metaphysics of opera from Monteverdi to the present day, and paying particular attention to the theories of Richard Wagner, the chapter suggests that operatic metaphysics serves to universalise (and mythologise) the subject matter and characters of opera. But I also suggest that the material reality of operatic performance constantly threatens to undermine the metaphysical apparatus of opera. And moreover, I suggest that the anti-humanism of musical modernism also negates the pretensions to "universal humanism" of conventional opera. Composers of the postwar avant garde who rejected the aesthetico-ideological apparatus of western art music therefore tended to avoid the form of opera altogether, seeking alternative ways of deploying the media from which opera is made. This anti-operatic tendency continues to fuel the energy of many contemporary forms of music theatre. But at the conclusion of this chapter I consider the work of three living composers, Helmut Lachenmann, Salvatore Sciarrino and Olga Neuwirth, who, in related ways, appear to have found a way to re-engage with the forms of opera without being sucked once again into its metaphysical sloughs.

3. THE SINGING BODY IN THE *TRAGÉDIE LYRIQUE* OF SEVENTEENTH- AND EIGHTEENTH-CENTURY FRANCE: VOICE, THEATRE, SPEECH, PLEASURE

SARAH NANCY

By considering the voice as the centre of the work, and naturalising the conditions of its presentation and production, the nineteenth-century grand operatic tradition, whose legacy is still very evident in repertoires and expectations today, has led to an interpretation of the singing body as either paradoxically absent in spite of its overwhelming effect on the listener, or present in a purely negative way. My hypothesis is that to acknowledge the reorganisation of values that takes place in France from the birth of the *tragédie lyrique* to its decline—from the so-called "classic age" to the Enlightenment—makes us witness the elaboration of the assumptions that have led to such an impasse. We move from a "literary" view of opera to a view of the genre as a "jewellery box" for the voice; from a conception of the performer as being devoted to the character, to a conception where the performer uses his/her body in order to serve his/her voice first; from a conception of pleasure made of a negotiation between his passions and his ethical and social "self" to a system of values where singing is considered the best way to arouse an emotion that can hardly be formulated. In other terms, this historical detour helps us to consider how music theatre links the aesthetic body to the public body, thus inviting us to reflect upon what philosopher Jacques Rancière calls the "Sharing of the Sensible" ("*partage du sensible*"), by referring to the way the aesthetic experience organises space, and thus affects the way we live together.

4. PERFORMING AFFECT IN SEVENTEENTH-CENTURY OPERA: PROCESS, RECEPTION, TRANSGRESSION

CLEMENS RISI

This chapter discusses the musical and theatrical representation of affect, as well as its transference to the listener, that was *the* central theme of the newly emerging performance genre around 1600: opera.

It starts from the notion that the transfer of affect occurs as a process between performers and perceiving listeners/spectators, and as such, it pertains to the paradigmatic moments of opera's performative dimension. It sheds light on this performative core of opera from two directions. Firstly, from a historical perspective, the article reconstructs the supposed mechanisms for the transfer of affect and the transgression of these rules, focusing on seventeenth-century physiological and anatomical knowledge. Secondly, by means of two examples from current productions (Monteverdi's *L'incoronazione di Poppea*, staged by Klaus Michael Grüber, conducted by Marc Minkowski, in Aix-en-Provence in 1999; and Purcell's *Dido and Aeneas*, staged by Sasha Waltz, conducted by Attilio Cremonesi, in Berlin in 2005), the article attempts to identify the causes as to why, at present, an increased interest in the performance of the affect-oriented music of the seventeenth century can be observed.

5. THE VIOLETTAS OF PATTI, MUZIO AND CALLAS: STYLE, INTERPRETATION AND THE QUESTION OF LEGACY

MAGNUS TESSING SCHNEIDER

This chapter attempts to view the history of operatic singing in the light of the history of acting, taking as its point of departure the claim that a musical performance in the theatre—if operatic singing is a stage language on a par with the actor's delivery—is also a theatrical performance. It is argued that the academic approach of theatre studies may be of use in the linking of the musicologists' traditional close readings of the operatic score with the study of musical performance practice, one of the traditional virtues of the theatre scholar being the trained ability to read a dramatic text less as a finished artwork than as a theatrical script containing an infinite variety of scenic possibilities. This point is demonstrated through a comparison of three of the most admired and influential Violettas in the history of opera, those of Adelina Patti, Claudia Muzio and Maria Callas. Through the ages, fans of the three sopranos have claimed that *their* idol was the one who actually realised Verdi's ideals, but through analyses of historical descriptions of their performances, it is shown how the singers, in fact, reflected the theatrical conventions of their own time to a very high degree, which their contemporaries have usually failed to recognise.

From the comparison of Patti, Muzio and Callas it becomes clear that different performances of an opera have such a profound impact not only on the psychological conception of the roles, but on such basic issues as the nature of character representation and the word-tone relationship, that it is virtually impossible to discuss these issues in relation to the score without considering the aspects of its performance.

6. THE TENOR IN DECLINE? NARRATIVES OF NOSTALGIA AND THE PERFORMATIVITY OF THE OPERATIC TENOR

PAMELA KARANTONIS

This chapter will examine some key concepts concerned with the performativity of the operatic tenor over the past one hundred years. Attendant to this are issues of masculinity, the visceral presence of the artist over issues of representation, genre transgression and the cultural power of vocal pedagogues. Also core to these issues is the experience of the listening audience, not only in the sense of live performance, but as consumers of the recording industries, cinema and the historical archive of the tenor. Much of the content of this chapter arises from the abundant examples of the tenor's *paratextual* appeal, which suggests that his celebrity goes well beyond the bounds of conventional repertoire. Underlying the celebration of the tenor's corporeality is the relevance of vocal pedagogic discourse, both as a quasi-science, but also as a culturally loaded site of perpetual myth-making about the tenor. This chapter concludes that the performativity of the tenor exists within a matrix of complicated and competing narratives about his decline and celebrity, within a culture in which the cultivated voice of the operatic tenor is somehow naturalised as overtly masculine yet fraught with desires and anxieties in its production and reception. What might be suggested, ultimately, is that there is an anxiety in the relationship of the listener to the tenor, when the pleasure of the listener is threatened by the inevitable aging and decline of their celebrated ideal.

7. *THE THREEPENNY OPERA*: PERFORMATIVTY AND THE BRECHTIAN PRESENCE BETWEEN MUSIC AND THEATRE

MICHAEL EIGTVED

This chapter will sketch out how the theories of what Peter Bürger has labelled the historical avant garde, of performativity and of theatricality, can be used to investigate music theatre. My thesis is that an analysis of the performativity involved in the kind of music theatre which Bertolt Brecht devised will reveal elements of the experience which are essential to the notion of what potential this music theatre possesses. The chapter uses Brecht/Weill's *Die Dreigroschenoper* (1928) as source material, taking off both from Brecht's writings on it and from an analysis of the historical opening night in August 1928 in Berlin. This process will also reflect on the problems and possibilities of investigating the performativity of historical performances. The chapter discusses in some depth Bertolt Brecht's ideas about the actor's "doubleness" in singing "songs" and how an analysis of the performativity in *Die Dreigroschenoper* can be used to discuss a renewed understanding of it. The chapter finally points out how these three different approaches to music theatre can be distinguished by their different perspectives on the transition from a spoken mode to a sung mode of performance.

8. THE *ACOUSMÊTRE* ON STAGE AND SCREEN: THE POWER OF THE BODILESS VOICE

JEONGWON JOE

This chapter considers a recent trend in operatic theatre, which exploits cinema's "castration anxiety", that is, the separation of voice and body. Unlike traditional live theatre in which the voice is embodied, in cinema, voice and body—sound and image—are separated in the process of recording, and they are preserved on, and reproduced from, physically separated tracks. In view of the psychoanalytical theory that interprets this anxiety as the origin of cinema's envy of a live medium, the voice-body separation in operatic theatre can be read as opera's "reversed envy": reversed in the sense that it is *opera's envy* of the cinematic separation of voice and body instead of *cinema's envy* of a live medium. In my chapter, I trace opera's envy of cinema's anxiety to cinema's ironic privileging of the voice/sound in spite of the seeming dominance of the visual in the cinematic medium. I support my argument by demonstrating a parallelism between what Slavoj Žižek calls an "uncanny autonomization of the voice" in sound film and "the uncanny aspects of operatic performance", as argued by Carolyn Abbate. By contextualising film theories in the recent discourse on opera performance, I show how those theories can provide a methodological perspective, from which the re-negotiated relationship between voice and body in live operatic theatre can be analysed, and in so doing, how they can expand and enrich the hermeneutic scope for analysing the opera-cinema encounter. I cannot over-emphasise that what I argue in this essay is *one possible interpretation* that may not have much, if anything, to do with the intentionality of the composer, the stage director, or the film director.

9. DANCING IN THE TWILIGHT: ON THE BORDERS OF MUSIC AND THE SCENIC

DAVID ROESNER

This chapter investigates the complex interaction of music and theatre, musical and theatrical performance and perception and particularly the dissolution of clearly definable borders between them on the basis of two different practices: Lars von Trier's meta-musical-theatre film *Dancer in the Dark* (2000), and composer-director Heiner Goebbels' experimental music-theatre production *Eraritjaritjaka* (2004). The methodological considerations that precede these investigations are based on Jens Schröter's notion of transformational intermediality and expand the idea of an intermedial relation that "consists in one medium representing another" into three types of relations, which I label with the metaphors "*Suchbild*" (picture puzzle), the "*Kippfigur*" (tilting phenomenon) and the "*Schwellenphänomen*" (liminal phenomenon). In my argument these notions are used to classify and distinguish different forms of cohesion or fusion between music and theatre in performance. I focus on productions which challenge or blur boundaries of clearly distinguishable media, genres and/or performance modes. They also question fixed dispositions with respect to both production process and perception and draw their particular appeal from this ambiguity.

10. TURKISH POST-MIGRANT "OPERA" IN EUROPE: A SOCIO-HISTORICAL PERSPECTIVE ON AURALITY

PIETER VERSTRAETE

This chapter aims to discuss the emergence of post-migrant forms of music theatre and opera *with*, *for* and *by* European Turkish artists and communities, by means of two recent productions: *Lege Wieg / Boş Beşik* by Hollands Diep in Dordrecht, and *Tango Türk* by the Neuköllner Oper in Berlin. Currently, transnational networks of similarly minded, multicultural venues are being formed in Germany, the Netherlands, the UK and Belgium. The label of "post-migrant", which is still fairly new and which stems from the German artistic scene, helps to contextualise these performances in relation to their social function to give access to and reflect upon migrant experiences within a growing multicultural Europe. Central to my argument is how music works as a vehicle to communicate aspects of social history in these performances, negotiating socio-cultural issues, among others, of cultural memory, tradition and the experience of modern subjectivity as constitutive of the post-migrant identity in the twenty-first century. Through the adaptation of "traditional" European music theatre conventions such as those of opera, these performances aim to include larger, heterogeneous audiences across generations and different cultural backgrounds. Hence, the chapter proposes theoretical concepts and historical contexts that enable an understanding of the hybrid experiences by the listeners in these performances. Ultimately, this chapter demonstrates how music theatre responds to and helps to shape this invisible space of "aurality" in relation to these heterogeneous audiences. I believe that it is in this shared, inter-subjective space that music theatre and the individual audience member can create meaning in relation to one another. The chapter aims then to disclose aurality as a social force, which, although it concerns *contemporary* listening cultures in the first place, is foremost tuned to history. It is in this historically determined space of aurality, which constitutes all of our experiences in music theatre or opera, that the listeners find each other in different aesthetic experiences giving access to different cultural memories that are as much about the modern individual today as about the collective.

11. "POWERFUL SPIRIT":
NOTES ON SOME PRACTICE AS RESEARCH

DOMINIC SYMONDS

My aim in this chapter is to take the paradigm of Practice as Research and to use it not as a methodology but as a critical theory. In doing this I will not only seek to upend—or perhaps more appropriately *level*—the perceived hierarchy between practical and theoretical enquiry, but also to use one (practice/theory) as the other (theory/practice) in a playful example of "critical impro". In particular, I will consider the development of music theatre as an extended research enquiry with which theoreticians (continue to) engage in their scholarly practice. I pick up on three particular aspects of Practice as Research and explore these in relation to Monteverdi's *L'Orfeo* (1607): I consider firstly the way that practical research findings are most vividly expressed in the language of their idiom (in this case, the language of the musical stage); secondly, that ongoing creative responses by collaborative or subsequent practitioners will refine and sometimes reveal new research knowledge; and thirdly, that the understanding borne out of practice will often challenge or contradict anticipated outcomes, leading to new insights. I suggest that *L'Orfeo* marks an early stage in what can be seen as an ongoing Practice as Research project; opera's development. I have suggested that powerful ideologies and paradigms of thought at the inception of that Practice as Research project, which caused early resistance to new findings being noticed, have more recently begun to shift so that valuable new insights in the area of music theatre can be explored by project participants.

NOTES ON CONTRIBUTORS

Michael Eigtved (University of Copenhagen)
Michael Eigtved studied musicology and cultural studies at the University of Copenhagen, finishing his MA in 1992. He completed his PhD at the Centre for Urbanity and Aesthetics, University of Copenhagen, working on the relationship between popular music theatre and urban life. Since 1999 he has been Associate Professor of Theatre and Performance Studies at the Department of Arts and Cultural Studies, University of Copenhagen; from 2011 he has also been Head of Studies at the department. He is co-founder of the Music Theatre Working Group and was also director of the Network for Music Theatre under the Danish Research Council (2001-06). He has published a number of books about music theatre, among others *Det populære Musikteater* (*Popular Music Theatre*) in 2003, and *Forestillinger* (*Performances*) in 2004. A textbook *Forestillings-analyse. En introduction.* (*Performance Analysis. An introduction*) came out in 2007, and most recently a book on revues/shows in Copenhagen from 1912-30, *Scala—A Spectacular Urban Revue* was published in 2012.

Jeongwon Joe (University of Cincinnati)
Jeongwon Joe is Associate Professor of Musicology at the University of Cincinnati's College-Conservatory of Music. She is the author of *Opera as Soundtrack* (Ashgate, forthcoming in 2013) and co-editor of *Wagner and Cinema* (Indiana University Press, 2010) and *Between Opera and Cinema* (Routledge, 2002). Her current projects include a monograph, *Western Opera's Diaspora in Korea During the Japanese Occupation (1910-1945)*. She is an associate editor of *The Journal of Film Music* and has served as a music consultant to Chanwook Park, the director of Cannes award-winning films *Oldboy* (2004) and *Thirst* (2009) and has served as a music consultant to the Cannes award-winning film *Night Fishing*, which won a Golden Bear at the 2011 Berlin Film Festival.

Bianca Michaels (Ludwig-Maximilians-Universität, Munich)
Bianca Michaels studied Theatre Studies, German Philology, and Musicology at the Universities of Erlangen, Mainz, Vienna (Austria),

and Stanford (US) and holds degrees from the Universities of Mainz and Amsterdam (NL). She currently holds the position of Senior Lecturer at the Ludwig-Maximilian-University in Munich where, in addition to her work in research and teaching, she also established and is now in charge of an advanced vocational training programme in theatre and music management. Her research focuses on contemporary music theatre, media opera, and media theory. Her latest area of research explores institutional aspects of theatre and its legitimisation, cultural policy and cultural governance. She has recently published articles on theatre and migration today and on cultural policy during the Weimar Republic.

Pamela Karantonis (Bath Spa University)
Pamela Karantonis is Senior Lecturer in Voice at Bath Spa University. She has a performance background in opera and completed her doctoral thesis, "Impersonation", at the School of Theatre, Film and Dance at The University of New South Wales, Sydney in 2004. She is a Convenor of the Music Theatre Working Group of The International Federation for Theatre Research. Pamela was joint editor and contributing author for *Opera Indigene: Re/presenting First Nations and Indigenous Cultures* (Ashgate, 2011) and was a guest speaker at the European Humanities Research Council Colloquium on *Opera and Politics* at Oxford University. Additionally she has presented papers at the Amsterdam School of Cultural Analysis and the University College London Institute in Paris. She is currently a co-editor for *Cathy Berberian: Pioneer of Contemporary Vocality* (Ashgate, due 2013).

Sarah Nancy (University Sorbonne Nouvelle-Paris 3)
Sarah Nancy is Associate Professor at the University Sorbonne Nouvelle-Paris 3 where she teaches seventeenth-century French Literature. Her publications include *La Voix féminine et le plaisir de l'écoute en France aux XVIIe et XVIIIe siècles* (*The female voice and the pleasure of listening in France in the 17th and 18th centuries*, Classiques Garnier, 2012, with an audio CD) and articles on the voice in different musical and literary genres and on the interpretation of sexual difference in language. Her research is inspired by her own singing practice. She was awarded the New Scholars Prize of the International Federation for Theatre Research in 2005.

Clemens Risi (Freie Universität Berlin)

Clemens Risi is Assistant Professor (*Juniorprofessor*) of Opera and Music Theatre at the Freie Universität Berlin and Acting Interim Chair for Theatre and Media Studies at the Friedrich-Alexander-Universität Erlangen-Nürnberg. He studied Musicology, Theatre Studies, and Business Administration in Mainz, Munich and Rome. He has been a member of the collaborative research centre "Kulturen des Performativen" (Cultures of the Performative) and the Cluster of Excellence "Languages of Emotion" at FU Berlin. Clemens has held Visiting Professorships at Brown University (2008) and the University of Chicago (2010). He has published widely about opera and music theatre from the seventeenth century to the present, and is the author of *Auf dem Weg zu einem italienischen Musikdrama (Towards an Italian music theatre*, Tutzing 2004). He is currently completing a book on *Opera in Performance* and a monograph for the Parma Verdi Prize about performance practice in mid-nineteenth-century Italian opera. Along with Gundula Kreuzer, he edited a special issue of *The Opera Quarterly* entitled "Opera in Transition" (27(2-3), 2011).

David Roesner (University of Kent)

David Roesner is Senior Lecturer in Drama and Theatre at the University of Kent. In his research he explores the musicality of theatre and the theatricality of music in historic and contemporary practices. Major publications include the article "The Politics of the Polyphony of Performance: Musicalization in Contemporary German Theatre" (*Contemporary Theatre Review* 18(1), 2008), which won him the Thurnau Award for Music Theatre Studies 2007, and two edited books: *Theatre Noise* (Cambridge Scholars Publishing 2011, with Lynne Kendrick) and *Composed Theatre* (Intellect 2012, with Matthias Rebstock). He also works as a theatre-musician/sound designer. Traces of his work and further publications can be viewed online at: http://kent.academia.edu/DavidRoesner.

Magnus Tessing Schneider (Stockholm University)

Magnus Tessing Schneider is author of *The Charmer and the Monument: Mozart's Don Giovanni in the Light of Its Original Production* and *The Bassi Legacy* (both forthcoming with the Hollitzer Wissenschaftsverlag). He specialises in the history of scenic-musical performance practice within Italian opera. A co-founder of the

Nordic Network for Early Opera, he made his debut as a stage director in 2007. He is currently employed as a post-doctoral fellow within the research project "Performing Premodernity: Exploring Cultural Heritage through the Drottningholm Court Theatre", a collaboration between Stockholm University, Drottningholm Palace Theatre and the University College of Opera in Stockholm.

Dominic Symonds (University of Lincoln)
Dominic Symonds is Reader in Drama at the University of Lincoln, and along with Pamela Karantonis he convenes the Music Theatre Working Group of the International Federation for Theatre Research (2010-2014). His research focuses on post-structuralist approaches to the musical stage. He is editor of *Studies in Musical Theatre* (Intellect) and founded the international conference "Song, Stage and Screen", both with George Burrows. He co-edited a special issue of *Contemporary Theatre Review*, "The Broadway Musical: New Approaches" (19(1), 2009, with Dan Rebellato), and is a regular contributor to the Harvard-Princeton Musical Theater Forum. His monographs *We'll Have Manhattan: The Early Work of Rodgers and Hart* (Oxford University Press) and *Broadway Rhythm: Imaging the City in Song* (University of Michigan Press), are forthcoming.

Nicholas Till (University of Sussex)
Nicholas Till is a theatre artist, an historian and theorist of opera and music theatre. He is Professor of Opera and Music Theatre, and Director of the Centre for Research in Opera and Music Theatre (CROMT) at the University of Sussex. Nick is also Leverhulme Research Fellow, working currently in the area of early opera and modernity, including a book on the origins of opera entitled *Opera, Myth and Modernity*. His publications include *Mozart and the Enlightenment: Truth, Virtue and Beauty in Mozart's Operas* (1992), *The Cambridge Companion to Opera Studies* (2012) and numerous articles on contemporary music and theatre. As a director and writer-director he has worked for companies including Glyndebourne Opera, The Royal Opera, English National Opera Studio and Stuttgart Opera and he is co-director of the experimental Music Theatre company Post-Operative Productions. His 2004 critical manifesto for a "post-operatic" Music Theatre has recently been translated into Italian.

Pieter Verstraete (Independent / Universities of Sabancı and Ankara) Pieter Verstraete is a freelance researcher based in Turkey. Since 2012, he has held an Honorary University Fellowship at the University of Exeter, where he was previously Lecturer in Drama. His current research on Turkish post-migrant theatre and opera in Europe was granted the support of both a Tübitak Fellowship at Ankara University and a Mercator-IPC Fellowship at Sabancı University in Istanbul. In 2009, he completed his PhD, entitled The "Frequency of Imagination: Auditory Distress and Aurality in Contemporary Music Theatre". He has co-edited and authored numerous works on sound, voice and aurality in theatre, the most recent being published in *Performance Research* (Routledge 2010) and *Theatre Noise* (Cambridge Scholars Publishing 2011). He is also a co-editor of *Cathy Berberian: Pioneer of Contemporary Vocality* (Ashgate, due 2013).

BIBLIOGRAPHY

PRIMARY REFERENCES

Adorno, Theodor W. and Max Horkheimer. 1973. *Dialectic of Enlightenment* (tr. J. Cumming). London, New York: Verso.

Adorno, Theodor W. 1976. *Introduction to the Sociology of Music* (tr. E. B. Ashton). Seabury Press: New York.

——1997. *Aesthetic Theory* (tr. R. Hullot-Kentor). Minneapolis: University of Minnesota Press.

——1998. *Quasi una Fantasia: Essays on Modern Music* (tr. R. Livingstone). London: Verso.

——1999. *Sound Figures* (tr. Rodney Livingstone). Stanford: Stanford University Press.

——2002. *Essays on Music* (ed. Richard Leppert, tr. S. H. Gillespie). Berkeley, Los Angeles, London: University of California Press.

Agamben, Giorgio. 1996. *L'Homme sans contenu*. Paris: Circé.

Aristotle. 1961. *Poetics* (tr. S.H. Butcher). New York: Hill and Wang.

Ashley, Robert. 1991. *Perfect Lives—An Opera*. San Francisco: Burning Books.

——2001. 'Robert Ashley at home, in conversation with Frank J. Oteri'. Online at: http://www.newmusicbox.org/24/images/Ashley_interview.pdf (consulted 03.03.05).

——n.d. 'Productions: Perfect Lives'. Online at: http://www.robertashley.org/productions/perfectlives.htm (consulted 30.11.2011).

Bacilly, Bénigne de. 1679, 1994. *L'art de bien chanter; augmenté d'un discours qui sert de réponse à la critique de ce traité* Paris: chez l'Auteur: Genève: Minkoff.

Barthes, Roland. 1968, 1984. (tr. and ed. S. Heath, 1984) *Image, Music, Text*. London: Fontana.

——1973. *Mythologies* (tr. A. Lavers). London: Paladin Books.

Bary, René. 1679. *Méthode pour bien prononcer un discours, & pour le bien animer. Ouvrage très utile à tous ceux qui parlent en public, & particulierement aux Predicateurs, & aux Avocats*. Paris: D. Thierry.

Becker, Heinz (ed.). 1981. *Quellentexte zur Konzeption der europäischen Oper im 17. Jahrhundert*. Kassel: Bärenreiter.

Benjamin, Walter. 1978. *Reflections* (ed. Peter Demetz, tr. E. Jephcott). New York: Schocken Books.

Bérard, Jean-Baptiste-Antoine. 1755, 1972. *L'Art du chant*. Paris: Dessaint & Saillant (original 1755 print). Genève: Minkoff.

Berberian, Cathy. 1966. 'La nuova vocalità nell'opera contemporanea' in *Discoteca* 62: 12.

Blair, Tony. 1996. 'Leader's Speech, Blackpool 1996'. Online at: http://www.britishpoliticalspeech.org/speech-archive.htm?speech=202 (consulted 20.1.13).

Bois, Yve-Alain and Rosalind Krauss. 1997. *Formless: A User's Guide*. New York: Zone Books.

Bourdieu, Pierre. 1986. *Distinction: A Social Critique of the Judgement of Taste* (tr. R. Nice). London: Routledge and Kegan Paul.

Brecht, Bertolt. 1918-1933, 1993. *Schriften zum Theater*. Frankfurt: Suhrkamp Verlag.

——1918-1956, 1964. *Brecht on Theatre: The Development of an Aesthetic* (ed. and tr. John Willett). New York: Hill and Wang.

——1928, 2004. *Die Dreigroschenoper* (commentary J. Lucchesi). Frankfurt: Suhrkamp Basis Bibliothek.

Bussotti, Sylvano. 2002. (forthcoming). 'Allegory actually' from *Disordine Alfabetico* (tr. F. Placanica) in Karantonis, Pamela and Pieter Verstraete *et al* (eds). *Cathy Berberian: Pioneer of Contemporary Vocality*. Farnham: Ashgate.

Calvé, Emma. 1922. *My Life* (tr. R. Gilder). New York and London: D. Appleton.

Christiansen, Rupert. 1984. *Prima Donna: A History*. Middlesex and New York: Harmondsworth.

Cordemoy, Géraud de. 1677. *Discours physique de la parole*. Paris: Michallet.

Cureau de la Chambre, Marin. 1647. *L'Art de connoistre les homes*. Paris: P. Rocolet.

Deleuze, Gilles and Félix Guattari. 1987. *A Thousand Plateaus: Capitalism and Schizophrenia* (tr. B. Massumi). New York and London: Continuum.

Derrida, Jacques. 1967. *L'écriture et la différence* (Collection Tel Quel). Paris: Seuil.

——1967. *La Voix et le phénomène: Introduction au problème du signe dans la phénoménologie de Husserl*. Paris: Presses Universitaires de France.

——1976. *Of Grammatology* (tr. G. Chakravorty Spivak,). Baltimore: Johns Hopkins University Press.

——1981. *Dissemination* (tr. B. Johnson). London: Athlone Press.

——2003. *The Problem of Genesis in Husserl's Philosophy* (tr. M. Hobson). Chicago and London: University of Chicago Press.

Erasmus. 1530, 1977. *La Civilité puerile*. Paris: Ramsay.

Gasset, José Ortega y.1968. *The Dehumanisation of Art and other Essays on Art, Culture and Literature* (tr. H. Weyl). Princeton: Princeton University Press.

Genette, Gérard. 1997. *Paratexts—Threshholds of Interpretation* (tr. J. E. Lewin). Cambridge: Cambridge University Press.

Goehr, Alexander. 1973. *Naboth's Vineyard*. London: Schott.

Green. Joseph. 1923. 'A Mournful Lamentation of the Sad and Deplorable Death of Mr. Old Tenor. 31st March, 1750', in *The Magazine of History With Notes and Queries* (Extra Number 90, Reprint). New York: William Abbatt.

Grimarest, Jean Léonor Le Gallois de. 1707, 2001. *Traité du recitative*. Paris: Le Fèvre in Chaouche, Sabine (ed.). *Sept traités sur le jeu du comédien et autres textes, de l'action oratoire à l'art dramatique (1657-1750)*. Reprint, Paris: Champion.

Hegel, George Wilhelm Friedrich. 1835, 1975. *Aesthetics: Lectures on Fine Art* Vol II (tr. T.M. Knox). Oxford: Clarendon Press.

Hirsch, Andreas. 1662, 1988. *Philosophischer Extract und Auszug aus deß Welt-berühmten Teutschen Jesuitens Athanasii Kircheri von Fulda Musurgia Universali*. Kassel: Bärenreiter-Antiquariat.

Kellogg, Clara Louise. 1913. *Memoirs of an American Prima Donna*. New York and London: G. P. Putnam's Sons.

Kircher, Athanasius. 1650. *Musurgia universalis sive ars magna consoni et dissoni*. Rome: Ex typographia Haeredum Francisci.

——1650.1995. "Musurgia Universalis. Ex Libro VII" (tr. B. Blackburn and L. Holford-Stevens) in *The Perfect Musician*. Special issue of *Practica Musica* 3: 64-7.

Lacan, Jacques. 1981. 'Les Psychoses' in *Le Séminaire. Livre 11*. Paris: Le Seuil.

Lachenmann, Helmut. 2002. 'Sounds are Natural Phenomena'. Excerpt from an interview with Klaus Zehelein and Hans Thomalia in liner notes to *Das Madchen mit den Schwefelholzern*. Staatsoper Stuttgart, cond. Lothar Zagrosek. Kairos. CD No. 0012282KAI.

——2008. 'Musique Concrète Instrumentale: Helmut Lachenmann, in conversation with Gene Coleman'. 7 April 2008. http://www.slought.org/content/11401/ (consulted 28.12.2010).

Le Cerf de la Viéville, Jean-Laurent. 1705, 1972. *Comparaison de la musique italienne et de la musique françoise*. Bruxelles: François Foppens / Reprint Genève: Minkoff.

Le Faucheur, Michel. 1657, 2001. *Traité de l'action de l'orateur ou de la prononciation et du geste* (Paris: A. Courbé) in Chaouche, Sabine (ed.). *Sept traités sur le jeu du comédien et autres textes. De l'action oratoire à l'art dramatique (1657-1750)*. Reprint, Paris: Champion.

Lloyd Webber, Andrew and Charles Hart. 1987. *The Phantom of the Opera*. London: Cameron Mackintosh and the Really Useful Theatre Company Ltd. Reprint editions of score through Hal Leonard, Milwaukee.

Ludlam, Charles. 2001. *The Mystery of Irma Vep and Other Plays*. New York: Theatre Communications Group.

Mann, Thomas. 1947, 1968. *Doctor Faustus* (tr. H. T. Lowe Porter). Harmondsworth: Penguin.

——1967, 1985. *Pro and Contra Wagner* (tr. A. Blunden). London: Faber and Faber, 1985.

Marinetti, Filippo. 1909-1933, 1971. *Selected Writings* (ed. and tr. R.W. Flint). New York: Farrar, Straus and Giroux.

Maugars, André. 1639, 1993. *Response faite à un curieux sur le sentiment de la musique d'Italie*. Lille: Cahiers GKC-La Musique éloquente.

Mersenne, Marin. 1636, 1986. *Harmonie universelle*. Paris: CNRS.

Metz, Christian. 1974. *Film Language* (tr. M. Taylor). New York: Oxford University Press.

——1982. *The Imaginary Signifier: Psychoanalysis and the Cinema* (tr. B. Brewster). Bloomington: Indiana University Press.

Monteverdi, Claudio. 1607, 1968. *L'Orfeo: favola in musica for soloists, chorus and orchestra* (ed. D. Stevens). London: Novello.

——1638, 1967. *Madrigali guerrieri, et amorosi. Libro ottavo* (Venetia 1638) in *Tutte le opere di Claudio Monteverdi* (ed. G. Francesco Malipiero), Vienna: Universal Edition.

——1642, 1967. *L'Incoronazione di Poppea* in *Tutte le opere di Claudio Monteverdi* (ed. G. Francesco Malipiero), Vienna: Universal Edition.

n.a. 'Relation des opera, representez à Venise pendant le Carnaval de l'année 1683' in *Mercure Galant*. March 1683. 243-245.

Neuwirth, Olga. 2003. 'Laughter. An exceptional state'. Liner notes to *Bählamms Fest* (Kairos). CD No. 0012342KAI.

Nietzsche, Friedrich. 1872, 1967. *The Birth of Tragedy*. (tr. W. Kaufmann). New York: Vintage Books.

——1886, 1986. *Human all Too Human: A Book for Free Spirits* (tr. R.J Hollingdale). Cambridge: Cambridge University Press.

——1889-1895, 1998. *Twilight of the Idols* (1889) *and The Anti-Christ* (1895). (tr. R. J. Hollingdale). London: Penguin.

——1899. *The Case of Wagner, Nietzsche Contra Wagner, The Twilight of the Idols, The Anti-Christ* (tr. Thomas Common). London: T. Fisher Unwin.

Obama, Barack. 2008. 'Barack Obama's New Hampshire Primary Speech'. Online at: http://www.nytimes.com/2008/01/08/us/politics/08text-obama.html?pagewanted=all&_r=0 (consulted 20.1.13).

Pavarotti, Luciano and William Wright. 1995. *My World*. London: Random House.

Purcell, Henry. 1689, 1889. *The Works of Henry Purcell*, Volume 3 – *Dido and Aeneas* ed. under the supervision of the Purcell Society (ed. W.H. Cummings). London: Novello.

Quantz, Johann Joachim. 1752. *Essai d'une méthode pour apprendre à jouer de la flûte traversière*. Berlin: C. F. Voss.

Raguenet, François. 1702. *Parallele des Italiens et des François en ce qui regarde la Musique et les Opéra*. Paris: J. Moreau.

Rancière, Jacques. 2000. *Le Partage du sensible*. Paris: La Fabrique.

——2009. *The Emancipated Spectator* (tr. G. Elliot). London: Verso.

Reich, Steve and Beryl Korot. 1998-2002. 'Three Tales: a documentary digital video opera'. Online at: http://www.stevereich.com/threetales_info.html (consulted 30.11.2011).

Rochemont de. 1754. *Réflexions d'un patriote sur l'opéra français, et sur l'opéra italien*. Lausanne

'Royal Opera House Muscat'. Online at http://www.rohmuscat.org.om/venue (consulted 28.10.2012).

Russolo, Luigi. 1913, 1973. 'The Art of Noises' in Apollonio, Umbro (ed.) *Futurist Manifestos*. Boston: MFA Publications.

Saint-Évremond, Charles Marguetel de Saint-Denis. 1677, 1990. 'Lettre sur les Opera' in *Œuvres Meslées*, (Vol. 11). Cambridge, Massachusetts: Omnisys.

——1676, 1979. *Les Opera*. Genève: Droz.

——1969. 'Eclaircissement sur ce qu'on a dit de la Musique des Italiens' in *Œuvres en prose*. Paris: Didier.

Schoenberg, Arnold. 1975. 'Mechanical Musical Instruments' in Stein, Leonard (ed.). *Arnold Schoenberg, Style and Idea: Selected Writings of Arnold Schoenberg* (tr. L. Black). London: Faber and Faber.

Schwarzkopf, Elisabeth. 1982. *On and Off the Record: A Memoir of Walter Legge*. London: Faber and Faber.

Shaw, George Bernard. 1932. *Music in London 1890-94* (Vols I-III). London: Constable.

——1937, 1950. *London Music In 1888-89 As Heard by Corno di Bassetto (Later Known As Bernard Shaw) With Some Further Autobiographical Particulars*. London: Constable.

Tetrazzini, Luisa. 1921. *My Life of Song*. London: Cassell.

Turner, Victor. 1986. 'Betwixt and Between: The Liminal Period in Rites de Passage' in *The Forest of Symbols*. Ithaca: Cornell University Press.

Vigarello, Georges. 1985. *Le Propre et le Sale*. Paris: Seuil.

Wagner, Cosima. 1878-1883, 1977. *Die Tagebücher—Volume 2* (ed. Martin Gregor-Dellin and Dietrich Mack). Munich: R. Piper and Co.

Wagner, Richard. 1849, 1993. 'The Art-Work of the Future' in *Richard Wagner, The Art-Work of the Future, and other works* (tr. W. Ashton Ellis). Lincoln and London: University of Nebraska Press.

——1851. 1995. *Opera and Drama* (tr. W. Ashton Ellis). Lincoln and London: University of Nebraska Press.

——1871. 1995. *Actors and Singers* (tr. W. Ashton Ellis). Lincoln and London: University of Nebraska Press.

Waltz, Sasha and Attilio Cremonesi. 2005. 'Liebe in Zeiten des Krieges': Sasha Waltz und Attilio Cremonesi im Gespräch mit Caroline Emcke' in *Staatsoper Unter den Linden* (prod.). *Dido & Aeneas*. Programme Booklet for premiere. 19 February 2005. Berlin Staatsoper Unter den Linden.

Young, Kirsty and Ian McMillan. 2010. 'Ian McMillan' on *Desert Island Discs*. Online at:
http://www.bbc.co.uk/radio4/features/desert-island-discs/castaway/89df5dc8#b00vr9l2 (consulted 20.1.13).

Žižek, Slavoj. 1996. ' "I Hear You with My Eyes"; or The Invisible Master' in Salecl, Renata and Slavoj Žižek (eds.). *Gaze and Voice as Love Objects*. Durham: Duke University Press: 90-128.

SECONDARY REFERENCES

Abbate, Carolyn. 1991. *Unsung Voices—Opera and Musical Narrative in the Nineteenth Century*. New Jersey: Princeton University Press.

——2001. *In Search of Opera*. Princeton: Princeton University Press.

——2004. 'Music—Drastic or Gnostic?' in *Critical Inquiry* 30(3): 505-536.

Abel, Samuel D. 1996. *Opera in the Flesh: Sexuality in Operatic Performances*. Boulder: Westview.

Agid, Philippe and Jean-Claude Tarondeau (eds.). 2010. *The Management of Opera: an International Comparative Study*. Basingstoke: Palgrave Macmillan.

Albert, Annibale (ed.) 1931. *Verdi intimo: Carteggio di Giuseppe Verdi con il conte Opprandino Arrivabene, 1861-1886*. Milan: Mondadori.

Allegue, Ludivine *et al* (eds.) 2009. *Practice-as-Research in Performance and Screen*. London: Palgrave Macmillan.

Ardoin, John. 1987. *Callas at Juilliard: The Master Classes*. New York: Alfred A. Knopf.

Arnold, Denis and Nigel Fortune (eds.). 1985. *The New Monteverdi Companion*. London and Boston: Faber and Faber.

Aufricht, Ernst Josef. 1966. *Erzähle, damit du dein Recht erweist*. Berlin: Propylän Verlag.

Auslander, Philip. 1999. *Liveness. Performance in a Mediatized Culture*. London and New York: Routledge.

Balme, Christopher. 2001. 'Pierrot encadré. Zur Kategorie der Rahmung als Bestimmungsfaktor medialer Reflexivität' in Leeker, Martina (ed.). *Maschinen, Medien, Performances. Theater an der Schnittstelle zu digitalen Welten*. Berlin: Alexander.

——2004. 'Intermediality: Rethinking the Relationship between Theatre and Media'. Online at:
http://epub.ub.uni-muenchen.de/13098/1/Balme_13098.pdf (consulted 18.01.2013).

Barnes, Jennifer. 2003. *Television Opera: The Fall of Opera Commissioned for Television.* Woodbridge: Boydell and Brewer.

Barrett, Estelle and Barbara Bolt (eds.). 2007. *Practice as Research: Approaches to Creative Arts Enquiry.* London and New York: I. B. Tauris.

Bentley, Eric (ed.). 1964. *The Threepenny Opera.* New York: Grove Press.

Birringer, Johannes. 1991. *Theatre, Theory, Postmodernism.* Bloomington: Indiana University Press.

Blue, Robert W. 2002. 'The Operas of Mikel Rouse: Dennis Cleveland downtown opera comes uptown'. Online at: http://usoperaweb.com/2002/april/rouse/htm (consulted 12.04.05).

Bonardi, Alain and Francis Rousseaux. 2002. 'Composing an Interactive Virtual Opera: The "Virtualis" Project' in *Leonardo* 35(3): 315-318.

Bordwell, David and Noël Carroll (eds). 1996. *Post-Theory: Reconstructing Film Studies.* Madison: University of Wisconsin Press.

Breslin, Herbert and Anne Midgette. 2004. *The King & I—The Uncensored Tale of Luciano Pavarotti's Rise to Fame by his Manager, Friend and Sometime Adversary.* Edinburgh: Mainstream.

Broadhurst, Susan. 1999. *Liminal Acts—A Critical Overview of Contemporary Performance and Theory.* London and New York: Cassel.

Brodsky, Seth. 2008. 'Helmut Lachenmann (1935-); DEU'. Online at: http://www.classicalarchives.com/composer/20003.html#tvf=tracks&tv=about (consulted 20.10.2011).

Bürger, Peter. 1982. *Theorie der Avantgarde.* Frankfurt: Suhrkamp Verlag.

Busch, Hans (ed.). 1978. *Verdi's Aida: The History of an Opera in Letters and Documents.* Minneapolis: University of Minnesota Press.

Butler, Judith. 1993. *Bodies that Matter.* London: Routledge.

Calcagno, Mauro. 2002. ' "Imitar col canto chi parla': Monteverdi and the Creation of a Language for Musical Theater' in *Journal of the American Musicological Society* 55(3): 383-41.

Cascardi, Anthony J. 1992. *The Subject of Modernity.* Cambridge: Cambridge University Press.

Celli, Teodoro. 1959. 'Great Artists of Our Time: 1. Maria Meneghini Callas' in *The Saturday Review* 42(5): 40-44, 60-63. (31 January 1959).

Celletti, Rodolfo. 1969, 1987. 'The Callas Debate' in Lowe, David A (ed.) *Callas As They Saw Her.* London: Robson.

Chapple, Freda and Chiel Kattenbelt (eds.) 2006. *Intermediality in Theatre and Performance* (2nd ed.). Amsterdam and New York: Rodopi.

Chion, Michel. 1982. *La Voix au Cinema.* Paris: Cahiers du Cinema.

Christiansen, Rupert. 2002. 'Karaoke on a Grand Scale' in *The Daily Telegraph*, 8 April 2002. Online at: http://www.telegraph.co.uk/culture/4727627/Karaoke-on-a-grand-scale.html (consulted 3.12.11).

Christiansen, Svend. 1975. *Klassisk skuespilkunst: Stabile konventioner i skuespilkunsten 1700-1900.* Copenhagen: Akademisk forlag.

Clements, Andrew. 1998. 'Music Theatre' in Sadie, Stanley (ed.). *The New Grove Dictionary of Opera—Volume 3.* London: Macmillan.

——2001. 'Music theatre' in Sadie, Stanley (ed.). *New Grove Dictionary of Music and Musicians* (2nd ed.). London: Macmillan.

Cone, John Frederick. 1981. *Adelina Patti: Queen of Hearts.* Portland, Oregon: Amadeus Press.

Cook, Nicholas. 1998. *Analysing Musical Multimedia*. Oxford: Oxford University Press.

Cooke, Mervyn. 2008. *A History of Film Music*. New York: Cambridge University Press.

Corse, Sandra. 1990. *Wagner and the New Consciousness: Language and Love in the Ring*. London and Toronto: Associated University Presses.

——2000. *Operatic Subjects: The Evolution of Self in Modern Opera* London and Toronto: Associated University Presses.

Cox, John. 1973. 'Preface' in Goehr, Alexander. *Naboth's Vineyard*. London: Schott.

Cremona, Vicky Ann et al. (eds.). *Theatrical Events*. Amsterdam: Rodopi.

Croft, John. 2009. 'Fields of Rubble: On the Poetics of Music after the Postmodern' in Heile, Björn (ed.). *The Modernist Legacy: Essays on New Music*. Farnham: Ashgate.

Csampai, Attila and Dietmar Holland (eds.). 1987. *Bertolt Brecht/Kurt Weill. Die Dreigroschenoper*. Reinbek bei Hamburg: Rohwohlt.

Cummings, Laurence. 2006. Programme notes. *L'Orfeo*. London: English National Opera.

Daiken, Melanie. 1980. 'Notes on Goehr's *Triptych*' in Northcott, Bayan (ed.). *The Music of Alexander Goehr*. London: Schott.

Dammann, Rolf. 1995. *Der Musikbegriff im deutschen Barock*. Laaber: Laaber-Verlag.

Dandrey, Patrick. 1990. 'La Phoniscopie, c'est-à-dire la science de la voix' in *La Voix au XVIIe siècle (Littératures classiques)* 12: 25-39.

De Boer, Aukje et al (eds.). 2009. *Turks Theater Bestaat Niet—Interviews met Turkse theatermakers en anderen*. Utrecht: Kunstfactor.

Dell, Matthias. "Minus + Minus = Plus". Interview with Shermin Langhoff.

Der Freitag. 30 July 2009. Online at: http://www.freitag.de/autoren/der-freitag/minus-minus-plus (consulted 20.11.2012).

Douglas, Nigel. 1992. *Legendary Voices*. London: Deutsch.

——1994. *More Legendary Voices*. London: Deutsch.

Duncan, Michelle. 2004. 'The Operatic Scandal of the Singing Body: Voice, Presence, Performativity' in *Cambridge Opera Journal*. 16(3): 283-306.

Dunn, Leslie C. and Nancy A Jones. (eds.). 1994. *Embodied Voices—Representing Female Vocality in Western Culture*. Cambridge: Cambridge University Press.

Elias, Norbert. 1973. *La Civilisation des mœurs*. Paris, Pocket Agora.

Fassmann, Kurt. 1958. *Brecht, eine Bildbiografie*. Munich: Kindler Verlag.

Fearn, Raymond. 1997. *Italian Opera Since 1945*. London: Routledge.

Feral, Josette. 2002. 'Foreword' in *SubStance* 31(2-3): 3-13.

Finter, Helga. 1997. 'Antonin Artaud and the Impossible Theatre. The Legacy of the Theatre of Cruelty' in *The Drama Review* 41(4): 15-40.

Fink, Robert. 1999. 'Going Flat: Post-Hierarchical Music Theory and the Musical Surface' in Cook, Nicholas and Everist, Mark (eds.). *Rethinking Music*. Oxford: Oxford University Press.

Fischer, Erik. 1999. ' "Die Oper". Der problematische Anweg zum Problem ihrer gattungstheoretischen Definition' in Bayerdoerfer, Hans-Peter (ed.). *Musiktheater als Herausforderung. Interdisziplinäre Facetten von Theater- und Musikwissenschaft*. Tuebingen: Niemeyer.

Fischer-Lichte, Erika. 1995. 'From Theatre to Theatricality. How to Construct Reality' in *Theatre Research International* 20(2): 97-105.

——2004. *Ästhetik des Performativen*. Frankfurt: Edition Suhrkamp.

——and Jens Roselt. 2001. 'Attraktion des Augenblicks—Aufführung, Performance, performativ und Performativität als theatrewissenschaftliche Begriffe' in *Paragrana* 10(1): 237-254.

——et al. 2005. *Diskurse des Theatralen*. Tübingen and Basel: A. Francke Verlag.

Flaßpöhler, Svenja, Tobias Rausch and Christina Wald (eds.). 2007. *Kippfiguren der Wiederholung: interdisziplinäre Untersuchungen zur Figur der Wiederholung in Literatur, Kunst und Wissenschaft*. Frankfurt: Peter Lang.

Fleck, Stefan. 2008. 'Die Dreigroschen Drehorgel' in *Das Mechanische Musikinstrument* 102: 22-32.

Fleeger, Jennifer Lynn. 2009. 'Opera, Jazz, and Hollywood's conversion to Sound'. PhD thesis. Iowa City: University of Iowa.Freeman, John. 2010. *Blood, Sweat and Theory: Research through Performance*. Faringdon: Libri.

Frith, Simon.1996. 'Music and Identity' in Hall, Stuart and Du Gay, Paul (eds.). *Questions of Cultural Identity*. London: SAGE Publications.

——1996. *Performing Rites: Evaluating Popular Music*. Oxford: Oxford University Press.

——2000. 'The Discourse of World Music' in Born, Georgina and Hesmondhalgh, David (eds.). *Western Music and its Others*. Berkeley: University of California Press.

——2004. 'What is Bad Music?' in Washburne, Christopher and Derno, Maiken (eds.). *Bad Music: The Music We Love to Hate*. New York: Routledge.

Fuegi, John. 1994. *The Life and Lies of Bertolt Brecht*. London: HarperCollins.

Galatopoulos, Stelios. 1976. *Callas: Prima Donna Assoluta*. London: Howard and Wyndham.

Garber, Marjorie. 1992. *Vested Interests*. New York, Routledge.

Goebbels, Heiner. 2002. 'Gegen das Gesamtkunstwerk. Zur Differenz der Künste' in Sandner, Wofgang (ed.). *Heiner Goebbels. Komposition als Inszenierung*. Berlin: Henschel.

——2004a. 'Performance as Composition. Heiner Goebbels interviewed by Stathis Gourgouris' in *PAJ—A Journal of Performance and Art* 26(78): 1-16.

——2004b. *Eraritjaritjaka. Musée des phrases*, based on texts of Elias Canetti. Online at http://www.heinergoebbels.com/en/archive/texts/material/read/533 (consulted 18.01.2013).

——2007. 'Manches merkt man sich bloß, weil es mit nichts zusammenhängt". Fragen beim Bau von Eraritjaritjaka' in Lechtermann, C., K. Wagner and H. Wenzel (eds.). *Möglichkeitsräume—Zur Performativität von sensorischer Wahrnehmung*. Berlin: Erich Schmidt Verlag.

——2012. '"It's all part of one concern". A "keynote" to composition as staging' in Rebstock, Matthias and David Roesner (eds.). *Composed Theatre. Aesthetics, Processes, Practices*. Bristol: Intellect.

Goldmark, Daniel, Lawrence Kramer and Richard Leppert (eds.). 2007. *Beyond the Soundtrack: Representing Music in Cinema*. Berkeley: University of California Press.

Gorbman, Claudia. 1987. *Unheard Melodies: Narrative Film Music*. London: BFI Publishing.

Grey, Thomas S. 2008. 'Leitmotif, temporality and musical design in *The Ring*' in Grey, Thomas (ed.). *The Cambridge Companion to Wagner*. Cambridge: Cambridge University Press.

Grover-Friedlander, Michal. 1999. '"The Phantom of the Opera": the Lost Voice of Opera in Silent Film' in *Cambridge Opera Journal* 11(2): 179-192.

Gualerzi, Giorgio.1986. 'The Divine Claudia' in *Opera* 37: 643–51.

Günther, Renate. 2002. *Marguerite Duras*. Manchester and New York: Manchester University Press.

Hatten, R. S. 1994. *Musical Meaning in Beethoven: Markedness, Correlation and Interpretation*. Bloomington: Indiana University Press.

Hayles, Katherine. 1999. *How We Became Posthuman: Virtual Bodies in Cybernetics, Literature and Informatics*. Chicago: University of Chicago Press.

Hegarty, Paul. 2003. 'Residue—Margin—Other: Noise as Ethics of Excess'. Online at: http://www.dotdotdotmusic.com/hegarty1.html (consulted 20.01.2011).

Heile, Björn. 2006. 'Recent Approaches to experimental music theatre and contemporary opera' in *Music and Letters* 87(1): 72–81.

Henderson, William J. 1938, 1968. *The Art of Singing*. Freeport, New York: Books for Libraries Press.

Herbert-Caesari. Edgar. 1958. *Tradition and Gigli, 1600-1955—A Panegyric.* London: Hale.

——1978. *The Voice of the Mind.* New York: Crescendo.

Heriot, Angus. 1974. *The Castrati in Opera.* New York: Da Capo Press.

Hewett, Ivan. 2002. 'Review of *Vampyrotheone; Instrumental-Inseln aus 'Bählamms Fest'; Hooloomooloo* by Olga Neuwirth' in *Tempo* 222: 36-38.

Hinton, Stephen (ed.). 1990. *Kurt Weill and The Threepenny Opera*. Cambridge: Cambridge University Press.

Hiss (Hiß), Guido. 2005. *Synthetische Visionen: Theater als Gesamtkunstwerk von 1800 bis 2000*. Munich: Epodium.

Jacobshagen, Arnold (ed.). 2002. *Praxis Musiktheater: Ein Handbuch*. Laaber Verlag.

Jahn, Hans-Peter. 2000. 'Shade Eaters: Through the Deserts of Salvatore Sciarrino's Music' (tr. C. Lindner). Sleeve notes to *Lo spazio inverso* by Salvatore Sciarrino (Kairos 0012132KAI).

Jellinek, George. 1960. *Callas: Portrait of a Prima Donna*. New York: Ziff-Davis Publishing.

Jelavich, Peter. 1993. *Berlin Cabaret*. Cambridge, Massachusetts: Harvard University Press.

Jesse, Horst. 1996. *Brecht in Berlin*. Munich: Verlag Das Freie Buch.

Joe, Jeongwon. 1998. 'Hans-Jürgen Syberberg's *Parsifal*: The Staging of Dissonance in the Fusion of Opera and Film' in *Music Research Forum* 13: 1-21.

——and Rose M. Theresa (eds.) 2002. *Between Opera and Cinema*. New York: Routledge.

—— 2013 (forthcoming). *Opera as Soundtrack.* Farnham: Ashgate.

Kahn, Douglas. 2001. *Noise Water Meat—A History of Sound in the Arts*. Cambridge, Massachusetts: MIT.

Kaiser, Michael. 2011. 'The Royal Opera House Muscat' in *The Huffington Post*, 11 October. Online at: http://www.huffingtonpost.com/michael-kaiser/the-royal-opera-house-mus_b_1004713.html (consulted 28.01.2013).

Karantonis, Pamela, et al (eds.) (forthcoming). *Cathy Berberian: Pioneer of Contemporary Vocality.* Farnham: Ashgate.

Kendrick, Lynne and David Roesner. 2011. *Theatre Noise: The Sound of Performance.* Newcastle Upon Tyne: Cambridge Scholars Publishing.

Kerman, Joseph. 1956. *Opera as Drama*. New York: Alfred A. Knopf.

Kershaw, Baz. 2007. *Theatre Ecology: Environments and Performance Events.* Cambridge: Cambridge University Press.

Kesting, Jürgen. 1986. *Die grossen Sänger I-III.* Düsseldorf: Claassen.

——1992. *Maria Callas* (tr. J. Hunt). London: Quartet Books.

Kesting, Marianne. 1996. *Bertolt Brecht* (Danish tr. I. Christensen). København: Gyldendal.

Kintzler, Catherine. 1991. *Poétique de l'opéra français de Corneille à Rousseau.* Paris: Minerve.

Kirby, Michael and Richard Schechner. 1995. 'An Interview with John Cage' in Sandford, Mariellen R. (ed.). *Happenings and Other Acts.* London and New York: Routledge.

Kirk, Elise K. 2001. *American Opera* (Music in American Life). Urbana: University of Illinois Press.

Kirle, Bruce. 2005. *Unfinished Show Business: Broadway Musicals as Works-in-Process.* Carbondale: Southern Illinois University Press.

Klein, Herman. 1903. *Thirty Years of Musical Life in London, 1870-1900.* New York: Century.

——1920. *The Reign of Patti.* London: T. Fisher Unwin.

——1931. *Great Women-Singers of My Time.* London: Routledge.

Knapp, Raymond. 2005. '"Selbst dann bin ich die Welt": On the Subjective-Musical Basis of Wagner's "Gesamtkunstwelt"' in *19th-Century Music* 29(2): 142-160.

Koestenbaum, Wayne. 1993. *The Queens' Throat—Opera, Homosexuality and the Mystery of Desire.* London: Penguin.

Kömürcü Nobrega and Suzan Onur. 2011. "We Bark from the Third Row: Berlin's Cultural Landscape and the Funding of Cultural Diversity Work" in *Jahrbuch Türkisch-deutsche Studien* (2): 91-112.

Kramer, Lawrence. 2002. *Musical Meaning: Towards a Critical History.* Berkeley, Los Angeles and London: University of California Press.

Krämer, Sybille. 1998. 'Form als Vollzug oder: Was gewinnen wir mit Niklas Luhmanns Unterscheidung von Medium und Form?' in *Rechtshistorisches Journal* 8(17): 558-73.

Lawrence, Amy. 1991. *Echo and Narcissus: Women's Voices in Classical Hollywood Cinema.* Berkeley, University of California Press.

Lebrecht, Norman. 2001. 'How to Kill Classical Music' in *The Daily Telegraph* (5 December 2001).

Lehmann, Hans-Thies. 1997. 'From Logos to Landscape: Text in Contemporary Dramaturgy' in *Performance Research* 2.1: 55-60. New York: Routledge.

——2006. *Post-dramatic Theatre* (tr. K. Jürs-Munby). Abingdon: Routledge.

Levin, David. (ed.) 1994. *Opera Through Other Eyes.* Stanford: Stanford University Press.

Lindenberger, Herbert. 1984. *Opera: The Extravagant Art.* Cornell: Cornell University Press.

Lister, David. 2011. 'The Week in Arts—Upstaged by the Ghost of Pavarotti' in *The Independent* (30 July 2011).

Louvat-Molozay, Bénédicte. 2002. *Théâtre et musique—Dramaturgie de l'insertion musicale dans le théâtre français 1550-1680.* Paris: Champion.

Lowe, David A (ed.) 1987. *Callas As They Saw Her.* London: Robson.

Luzio, Alessandro (ed.) 1947. *Carteggi verdiani I-IV.* Rome: Accademia nazionale dei lincei.

Mackendrick, Alexander. 2004. *On Film-making: An Introduction to the Craft of the Director* (ed. Paul Cronin). New York: Faber and Faber.

Maguire, Jan. 1968. 'Callas, Serafin, and the Art of Bel Canto' in *The Saturday Review* 51(3): 47-9.

Matheopoulos, Helena. 1986. *Bravo—Today's Great Tenors, Baritones and Basses Discuss their Roles*. London: Weidenfeld and Nicolson.

Matthews, Peter. 2000. 'Review of Dancer in the Dark' in *Sight and Sound*. Online at: http://old.bfi.org.uk/sightandsound/review/339 (consulted 18.01.2013).

McClary, Susan. 1991. *Feminine Endings: Music, Gender and Sexuality*. Minneapolis and London: Minnesota University Press.

McCullough, Christopher. (ed.) 1998. *Theatre Praxis: Teaching Drama through Practice*. London: Palgrave Macmillan.

McMillin, Scott. 2006. *The Musical as Drama*. Princeton: Princeton University Press.

Merlin-Kajman, Hélène. 1994. *Public et littérature en France au XVIIe siècle*. Paris: Les Belles lettres.

Michaels, Bianca. 2006. 'Opera for the Media Age: Composer Robert Ashley on Television Opera' in *Opera Quarterly* 22 (3-4): 534-537.

Michaels, Sean. 2010. 'Cage Against the Machine: pop stars to stage silent X Factor protest' in *The Guardian* (6 December 2010). Online at: http://www.guardian.co.uk/music/2010/dec/06/cage-against-machine-x-factor (consulted 18.11.2011).

Miller, Richard. 1997. *National Schools of Singing: English, French, German and Italian Techniques of Singing Revisited* (Revised edition). Lanham: Scarecrow Press.

Monaldi, Gino. 1929. *Cantanti celebri (1829-1929)*. Rome: Edizione Tiber.

Morris, Christopher. 2010. 'Digital Diva: Opera on Video' in *Opera Quarterly* 26(1): 96-119.

Murray, Kathleen. 2003. 'Beyond Genre. Towards a Playful Grammar of Musicals'. Online at: http://beard.dialnsa.edu/~treis/pdf/Towards%20a%20Playful%20Grammar%20of%20Musicals.pdf (consulted 28.02.2006).

n.a. 2004. "The Cruel and Crazy World of Lars von Trier" *New Zealand Herald* 4 May 2004. http://www.nzherald.co.nz/lifestyle/news/article.cfm?c_id=6&objectid=35646 72 (consulted 18.01.2013)

Nicholls, David. 1998. 'Ava++nt-garde and experimental music' in Nicholls, David (ed.). *The Cambridge History of American Music*. Cambridge: Cambridge University Press.

Paech, Joachim. 1997. 'Paradoxien der Auflösung und Intermedialität' in Warnke, Martin, et al (eds.). *HyperKult. Geschichte, Theorie und Kontext digitaler Medien*. Basel and Frankfurt: Stroemfeld / Nexus.

Pamuk, Orhan. 2005. *Istanbul: Memories and the City*. London: Faber and Faber.

Parker, Roger. 1998. 'On Reading Nineteenth-Century Opera: Verdi through the Looking-Glass' in Groos, Arthur and Parker, Roger (eds.). *Reading Opera*. Princeton: Princeton University Press.

Pavis, Patrice. 1980. 'Voix' in *Dictionnaire du théâtre: termes et concepts de l'analyse théâtrale*. Paris: Editions Sociales.

Pirrotta, Nino. 1982. *Music and Theatre from Poliziano to Monteverdi* (Cambridge Studies in Music). Cambridge: University of Cambridge Press.

Poizat, Michel. 1986. *The Angel's Cry: Beyond the Pleasure Principle in Opera* (tr. A. Denner). Ithaca and London: Cornell University Press.

Porter, Andrew and David Rosen. 1984. *Verdi's Macbeth: A Sourcebook*. Cambridge: Cambridge University Press.

Potter, John (ed.). 2000. *The Cambridge Companion to Singing*. Cambridge: Cambridge University Press.

Quignard, Pascal. 1987. *La Leçon de musique*. Paris: Hachette.

———1996 *La Haine de la musique*. Paris: Calmann-Lévy.

Rajewsky, Irina. 2002. *Intermedialität*. Tübingen and Basel: UTB.

Rasponi, Lanfranco. 1984. *The Last Prima Donnas*. London: Victor Gollancz.

Rebellato, Dan. 2009. ' "No Theatre Guild Attraction Are We": *Kiss Me, Kate* and the politics of the integrated musical'. *Contemporary Theatre Review* 19(1): 61-73.

Rebstock, Matthias and David Roesner (eds.). 2012. *Composed Theatre: Aesthetics, Practices, Processes*. Bristol: Intellect.

'REF Expert Advisory Groups'. 2010. London: Higher Education Funding Council for England. Online at: http://www.hefce.ac.uk/research/ref/resources/Summary_EAG_mgs.pdf (consulted 17.11.2011).

Reinelt, Janelle. 2002. 'The Politics of Discourse: Performativity meets Theatricality' in *SubStance* 31(2-3): 201-215.

Restagno, Enzo. 2002. (ed.). *Omaggio a Salvatore Sciarrino*. Torino: Divisione Servizi Culturali della Città di Torino.

Richards, John B. 1968. 'Claudia Muzio' in *The Record Collector* 17(9): 196-239.

Riley, Shannon Rose and Lynette Hunter (eds.). 2009. *Mapping Landscapes for Performance as Research: Scholarly Acts and Creative Cartographies*. Basingstoke: Palgrave Macmillan.

Risi, Clemens. 2005. 'The Operatic Stage as an Experimental Space for Affections. About the Concepts of Affections Asserted by Athanasius Kircher and Claudio Monteverdi' in Helmar Schramm, Ludger Schwarte and Jan Lazardzig (eds.). *Collection—Laboratory—Theater. Scenes of Knowledge in the 17th Century*. Berlin: Walter de Gruyer.

———2007. 'Erfahrung des Heiligen in der Oper? Zur religiösen Dimension der Affektdarstellung und -übertragung im Musiktheater des frühen 17. Jahrhunderts' in Ingrid Kasten and Erika Fischer-Lichte (eds.). *Transformationen des Religiösen. Performativität und Textualität im geistlichen Spiel*. Berlin and New York: Walter de Gruyter.

Roesner, David. 2010a. 'Musicking as mise en scène' in *Studies in Musical Theatre* 4(1): 89-102.

———2010b. 'Musicality as a paradigm for the theatre—a kind of manifesto' in *Studies in Musical Theatre* 4(3): 293-306.

Şahin, Nevin. 2009. *Contested Belongings: Understanding the Meaning of Turkish Classical Music Among Young Women in Germany*. PhD Thesis. Middle East Technical University. September, 2009.

Salzman, Eric and Thomas Desi. 2008. *The New Music Theater: Seeing the Voice, Hearing the Body*. New York and Oxford: Oxford University Press.

Sandner, Wolfgang. (ed.). 2002. *Heiner Goebbels. Komposition als Inszenierung*. Berlin: Henschel.

Savage, Karen 2010. 'Fading—Feminism—Practice—Process: the fade as a "cite" for feminine écriture'. PhD thesis. Portsmouth: University of Portsmouth.

——and Dominic Symonds. 2010. 'Projecting the voice: stages of intermediality'. Paper presented at *Song, Stage and Screen V*. (University of Winchester, 3-5 September 2010).

Scharlau, Ulf. 1969. *Athanasius Kircher (1601-1680) als Musikschriftsteller. Ein Beitrag zur Musikanschauung des Barock (Studien zur hessischen Musikgeschichte 2)*. Kassel: Bärenreiter-Antiquariat.

Schepelern, Peter. 2005. 'Film according to Dogma: Ground Rules, Obstacles, and Liberations' (tr. R. Christensen) in Nestingen, Andrew and Elkington, Trevor G. (eds.). *Transnational Cinema in a Global North: Nordic Cinema in Transition*. Detroit: Wayne State University Press.

Schneider, Rebecca. 2001. 'Archives—Performance Remains' in *Performance Research* 6(2): 100-7.

Schröter, Jens. n.d. 'Intermedialität'. Online at: http://www.theorie-der-medien.de/text_detail.php?nr=12 (consulted 14.12.2010).

——2002. 'Intermedialität, Medienspezifik und die universelle Maschine'. Online at: http://www.theorie-der-medien.de/text_druck.php?nr=46 (consulted 14.12.2010).

Sciarrino, Salvatore. 1981. 'L'impossibità di divenire invisibili'. Programme notes to *Vanitas*. Milan: Piccola Scala.

——2001. *Carte da Suono*. Rome: CIDIM and Palermo: Novecento.

Senelick, Laurence. 2000. *The Changing Room—Sex, Drag and Theatre*. London: Routledge.

Sheppard, William Anthony. 2001. *Revealing Masks: Exotic Influences and Ritualized Performance in Modernist Music Theater*. Berkeley: University of California Press.

Silverman, Kaja. 1988. *Acoustic Mirror: The Female Voice in Psychoanalysis and Cinema*. Bloomington: Indiana University Press.

Sjogren, Britta. 2006. *Into the Vortex: Female Voice and Paradox in Film*. Urbana and Chicago: University of Illinois Press.

Smith, Hazel and Roger T. Dean (eds.). 2010. *Practice-Led Research, Research-Led Practice in the Creative Arts*. Edinburgh: Edinburgh University Press.

Smith, Steve. 2011. 'A Fresh Stamp on a Veteran Composer's Work'. Online at: http://www.nytimes.com/2011/11/09/arts/music/robert-ashleys-legacy-assessed.html?_r=1 (consulted 30.11.2011).

Szondi, Peter. 1987. *Theory of the Modern Drama* (tr. M. Hays). Minneapolis: University of Minnesota Press.

Tambling, Jeremy. 1997. 'Towards a Psychopathology of Opera' in *Cambridge Opera Journal* 9(3): 263-279.

Taussig, Michael. 1993. *Mimesis and Alterity: A Particular History of the Senses*. London and New York: Routledge.

Taylor, Millie. 2009. 'Integration and distance in the works of Stephen Sondheim' in *Contemporary Theatre Review* 19(1): 47-60.

'The Royal Opera House Muscat'. Online at: http://www.huffingtonpost.com/michael-kaiser/the-royal-opera-house-mus_b_1004713.html (consulted 28.10.2012).

Tomlinson, Gary. 1998. *Metaphysical Song: An Essay on Opera*. Princeton and Chichester: Princeton University Press.

Van Leeuwen, Theo. 1999. *Speech, Music, Sound*. Basingstoke and London: Macmillan.

Vennard, William. 1967. *Singing—The Mechanism and the Technic* (Revised ed.). New York: Carl Fischer.

Vernon, Polly. 'I didn't like being a celebrity. It's a service job. Like washing toilets' in *The Observer* (8 July 2007).

Verschaeve, Michel. 1997. *Le Traité de Chant et de mise en scène baroques*. Paris: ZurfluH.

Vinay, Gianfranco. 2005. 'Poétique et dramaturgie musicale de "l'action invisible": Vanitas, Lohengrin et "la nuit sauvée"' in Ferrari, Giordano (ed.). *L'Opéra eclatée: la dramaturgie musicale entre 1969 et 1984*. Paris: L'Harmattan.

Vivarelli, Nick. 2011. 'Zeffirelli brings opera to Middle East' in *Variety* (17 September 2011).

Vivès, Jean-Michel. 2002. 'La voi(x)e du féminin: entre regard et invocation' in Jacques André and Anne Juranville (eds.). *Fatalités du feminine*. Paris: P.U.F.

Wakin, Daniel J. 2012. 'Latest Met Aria: Bad Opera News is No News' in *The New York Times* (21 May 2012).

Whenham, John. (ed.). 1986. *Claudio Monteverdi: Orfeo* (Cambridge Opera Handbooks). Cambridge: Cambridge University Press.

Willet, John. 1998. *Brecht in Context*. London: Methuen.

Williams, Bernard. 1998. 'Opera' in Sadie, Stanley (ed.) *The New Grove Dictionary of Opera* (Volume 3). London: Macmillan.

Wiseman, Richard. 2011. 'Can you spot the hidden face?' Online at: http://richardwiseman.wordpress.com/2011/12/13/can-you-spot-the-hidden-face/ (consulted 15.01.2013).

Wisneski, Henry. 1976. *Maria Callas: The Art Behind the Legend*. London: Robert Hale.

Wyss, Monika (ed.). 1977. *Brecht in der Kritik*. Munich: Kindler Verlag.

Yew, Christoph. 2010. *The Turk on the Opera Stage: A History of a Musical Cliché*. Munich: GRIN Verlag.

Žižek, Slavoj. 2004. *Organs Without Body: On Deleuze and Consequences*. New York: Routledge.

——and Mladen Dolar. 2002. *Opera's Second Death*. New York: Routledge.

LIVE AND RECORDED WORKS

Bixio, Cesare Andrea. 'Mamma', Beniamino Gigli (Tenor), Dino Olivieri (Cond.). *The Gigli Collection, Number 10—Milan and London Recordings 1938-1940* (Naxos Historical Collection). CD 8.110271.

Boublil, Alain and Claude-Michel Schönberg. 1985. *Les Misérables*. Performance. London: Barbican Theatre.

Brignone, Guido (dir.). 1941. *Mamma*. Motion picture. Cinecittá, Italy/Germany.

Brodzsky, Nicholas and Sammy Cahn. 1950. 'Be My Love'. Los Angeles: RCA Victor. CD 20-1561.

Christie, William. (cond.) and Pier Luigi Pizzi (dir.). 2008. *L'Orfeo*. Performance at the Teatro Real de Madrid: Teatro Real/La Fenice, Les Arts Florissants and Les Sacqueboutiers de Toulouse.

Cummings, Laurence (cond.) and Shi-Zheng, Chen (dir.). 2006. *L'Orfeo*. Performance at The Coliseum, London: English National Opera.

Denver, John and Domingo, Placido. 1981. *Perhaps Love*. New York: Columbia. ASIN: B0000025MK Cassette and CD Release: Sony, 1990.

Hanly, Francis (dir.). 2005. *Pavarotti—The Last Tenor* . Documentary film. London: Decca. (Reproduced from Arena Edition, 2004). NTSC 07431023 DH.

Harnoncourt, Nikolaus (cond.) and Jean-Pierre Ponnelle (dir.). 1978. *L'Orfeo*. Performance at the Zurich Opera House. The Monteverdi Ensemble of the Zurich Opera House.

Lara, Agustin. 1932, 1958. 'Granada', Mario Lanza (Tenor). *Mario Lanza at His Best*. Re-mastered 1998. London: Castle Pulse, 1998: PLSCD205.

Morley, Brendan. 2003. *The Ten Tenors—One is Not Enough*. Fortitude Valley: Teldec CD 5046647952.

Musilli, John (dir.). 1981. *Mario Lanza: The American Caruso*. Documentary film. New Jersey: Kultur. VHS.

Muziektheater Hollands Diep. 2010. *Lege Wieg and Boş Beşik—Making Of*. DVD. Interviews by Loesje Clement. Camera/Editing/DVD by Kiki Petratou. Dordrecht: Muziektheater Hollands Diep, 2010.

Riedelsheimer, Thomas. 2004. *Touch the Sound—A Sound Journey with Evelyn Glennie*. Filmquadrat/Skyline Productions.

Savall, Jordi. (cond.) and Gilbert DeFlo (dir.). 2002. *L'Orfeo*. Performance at the Gran Teatre del Liceu, Barcelona: Le Concert des Nations and La Capella Reial de Catalunya.

Thorpe, Richard. 1951. *The Great Caruso*. Hollywood: MGM.

Wood, Sam. 1935. *A Night at the Opera*. Hollywood: MGM.

INDEX

0090 Festival, Antwerp, 205
"4'33'"" (John Cage 1952), 221
476 Players Theatre, London, 206n
à la Turca, 185; "Turkish" operas,
  205n
Abbate, Carolyn, 45-6, 60, 151, 162-
  3, 164n, 220, 235, 249
Abel, Sam, 152, 249
Acousmêtre, 149-164, 234
Adorno, Theodor W., 18, 24n, 39, 47-
  50, 55, 62-3, 64n, 245
aestheticity, 136
affect, 21-2, 65, 79-101, 231-2, 256
Agamben, Giorgio, 58, 63, 75, 245
agréments, 68
Alagna, Roberto, 127
Ali Pasha von Janina (Albert
  Lortzing 1828), 205n
alienation (*Verfremdung*), 48-51,
  136, 145, 199-200
Allons les gars (1991), 205
Altan, Sinem, 186, 207n; *Türkisch für
  Liebhaber* (2009), 207n; *Tango
  Türk* (2010), 10, 186, 193-4, 196-
  7, 200-4, 236
Andersen, Hans Christian, 53-5
Anderson, Laurie, 28, 66
animal spirits/*spiritus animales*, 81-2,
  101n
anti-humanism, 49-51, 230
Araiza, Francisco, 122-3
Arcola Theatre, London, 205n
Arianna (Claudio Monteverdi 1608),
  80-2
Aristotle, 40, 67, 76n, 134, 245
Armide (Jean-Baptiste de Lully
  1686), 72, 77n
Ashley, Robert: *Perfect Lives* (1978-
  1983), 21, 25, 27-32, 37-8n, 229,
  245, 255, 258
Aşik (Turkish tradition), 194
Atatürk, Mustafa Kemal, 198, 200-1,
  207n

Atys (Jean-Baptiste de Lully 1676),
  67, 76n
Aufricht, Ernst Josef, 138-143, 145-6,
  147-8n, 249
aurality, 15, 185-207, 236, 243
Auslander, Philip, 26, 28-9, 249
Bach, Johann Sebastian, 154, 176,
  180
Bacilly, Bénigne de, 71, 245
Bahn, Roma, 140
Bählamms Fest (Olga Neuwirth
  1998), 60, 63, 247, 253
Bakhtin, Mikhail, 174-5
Balatri, Filipo, 70
Ballhaus Naunynstrasse, Germany,
  205n
Balme, Christopher, 27, 166-7, 179,
  249
Baroni, Leonora, 71
Barthes, Roland, 40, 44, 54, 161, 225,
  245
Bary, René, 71-2, 245
Bataille, Georges, 59
Battersea Arts Centre, 24n
Bazin, André, 153
Beckett, Samuel, 19
becoming animal, 58-60
Beethoven, Ludwig van, 24n, 41-2,
  253
Beggar's Opera, The (John Gay
  1928), 139
Belle et la Bête, La (Philip Glass
  1994), 152, 159-160, 163, 164n
bel canto, 14, 42, 58
Benjamin, Walter, 28, 62, 64n, 245
Berberian, Cathy, 17, 24n, 219-220,
  227n, 240, 243, 245-6, 253
Berg, Alban, 50, 51, 150; *Lulu*
  (1935), 150, 163n; *Wozzeck*
  (1925), 51
Bieito, Calixto, 19

Birtwistle, Harrison, 50, 152, 160, 163; *Mask of Orpheus, The* (1986), 152, 160, 163
Bizet, Georges: *Carmen* (1875), 47-8, 149
Björk, 168, 171, 174-6, 183n; *Dancer in the Dark* (2000), 10, 168, 170, 172-5, 177, 182-3n, 235, 255
Björling, Jussi, 123, 128
Black on White (Heiner Goebbels 1997), 176
Blair, Tony, 224, 227n, 245
Blau, Herbert, 17
body politic, 75
Bono, 120
Boublil, Alain and Claude-Michel Schönberg: *Misérables, Les* (1985), 127, 259
Bourgeois Gentilhomme, Le (Jean-Baptiste de Lully 1670), 205
Brandt-Sigurdsson, Gunnar, 194, 206n
Brecht, Bertolt, 18, 22, 28, 131-148, 154, 158, 164n, 234, 246, 251-5, 258-9; and epic theatre, 132-3, 136-7, 141-2, 145, 158; *Threepenny Opera, The* (1928), 131-148, 234, 246, 250, 251-3; *Mahagonny (Aufstieg und Fall der Stadt Mahagonny)* (1930), 131
Breslin, Herbert, 121, 250
Brook, Peter, 19, 227n
Bunraku, 14
Burlesque on Carmen (Charlie Chaplin 1915), 149
Burst (Battersea Arts Centre), 24n
Bussotti, Sylvano, 17, 24n, 227n, 246
Bürger, Peter, 133-4, 234, 250
Cage, John, 50, 52, 62, 219, 221, 254-5; "4'33'"" (1952), 221; *Water Walk* (1959), 52; Cage Against the Machine (2010), 221, 227n, 255
Caine, Michael, 120
Callas, Maria, 103-117, 121, 150, 163, 163-4n, 232-3n, 249-50, 252-5, 258; *Galas* (Charles Ludlam, 1983), 150

Campra, Andre: *Hésione* (1700), 73
Can, Kerem, 195, 202
Carmen (Georges Bizet 1875), 47-8, 149; (Cecil B. DeMille 1915), 149
Carreras, José, 13, 121, 126
Carrington, Leonora, 60
Cartens, Caroline, 194
Caruso, Enrico, 121, 126, 128, 129n; *Great Caruso, The* (Richard Thorpe 1951), 126; *Mario Lanza: The American Caruso* (John Musilli 1983), 128, 259
castration, 120; anxiety of, 151-4, 156, 161, 164n, 234
castrato / castrati, 70, 121-2, 225, 253
chaconne, 97
Chaplin, Charlie, 158; *Burlesque on Carmen* (1915), 149; *Gold Rush, The* (1925), 158
Chion, Michel, 153-4, 156, 161, 250
civilising process, 7
CNN opera, 25
Cocteau Trilogy (Philip Glass), 159-60, 164n
Coliseum, 13, 259; English National Opera, 13, 220, 242, 251, 259
Comolli, Jean-Louis, 153
Cook, Nicholas, 46, 165-6, 251-2
Cordemoy, Géraud de, 73, 246
counter-tenor, 121-2
Couperin, François, 72
Cremonesi, Attilio, 9, 79, 96, 97, 101n, 232, 249
critical impro, 213, 237
cross-gender performance, 121, 257
cultural diversity, 185-207, 236
Cureau de la Chambre, Marin, 68, 246
cycle of enquiry, 217
Dancer in the Dark (Lars von Trier 2000), 10, 168, 170, 172-5, 177, 182-3n, 235, 255
Danchet, Antoine: *Hésione* (1700), 73
Dandrey, Patrick, 69, 255
Davies, Peter Maxwell: *Eight Songs for a Mad King* (1969), 52, 57

De Beer, Lotte, 186; *Tango Türk* (2010), 10, 186, 193-4, 196-7, 200-4, 236
declamation, 68, 85, 97, 108, 115
deixis, 223
Deleuze, Gilles, 174, 259; and Félix Guattari, 58-59, 63, 210, 221, 226n, 246
Delunsch, Mireille, 9, 87-9
Deluy, Clementine, 9, 96
DeMille, Cecil B.: *Carmen* (1915), 149
Democratisation, 187, 190, 198-9, 202
Denver, John, 126, 259
Derrida, Jacques, 40-1, 64n, 209-10, 226n, 246; *eidos*, 210, 222, 226n
Desi, Thomas and Eric Salzman, 188, 228n, 256
discourse, 12-4, 20, 23, 25-6, 28, 34, 36, 74, 123, 151, 166, 187, 197, 215, 217, 219, 221, 229, 231, 233, 235, 252, 256
diskutierbarheit (discussability), 134
diva, 19, 22, 76, 105, 120-1, 255
doctrine of affections, 84
Dogma (film style), 172, 183n, 257
Dolar, Mladen, 11, 13-4, 16, 24n, 216, 226n, 259; and Slavoj Žižek, 11, 16, 24n, 216, 226n, 259
Domingo, Placido, 11, 13, 121, 126, 259
Don Giovanni (Wolfgang Amadeus Mozart 1787), 241
dramma per musica, 214, 216
Dreigroschenoper, Die (*Threepenny Opera, The*) (Bertolt Brecht and Kurt Weill 1928), 131-148, 234, 246, 250, 251-3
Dubos, Jean-Baptiste, 67
Duncan, Michelle, 65, 75, 251
DuPar, Edwin B., 9, 149
Duras, Marguerite, 10, 154-158, 253; *Nathalie Granger* (1972), 10, 154-5; *Femme du Gange, La* (1973), 154
Eight Songs for a Mad King (Peter Maxwell Davies 1969), 52, 57

emancipated spectator (Rancière), 190, 248
embodied knowledge, 211-2, 214, 223, 225, 227n
emergence, 176, 181, 222
Engels, Erich, 131, 140, 147n
English National Opera, 13, 220, 242, 251, 259
Entführung aus dem Serail, Die (Wolfganag Amadeus Mozart 1782), 205n
epic theatre, 132-4, 136-7, 139, 141, 145, 158
Eraritjaritjaka (Heiner Goebbels 2004), 176-80, 183n, 235, 252
Ersoy, Özgür, 207n
falsetto, 61, 121-3, 127
Femme du Gange, La (Marguerite Duras 1973), 154
fetish (Freudian), 13-14, 65, 124, 126, 154, 156, 214
FIFA, 14
fin de siècle, 16, 18, 112
Fischer-Lichte, Erika, 132, 135-137, 251-2, 256
Fleeger, Jennifer Lynn, 163n, 252
fliegender Holländer, Der (Richard Wagner 1843), 61
Florentine Camerata, 66, 210, 214-5, 218, 223-5
Fragmentation of the subject, 28, 202
Frankenstein, The Modern Prometheus (Libby Larson 1990), 150
Freischütz, Der (Carl Maria von Weber 1821), 61
Freud, Anthony, 12, 19, 23n
Freud, Sigmund, 40, 153, 156, 221
Frith, Simon, 123, 126, 191, 197, 202, 252
Futurists, 49
Galas (Charles Ludlam, 1983), 150
Galás, Diamanda, 66
Garajistanbul, Istanbul, 205
Garcia, Manuel, 122
Gay, John: *Beggar's Opera, The* (1928), 139
Gelb, Peter, 13, 24n

gender politics, 22, 44, 120, 156,
    164n, 201, 255, 257
Gerron, Kurt, 140-1, 144-5
Gesamtkunstwerk (Total work of art),
    18, 158, 165, 177, 189, 226n,
    252-3
gest, 132, 137
Gestalt, 209
Gesture, 44-6, 52, 55, 57, 71, 73, 87,
    90, 96, 105-6, 158, 180, 194, 224
Gigli, Beniamino, 124-5, 253, 259
Glass, Philip, 50; *La Belle et la Bête*
    (1994), 152, 159-60, 163, 164n;
    Cocteau Trilogy, 159-60, 164n
Glennie, Evelyn, 259
Gluck, Christoph Willibald, 13, 24n,
    205n; *La Rencontre imprévue ou
    Les Pélerins de la Mecque* (1764),
    205n
Goebbels, Heiner, 148, 167, 176-80,
    183n, 235, 252, 257; *Black on
    White* (1997), 176; *Eraritjaritjaka*
    (2004), 176-80, 183n, 235, 252
Goehr, Alexander, 152, 157-8, 163,
    164n, 246, 251; *Triptych* (1968-
    1971), 152, 157-8, 163; *Naboth's
    Vineyard* (1968), 152, 157-8,
    164n, 246, 251; *Sonata About
    Jerusalem* (1971), 152, 157
Gold Rush, The (Charlie Chaplin
    1925), 158
Great Caruso, The (Richard Thorpe
    1951), 126
grimace, 71-2, 77n
Grimarest, Jean-Léonor Le Gallois
    de, 68, 246
Grüber, Klaus Michael, 9, 79, 87-90,
    232
Guangzhou Opera House, 11
Guattari, Félix, and Gilles Deleuze,
    58-59, 63, 210, 221, 226n, 246
Gästarbeiter, 192
Hadid, Zaha, 11
Handel, George Frideric: *Tamerlano*
    (1719), 205
Harnoncourt, Nikolaus, 220-1, 259
Hauptmann, Elisabeth, 139, 147n
Haus der Kulturen der Welt, Berlin,
    205n

Hebbel am Ufer Theater, Berlin, 205n
Hegarty, Paul, 183n, 253
Hegel, Wilhelm Friedrich, 11, 40-1,
    43, 246
Heimathafen Neukölln, 205n
Heldentenor, 123-4
Herbert-Caesari, Edgar: *Voice of the
    Mind, The* (1978), 125, 253
Hésione (Andre Campra, Antoine
    Danchet 1700), 73
het Energiehuis, Dordrecht, 186, 199
het Muziektheater, Amsterdam, 206n
Hoffman, Dustin, 120
Hogerzeil, Cilia, 10, 186, 195; *Lege
    Wieg / Boş Beşik* (2010), 10, 186,
    193-5, 197-9, 204, 206-7n, 236,
    259
Holland Opera (Xynix Opera), 205n
Hollands Diep, Dordrecht, 186, 191,
    193, 195, 203, 236, 259
HTIB, Turkish Workers Union in The
    Netherlands, 206n
humoral pathology, 81
hypermedium, 190
Hüzün, Turkish notion of, 201-3
Imece choir, Berlin, 206n
Incoronazione di Poppea, L' (Claudio
    Monteverdi 1642), 9, 79, 85, 87-
    90, 96, 232, 247
inégalités, 68
instrumental theatre, 52
Intercultural Centre De Centrale,
    Ghent, 205n
interculturality, 185-207, 236
intermediality, 165-167, 177, 179,
    181, 227n, 250, 257
International Federation for Theatre
    Research, 5, 14, 23n, 25, 240, 242
Italian opera, 69-71, 73, 109, 220,
    241, 252
Jelinek, Elfriede, 60-1
Jones, Simon, 211, 214
jouissance, 66, 128, 214, 225
Kagel, Mauricio, 52, 176
Kershaw, Baz, 210, 213, 222, 254
Kintzler, Catherine, 67, 254
Kircher, Athanasius, 79-84, 101n,
    246-8, 256; *Musurgia universalis*
    (1650), 79-80, 101n, 246-7

Kirle, Bruce, 19, 219, 254
Koestenbaum, Wayne, 123, 254
Korot, Beryl, 32, 38n, 248
Kramer, Laurence, 46, 253
Kraus, Alfredo, 59, 124-5, 147n, 245
La Mettrie, Julien Offray de, 74
La Scala, 11, 106
Lacan, Jacques, 59, 66, 247
Lachenmann, Helmut, 53-7, 59, 61-4,
    230, 247, 250; *Das Mädchen mit*
    den Schwefelhölzern (1997), 53-5,
    57, 63, 247
Ladvocat, Louis , 67
Lamento della Ninfa (Claudio
    Monteverdi 1614?), 82, 84
Langhoff, Shermin, 185, 205n, 251
Lanza, Mario, 123, 126, 128, 259;
    Toast of New Orleans, The
    (1950), 126; *Great Caruso, The*
    (1951), 126, 259
Larson, Jonathan: *Rent* (1996), 223
Larson, Libby: *Frankenstein, The*
    Modern Prometheus (1990), 150
Lawrence, Amy, 156, 164n, 254
Le Cerf de la Viéville de Fréneuse,
    Jean-Laurent, 69-70, 72-3, 77n,
    247
Le Faucheur, Michel, 74, 247
Lege Wieg / Boş Beşik (Seung Ah-Oh,
    Cilia Hogerzeil 2010), 10, 186,
    193-5, 197-9, 204, 206-7n, 236,
    259
Lehmann, Hans-Thies, 24n, 189,
    206n, 210, 254
Lems, Arnout, 194
Lenya, Lotte, 138-40, 143-4, 147-8n
Lepage, Robert, 12, 167
Lévi-Strauss, Claude: *tristesse*, 201
listener, 22, 47, 57, 59, 61, 65-6, 72-
    6, 79-81, 83, 122-4, 128, 186,
    188, 197, 200, 216, 231-3, 236
liveness, 26, 28, 35, 249
Lloyd Webber, Andrew, 19, 223, 224,
    227n, 247; *Phantom of the Opera,*
    The (1986), 223, 224, 227n, 247
LOD, Ghent, 205n
logocentrism, 206n, 212, 223
Lortzing, Albert: *Ali Pasha von*
    Janina (1828), 205n

Lost Highway (David Lynch 2003),
    61; *Lost Highway* (Olga Neuwirth
    2003), 61
Louvat-Molozay, Bénédicte, 67, 254
Ludlam, Charles: *Galas: A Modern*
    Tragedy (1983), 150
Lully, Jean-Baptiste de, 67, 72-3; *Atys*
    (1676), 67, 76n; *Armide* (1686),
    72, 77n; *Persée* (1682), 73;
    Bourgeois Gentilhomme, Le
    (1670), 205
Lulu (Alban Berg 1935), 150, 163n
Lynch, David, 10, 61, 161-3, 164n;
    Mulholland Drive (2001), 10,
    161-3; *Lost Highway* (2003), 61
Lyric Opera of Chicago, 12
lyrico-spinto, 123
machismo, 120
Mackeben, Theo, 139
Mackintosh, Cameron, 19, 247
Mädchen mit den Schwefelhölzern,
    Das (Helmut Lachenmann 1997),
    53-5, 57, 63, 247
Magic Flute, The (Wolfgang
    Amadeus Mozart 1791), 223-4
Mahagonny (Aufstieg und Fall der
    Stadt Mahagonny) (Bertolt Brecht
    and Kurt Weill 1930), 131
Makam (Eastern compositional
    mode), 200
Mamma (Guido Brignone 1941), 125,
    258
Mann, Thomas, 42-3, 51, 247; *Doctor*
    Faustus (1947), 51, 247
Mario Lanza: The American Caruso
    (John Musilli 1983), 128, 259
Marino, Luis, 127
Marriage of Figaro, The (Wolfgang
    Amadeus Mozart 1786), 45
Martinelli, Giovanni, 9, 149, 163n
masculine, 46, 60, 119-29, 233
Mask of Orpheus, The (Harrison
    Birtwistle 1986), 152, 160, 163
materiality, 17, 44, 47, 53-4, 59-60,
    63, 95, 136, 167, 214
Maugars, André, 71, 77n, 247
May, Brian, 120
McLuhan, Marshall, 210
media opera, 21, 25-38, 229, 240

mediality, 21, 26-7, 29, 34-37, 38n,
    136, 165-83, 227n, 229, 235, 250,
    257
mediatisation, 22, 29, 35
Méliès, George: *La Damnation du
    Docteur Faust* (1904), 149
Merlin-Kajman, Hélène, 74, 251
Mersenne, Marin, 69, 77n, 247
Metropolitan Opera House, 12-3, 15,
    20, 24n, 37n, 122
Metz, Christian, 148-9, 158, 243
Meyerbeer, Giacomo: *Robert le
    Diable* (1831), 61
mimesis, 21, 39, 62-3, 64n, 230, 258
minimalism, 50, 53
Minkowski, Marc, 9, 77, 87-9, 232
Misérables, Les (Alain Boublil and
    Claude-Michel Schönberg 1985),
    127, 258
modernisation project, Turkey, 187,
    198-200
modernism, 48-53, 56, 114-5, 125,
    188-9, 251, 257
modernity, 16, 40-1, 49-50, 59, 63,
    204, 242, 250
Monteverdi, Claudio, 9, 16, 24n, 79-
    80, 82, 84-5, 87-90, 96-7, 103,
    101n, 108, 213, 216-25, 226-7n,
    230, 232, 237, 247, 249-50, 256-
    9; *L'Orfeo* (1607), 16, 213, 215-6,
    220-3, 225, 237, 247, 251, 258-9;
    Arianna (1608), 80-2; *Lamento
    della Ninfa* (1614?), 82-4;
    L'Incoronazione di Poppea
    (1642), 9, 79, 85, 87-90, 96, 232,
    247
Moss, David, 61
Mozart, Wolfgang Amadeus, 21, 45,
    103, 205n, 241-2; *Entführung aus
    dem Serail, Die* (1782), 205n;
    Marriage of Figaro, The (1786),
    45; *Don Giovanni* (1787), 241;
    Magic Flute, The (1791), 223-4
Mualem, Michal, 9, 96
Mueller, Heiner, 19
Mulholland Drive (David Lynch
    2001), 10, 161-3
multiculturality, 185-207, 236
multimedia, 12, 28-9, 46, 165-6, 251

Mulvey, Laura, 156, 164n
Murray, Kathleen, 174-6, 183n, 256
Music Theatre Working Group, 5, 12,
    14-5, 21-3, 23n, 239-40, 242
musicalisation, 24n, 170, 189, 206n,
    223
musicality, 127, 210, 224; in theatre,
    210, 241, 257
musicking, 15, 257
Musiktheater, 15, 191, 206n, 251,
    253, 256
Musurgia universalis (Athanasius
    Kircher 1650), 79-80, 101n, 246-
    7
Muzio, Claudia, 103-17, 232-3, 253,
    256
Naboth's Vineyard (Alexander Goehr
    1968), 152, 157-8, 164n, 246, 251
narrative, 16, 18, 23, 24n, 42-4, 47,
    50, 52-4, 56-8, 64n, 120, 123-4,
    134, 138, 150, 160, 167, 170, 172,
    174, 177, 179-80, 193, 197, 202,
    209, 218, 220, 223, 225, 233, 249,
    253
Nathalie Granger (Marguerite Duras
    1972), 10, 154, 155
Neher, Carola, 140
Neher, Caspar, 142
Neuköllner Oper, 10, 186, 191, 193,
    204, 207n, 236
Nelson, Robin, (5), 212, 214-5
Neuwirth, Olga, 53, 59-64, 64n, 230,
    247, 253; *Bählamms Fest* (1998),
    60, 63, 247, 253; *Lost Highway*
    (2003), 61
New Music (contemporary), 54, 251;
    (seventeenth century), 216, 217
New musicology, 15
NFPK+ Netherlands Fund for
    Performing Arts, The Hague, 186
Nietzsche, Friedrich, 39-40, 43-4, 47,
    224, 230, 248
noncoincidence, 175-6
Nono, Luigi, 55, 59, 63
Obama, Barack, 224, 227n, 248
Oh, Sueng-Ah, 186, 199; *Lege Wieg /
    Boş Beşik* (2010), 10, 186, 193-5,
    197-9, 204, 206-07n, 236, 259
Olivinn, Berlin, 207n

Öngören, Vasıf, 206n
Opera News, 13, 24n
Opera North, 13
Orfeo, L' (Claudio Monteverdi 1607), 16, 209-28, 237, 247, 251, 258-9
Orientalism, 185, 198, 200
Oslo Opera House, 11
Otter, Anne Sofie von, 9, 87-9
paratext, 14, 120, 124, 233, 246
PARIP (Practice as Research in Performance project, University of Bristol), 211
parody, 19, 51, 53, 56-7
Parsifal (Richard Wagner 1882), 156
Patti, Adelina, 103-117, 232-3, 250-4
Paulsen, Harald, 139-141, 144-5
Pavarotti, Luciano, 13, 119-121, 124, 127-9, 248, 250, 254, 259
Pepusch, J. C., 139
Perfect Lives (Robert Ashley 1978-1983), 21, 25, 27-32, 37-8n, 229, 245, 255, 258
performance practice, 18, 21-2, 100, 103-4, 116, 211, 214, 221, 232, 241
performativity, 15, 21-2, 52, 79, 83-4, 119, 121, 124-28, 131-48, 165, 178, 182-3n, 210, 214, 219, 223, 225, 227n, 232-4, 241, 251-3, 256-7
Phantom of the Opera, The (Andrew Lloyd Webber 1986), 223, 224, 227n, 247
resonance, 81-2, 107
Rimini Protokoll, Germany, 205n
Ring Cycle (Richard Wagner), 13, 42-3
Robert le Diable (Giacomo Meyerbeer 1831), 61
Rochemont de, 69, 248
Roesner, David, 22, 24n, (169-187), 182n, 210, 213, 218, (235, 241), 252, 256-7
Roselt, Jens, 136-7, 252
Rosselli, John, 121-2, 129n
Rossini, Gioachino, 15, 42, 58, 111, 116, 129n, 205n; *Il Turco in Italia* (1814), 205n; *Guillaume Tell* (1829), 120

Royal Opera House, Covent Garden, 11, 13
Royal Opera House, Denmark, 11
Royal Opera House, Muscat, 11-2, 23n, 248, 257
Saint-Évremond, Charles-Marguetel de, 69, 77n, 248
Salzman, Eric and Thomas Desi, 188, 228n, 256
Schechner, Richard, 17, 52, 254
Schneider, Rebecca, 17, 127, 257
Schoenberg, Arnold, 49-50, 56, 248; *Erwartung* (1909), 56; *Von Heute auf Morgen* (1929), 50; *Moses und Aron* (1932), 50
Schönberg, Claude-Michel and Alain Boublil: *Les Misérables, Les* (1985), 127, 259
Schröter, Jens, 167, 182n, 235, 257
Sciarrino, Salvatore, 53, 55-9, 61-64, 64n, 230, 253, 256-7; *Lohengrin* (1984), 56, 258; *Perseo e Andromeda* (1990), 57; *Luci miei traditrici* (1998), 58;
Scratch (Battersea Arts Centre), 24n
semioticity, 136-7
Sévigné, Marie de Rabutin-Chantal, Marquise de, 67
Silverman, Kaja, 151, 153, 156, 164n, 257
singing technique, French, 66-72, 74-5, 76n, 121, 124-5, 129n, 255; Italian, 69-71, 73, 105-6, 108-9, 121-6, 129n, 241, 252, 255
Sonata About Jerusalem (Alexander Goehr 1971), 152, 157
Sondheim, Stephen , 19, 257
Spohr, Louis: *Zemire und Azor* (1819), 205n
STIPT, Foundation for Intercultural Projects concerning Theatre, The Netherlands, 206n
storytelling, 194
Stravinsky, Igor: *Soldier's Tale, The* (1918), 223
Striggio, Alessandro, 216, 219
subject, 40-41, 47-51, 53-6, 58-64, 66, 75, 97, 100, 128, 164n, 166,

186, 202, 236, 251, 254;
    fragmentation of, 28, 202
surrealism, 59-60, 125
Sutherland, Dame Joan, 121
Syberberg, Hans-Jürgen *Parsifal*
    (1982), 10, 154-6, 164n, 253
sympathetic strings, 81
Szondi, Peter, 61, 258
Talimhane Tiyatrosu, Istanbul, 205n
Tamerlano (George Frideric Handel
    1719), 205
Tango Türk (Sinem Altan, Lotte De
    Beer 2010), 10, 186, 193-4, 196-
    7, 200-4, 236
Taymor, Julie: *Oedipus Rex* (1992),
    10, 151-2
Te Kanawa, Kiri, 126
Tebaldi, Renata, 121
telos, 206n
television opera, 25, 27-34, 36, 250,
    255
temperament theory, 81, 83
tenore di forza, 125
tenore robust, 123
Terziyan, Sesede, 195
Great Caruso, The (1951), 126, 259
Threepenny Opera, The
    (*Dreigroschenoper, Die*) (Bertolt
    Brecht and Kurt Weill 1928),
    131-148, 234, 246, 250, 251-3
Toast of New Orleans, The (1950),
    126
Voice of the Mind, The (Edgar
    Herbert-Caesari 1978), 125, 253
Theater am Schiffbauerdamm, 138-9,
    142-3, 146n
theatre ecology, 213, 254
theatricality, 28-9, 135, 137, 168,
    189, 234, 241, 252, 256
thought experiment, 213
Three Tenors, The, 14, 121, 124
Tiyatrom, Berlin, 205n
Tomlinson, Gary, 39, 40, 43, 258
Total work of art (*Gesamtkunstwerk*),
    18, 158, 165, 177, 189, 226n,
    252-3
Touch the Sound (Thomas
    Ridedelsheimer 2004), 181n,
    183n, 259

traditionalism, 13, 187, 197, 201
transnational, 201, 204, 236, 257
Trier, Lars von, 167-8, 170-2, 176,
    183n, 235, 255; *Dancer in the
    Dark* (2000), 10, 168, 170, 172-5,
    177, 182-3n, 235, 255
Triptych (Alexander Goehr 1968-
    1971), 152, 157-8, 163
Tristan und Isolde (Richard Wagner
    1865), 16
Tschaikowsky, Peter Ilyich: *Swan
    Lake* (1876), 11
Türkenoper ("Turkish" opera), 185
Türkisch für Liebhaber (Sinem Altan
    2009), 207n
Tüzemen, Begüm, 200, 207n
Uelum Theater, Ulm, 205n
Ugolin, Aurore, 9, 96, 100
unfinalisabilty, 176
Uyar, Nurhan, 200, 204, 206n
Valetti, Rosa, 139-40
van der Harst, Jennifer Claire, 194
Varopoulou, Helene, 206n
Vegter, Anne, 194, 206n
Verdi, Giuseppe, 103-4, 106-8, 110-2,
    114-17, 120, 128, 165, 232, 241,
    249-50, 256; *Traviata, La*
    (1853), 12, 104, 106-7, 111-4,
    117
Verfremdung (alienation), 48-51, 136,
    145, 199-200
virtual opera, 29, 37n, 250
Vitaphone, 9, 149, 163n
vocal pedagogy, 123
VocaalLAB, Zaandam, 186
Voice, autonomisation of, 151, 162-3;
    and breath, 57-8, 68-73, 110-11,
    114, 129n; embodied-ness/
    disembodied-ness of, 46-7, 54,
    64, 150-1, 153-4, 156-8, 160-2,
    164n, 234, 251; and masculinity,
    119-29, 233; materiality of, 47,
    54, 97, 214
Wagner, Richard, 13, 16, 18, 24n, 39,
    41-4, 46-8, 50, 53-5, 56-7, 61,
    64n, 120, 156, 158, 165, 189, 210,
    219, 223-4, 230, 239, 247-9, 251,
    253-4; *Gesamtkunstwerk* (Total
    work of art), 18, 158, 165, 177,

189, 226n, 252-3; *fliegender Holländer, Der* (1843), 61; *Tristan und Isolde* (1865), 16; *"Liebestod"*, 16; *Ring Cycle*, 13, 42-3, 252; *Parsifal* (1882), 156, 253
Waltz, Sasha, 9, 79, 90, 96-8, 100, 101n, 232, 249
Water Walk (John Cage 1959), 52
Watson, Russell, 126-7
Weber, Carl Maria von, 61, 205; *Abu Hasresan* (1811), 205; *Freischütz, Der* (1821), 61
Weill, Kurt, 28, 133, 137, 139-41, 143, 146, 147-8n, 158, 224, 234, 251, 253; *Lindbergflug, Der* (1929), 28; *Dreigroschenoper, Die* (*Threepenny Opera, The*) (Bertolt Brecht and Kurt Weill 1928), 131-148, 234, 246, 250, 251-3; *Mahagonny (Aufstieg und Fall der Stadt Mahagonny)* (Bertolt Brecht and Kurt Weill 1930), 131

Welsh National Opera, 13
Werkstatt der Kulturen, Berlin, 205n
Wilms, André, 176, 178-80
Wilson, Robert, 19, 160
working class, 121
World Cup, 14, 121, 124
Wozzeck (Alban Berg 1925), 51
writing proper to making, 213-16, 223
Wunderlich, Fritz, 119, 123, 128
X Factor, 221, 227n, 255
YeDo ensemble (Yeniliğe Doğru), 207
Yeni Kusak Theatre, Istanbul, 205n
Zaimoğlu, Feridun, 205n
Zeffirelli, Franco, 11-2, 23n, 258
Zeitoper, 139
Žižek, Slavoj, 11, 16, 24n, 59, 151, 161-2, 164n, 216, 226n, 235, 249, 258; and Mladen Dolar, 11, 16, 24n, 216, 226n, 258